SCOTTISH IDENTITY

A CHRISTIAN VISION

Bob —
Thank you for being
with me in alongside ministry.
Your vision, sensitivity, & wisdom
spur us on. Your integrity
and love for Christ help to
make clear paths for
alongside. Thank you for
your leadership!
Lovingly,
Marfie

SCOTTISH IDENTITY

A CHRISTIAN VISION

William Storrar

The Handsel Press

Published by
The Handsel Press Ltd.
139 Leith Walk, Edinburgh EH6 8NS

ISBN 0 905312 44 9
1 871828 01 5 (pbk)

British Library Cataloguing in Publication Data
Storrar, William
    Scottish identity
    1. Scots. National identity. Christian viewpoints
    I. Title
    261.7

    ISBN 0-905312-44-9
    ISBN 1-871828-01-5 pbk

Typeset by Trinity Typesetting, Edinburgh
Printed in Great Britain by
Bell and Bain Ltd., Glasgow

CONTENTS

FOREWORD

The Rt Hon Sir David Steel MP

Scottish Identity: a Christian Vision is a disturbing book, as I expect its author intended it to be. Disturbing, and exciting, because it is the first effort I have seen to deploy in depth the philosophical arguments behind the historic campaign for Scottish self-government. Reading, as I had to, the word-processed script on concertina'd paper which occasionally flowed from my grasp, I do not claim to have followed all of Willie Storrar's chain of thoughts - especially those where he delves into theology - but I look forward enormously to reading it again in manageable book form.

He starts by identifying the continuous though evolving constitutional tradition based on the principle of the limited sovereignty of the state under the law of God. He is right to do so. The English constitutional tradition rests heavily on the sovereignty of the Queen in Parliament. Thus the nation state can readily become imbued with what the author describes as 'triumphant secular patriotism', while in Scotland sovereignty has always resided in the people. It is the re-assertion of that sovereignty in the Claim of Right approved by the Scottish Convention of 1989 which makes this book timely in appearance and so important.

There is a further gulf between Mr Storrar's vision and the prevailing orthodoxy in power. He does not give us the full quotation but I know what he is aiming at: 'There is no such thing as society; only the individuals that compose it.' Mrs Thatcher's most unguarded insights come not in her prepared speeches, not even in the sermon on the Mound, but in throw-away answers like that one in a television interview at the last general election.

Here the author delivers a trumpet blast against her monstrous vision: 'Her individualist vision of human identity is a grave distortion of the Biblical view of humanity, where individual human personhood is found only in dependent relationship with God and other people. It is incompatible with the understanding of human identity found in Scottish social thought, where society is paramount.'

He sketches a third difference, namely: 'Her dualist vision of Church and State is totally alien to ... the Scottish Christian tradition which recognises no fundamental cleavage between the secular affairs of this earthly world and the spiritual concerns of "another country".' In other words - as he demonstrates in the historical section of his book - the Church has always been directly involved in politics in Scotland, with the very organisation of the polity.

These three currents established early on - Scottish sovereignty, stress on society, and the Church's proper involvement - explain precisely why Scotland is at present governed by such an alien and minority tradition.

But what are we to do about it? Mr Storrar is rightly suspicious of some brands of nationalism - including the English nationalism of Margaret Thatcher - and warns us of those strands which led to Nazi horrors and the Afrikaner nationalism of apartheid South Africa. Willie Storrar as an ordained minister of the Kirk would naturally wish Scotland to return to her influence. He quotes a telling passage from Moderator John Baillie's address to the 1943 General Assembly: 'The life of our Scottish community has largely slipped its Christian moorings.' He then goes on to lament the failure of John MacCormick's all-party Covenant movement to translate millions of signatures in favour of self-government within the UK into political change in the early 1950s and deduces that from then arose the more separatist push of the SNP. Here he is too kind and dwells not on some of the uglier manifestations and sloganising of nationalism as represented by some sections of the SNP over the years. Rather he chooses to quote their more reputable representatives.

Yet artificial sop-ridden 'devolution' proposals in response to rises in nationalist fervour have failed. Mr Storrar somewhat unfairly lays too much blame at the door of the Church for the referendum debacle of 1979. The chief fault lay in the lack of proper foundation for the proposals.

A decade on, that fatal flaw has been widely recognised. Hence this time unlike the 1950s energy is not being channelled into politically powerless signatures. Instead a Scottish Convention has been called with substantial muscle from MPs, councillors, trades unions and churches, beginning as I've said with a united commitment to Scotland's Claim of Right. Detailed proposals will follow from that sure foundation, and if these find general acceptance, the political struggle will take place at the next election to ensure their supremacy in Scotland, regardless of the other political struggle for government at Westminster.

'Nations are chameleon-like communities,' the author avers, 'they change their colour according to the historical landscape in which they are to be found.' Scotland's is changing. No longer do Scots bestride the globe as explorers, missionaries, engineers or governors. What Dean Acheson said about England losing her Empire is even more true of Scotland. We have yet to find a role. Might it be in Europe? With our Roman-Dutch tradition in law, our links with the ancient universities of Italy and our auld alliance with France, we are more genuinely a European country than is our larger southern neighbour.

The late John P. Macintosh used to talk of our feelings of dual nationality - Scottish and British. I am not sure that it isn't triple - Scottish, British and European, with the feeling for and emphasis on each part varying from time to time.

Certainly the early 1950s and the late 1970s provided examples of a failure of Scottish organisation and Scottish nerve respectively. The last decade of the twentieth century may prove the decade in which the Scots overcome both obstacles. If that proves to be, this volume will have largely provided the guidance and inspiration to make it so.

PREFACE by the author

I enjoy a tiny footnote in the history of Scottish Catholicism, of which I am very proud as a Scottish Calvinist minister. For a few short months I was the first Rector's Assessor to the first Catholic Rector in the history of that good Calvinist foundation, the University of Edinburgh. It was sufficient time to grant me the privilege of conversations on the theme of this book with the said Rector, Father Anthony Ross. He directed me to a collection of essays on Hugh MacDiarmid and told me to try to hold together what Scottish Christians of both traditions had rarely done, creation and redemption in our vision of humanity. I have tried. Anthony Ross has also provided the text on which my all too sermonic vision is based. In his own Christian vision of Scotland, an essay called *Resurrection*, published in 1970, he wrote:

> Before deciding what it is to be Scottish we need to re-
> examine our ideas as to what it is to be human, and to
> be Christian, and make at the start an act of contrition
> for ourselves and the community in which we live.

This gives the book its structure. I have seen the question of human and Christian identity in Scotland as central to re-thinking what it means to be Scottish. After an initial trumpet blast, not at a particular politician (who will in due course pass on) but at her vision which may yet survive, the first main section of the book offers the act of contrition for the Christian tradition and community of which I am part. It makes some judgements on the several historic Christian visions of our past, acknowledging their strengths and continuing legacy but seeking a more critical Christian understanding of their weaknesses.

If I write mainly of the Church of Scotland, it is not in a narrow denominational spirit. It is the branch on which I sit but not the tree to which I belong. I am a minister - but I understand fully why Tom Nairn uttered his famous diatribe (quoted in the book) against my ilk; as chapter five argues, the minister in question has become the substitute 'Scottish Christ', and only when we share the vision of the other, true, Christ do we enter the prism which shows up the true colours of church and nation.

Part Two takes MacDiarmid's advice and attempts the impossible, measuring Scotland, and all nations, against the scale of the Infinite - in my case, the God of Scripture and the orthodox Christian faith. It seeks to offer a Biblical and theological understanding of nationhood. Finally, Part Three takes up Ross' challenge and suggests some opening lines of thought for a Christian re-thinking of our human, Christian and national identities in Scotland.

The final chapter is a meditation on a recent event in Scotland, in the light of another woman's vision of Christ and nation, suggesting to me that the only Christian vision of Scotland for our time is a crucified vision of a humble nation. If I have not dealt in greater detail with Scottish nationalism, devolution, independence or some of the recurring issues of the Scottish identity debate - the divided self, the language question and so on - it is in part because Ross' questions seem the necessary prelude for such discussion and partly because my own conviction is that the political question is the key one for modern Scottish nationhood; and politics is about compromise, dialogue and the construction of alliances for limited, agreed ends - so I have kept my options open! And, I hope, my cross-party friendships!

This book was Jock Stein's idea and would never have been completed without his faith, hope, charity - and editing! It carries a supplementary dedication here to him, and to Margaret. I am indebted to all who have discussed the ideas in it with me over the years, especially Professor Duncan Forrester, Steven Mackie, David Wright, Professor Alan Lewis, Professor Christopher Harvie, Professor Douglas Kelly, Peter Bisset, the students in the 'Church and Society in Scotland' classes at Glasgow University, 1984-88, Ralph Smith and the Church of Scotland Audio-Visual Unit, the Carberry Conversationalists on Christianity and Scottish Identity, and above all to Ian Maxwell, Elliot Wardlaw, Gareth Davies and Fearghas MacFhionnlaigh, whose community of minds and hearts constitute my 'presbytery of relief'. Any wisdom is theirs, the folly and mistakes my own.

I wish to record my gratitude to my parents, Ian and Elizabeth Storrar, my sister Fiona, Allan Frazer, Alexa Sinclair, Douglas Grant and the Handsel Press, the Novum trust (who funded a period of research for this book), the Carberry Tower staff, Jack Beaumont, Victor Laidlaw and St Catherine's Argyll Church, Edinburgh, and my own congregation of St John's, Carluke, for their support. And to the Rt Hon Sir David Steel MP, for gracing this book with a gracious Foreword, my sincere thanks.

Finally, Jo, my jo, whose love and help have blessed me in this, as in all else. This book is for you, and for the three little American Scots who share our life together:

> As though explaining the idea of dancing
> Or the idea of some other thing
> Which everyone has known a little about
> Since they were children, which children learn
>   themselves
> With no explaining, but which children like
> Sometimes to hear the explanations of,
> I want to tell you something about our country,
> or my idea of it...

(Robert Pinsky, *An Explanation of America*)

William F. Storrar, November 1989

INTRODUCTION

Chapter 1

SCOTLAND - Whose Vision?

In the 1920s a composer suggested to a poet friend that he write a poem about a drunk man looking at the thistle. That image caught the poet's imagination and generated his literary masterpiece, *A Drunk Man looks at the Thistle*. The poet was Hugh MacDiarmid and the poem was his cosmic vision of Scotland and Scottish vision of the cosmos. In this visionary work, MacDiarmid's drunk man reflects:

> He canna Scotland see wha yet
> canna see the Infinite
> and Scotland in true scale to it.

The intellectual and cultural struggle to measure Scotland on such a scale has helped keep Scottish nationhood alive in the twentieth century. MacDiarmid himself died in 1978, surely a loss of vision to every Scot. As we prepare to enter the twenty-first century, we have lost the visionary, but not his inspiration to seek a worthier vision of Scotland; a vision that is universal and not parochial, humane and not mundane, bound by the Infinite and not the Kailyard.

Where shall we find such a vision to help us make sense of what is happening in Scotland today? As we wrestle daily with the collapse of the old industrial Scotland, the growing crisis of Scottish democracy and the debate about Scotland's future within the United Kingdom and Europe, where can we find that clarity of vision without which we perish as a nation? In the late 1980s, Scottish political leaders of different parties began to describe their policies as visions of Scotland. Whether they prove to be visions or illusions, we should at least consider them. As Robert Burns wrote, quoting the Scottish Common Sense philosophical conviction of his time, we can only see ourselves as others see us. It is only in a common dialogue with our history and with others in society that we can discover our own individual identity. But how do we see ourselves as Scots?

Whatever the popular caricature, it is certainly not thistles and tartans that constitute our national identity. The genius of the Scottish identity is our capacity to burst into new forms of national life. Continuity is essential in any sense of identity. But ours is the continuity of precedent, not tradition, as Hugh MacDiarmid put it. Not for us the unbroken traditions of our southern neighbour to instil a sense of nationhood. It is the precedent of dramatic change that gives the Scots our common sense of nationhood. It is those moments of historic change that define who we are as Scots; the medieval Wars of Independence, the Reformation, the Unions of Crown and Parliament, the Enlightenment, the Industrial Revolution, the end of Empire. There is no contradiction in basing our sense of national identity on the wildly different identities of our past. It is our very capacity to re-form our identity that gives us our sense of continuity with that past; reformed and yet always reforming, as our Calvinist forbears put it. The precedent of change breathes life into our contemporary sense of Scottish identity. It is not the preservation of the status quo that makes Scotland a nation. Such a view fails to understand the characteristic trait of our nationhood. Scotland is a nation today only in as much as it can re-cast its own identity. There is plenty of precedent for that.

However, the Scottish taste for a changing national identity is not thrawn or mindless. If there is to be a re-formed national identity, then it must be on the foundation of common assent to first principles, to be acceptable to the Scots. Defy a foreign invader, resist a monarch, disrupt a national Kirk, yes! But only with an accompanying commentary, a Declaration of Arbroath, a National Covenant, a Claim of Right, justifying such changes before the universal court of God, truth and conscience. Through changing cultural epochs in our national identity, Catholic, Reformed, and secular, we find a profound continuity in such fundamental principles. From the Declaration of Arbroath in

1320 to the Articles Declaratory of the Church of Scotland in 1926, for example, we can identify one continuous though evolving constitutional tradition based on the principle of the limited sovereignty of the state under the law of God: reaffirmed by the Church of Scotland 1989 General Assembly in a deliverance on the government of Scotland.

This principled approach is borne out by the kind of national institutions that survived the union with England in 1707, the Church, the Law and the educational system. Each institution is based on the notion of first principles. The national Reformed Kirk asserts the primacy and sovereignty of the Word of God. The Scottish legal system is founded on the notion of underlying legal principles derived from the divine law. And our Scottish educational tradition is committed to the importance of a general education grounded in a philosophical cast of mind that establishes first principles as the root of all branches of knowledge. If our Scottish identity has been based on dynamic precedent, not static tradition, then it has always had to be principled precedent. Nothing less would do. Nothing less will do today. Ironically, no one saw this more clearly in the late 1980s than the Prime Minister, Mrs Margaret Thatcher.

In response to a major electoral setback in Scotland at the 1987 General Election, when the number of its Scottish MPs fell to ten, the Conservative Government led by Mrs Thatcher saw the task before it as one of pressing on with radical change in Scotland rather than seeking a consensus approach acceptable to an electorate that had voted overwhelmingly for other parties. In a speech entitled *Time for a Change*, made in September 1987, the Secretary of State for Scotland, Malcolm Rifkind, declared:

> The challenge facing Scottish Conservatives and the Government is formidable but it is a challenge of our own making. Quite consciously and deliberately we are determined to change many of the attitudes and policies that have dominated Scotland for years and which are responsible for much of Scotland's social, economic and industrial problems. Such an objective is bound to be highly controversial and full of political risk but it is essential if Scots and Scotland are to realise their full potential.

These words come from a collection of Rifkind's speeches called *A Vision of Scotland*. His commitment to radical change could hardly have been more clearly stated. But, perhaps sensing this distinctive trait of our national identity, that only change grounded in first principles could ever be acceptable to the Scots, something more was offered in its defence.

A Trumpet Blast against a Montrous Vision

Hugh MacDiarmid and Margaret Thatcher are unlikely bed-fellows. And yet it was Mrs Thatcher who responded to MacDiarmid's challenge that Scotland can only be seen in true scale to the Infinite. When Margaret Thatcher addressed the General Assembly of the Church of Scotland, a body concerned with the moral and spiritual welfare of the nation of Scotland, in May 1988, she chose to speak in the light of her own fundamental beliefs as a Christian. In that address, we can discern three underlying convictions shaping her view of the universe.

Individualism lies at the heart of her vision of human life. Mrs Thatcher stated on another occasion that there is no such thing as society, only individuals. She believes passionately in the primacy of individuals, their individual responsibility, choices and potential. As human beings, we exist first as separate individuals endowed by God with the right to make individual choices about our individual responsibilities, according to our own individual judgements. This is the principle shaping her social vision.

The individual soul also lies at the heart of her spiritual vision. The Church chiefly serves the invisible heavenly country above, which extends its boundaries soul by soul, not group by group, within the social structures of society. In her address Mrs Thatcher drew on the hymn, *I vow to thee my country*, as the source of this insight. In it, she found a clear division between the State's concern for the affairs of our earthly country and the Church's concern for a heavenly country, with its unseen King and hidden warfare for individual souls. The primacy of the individual soul shapes her religious vision.

The hymn also furnished her with her national vision. As she said, 'It begins with a triumphant assertion of what might be described as secular patriotism, a noble thing indeed in a country like ours:

"I vow to thee my country all earthly things above;
entire, whole and perfect the service of my love." '

Once again it is the individual who owes a mystical loyalty to his or her country. (For her that country is the Britain created in part by the Union of 1707, but a Britain understood in terms of her own confessed English nationalism.) Individual love of country is the third principle inspiring the vision she offered Scotland in her Assembly address.

From these three principles we can gain our own insight into Mrs Thatcher's view of the universe, MacDiarmid's Infinite. It is essentially a double-decker universe, made up of separate individuals living on two levels. Down below, in the earthly country, live self-motivated individuals regulated by the market place, inspired by love of country and ruled by the sovereign State. Up above, in the heavenly country, live individual souls inspired by the life of faith and ruled by an unseen King. All traffic between the two levels is handled by the Church, taking no group bookings and handling only individual passengers; offering guided tours of the religious wing of our national heritage while you wait. As Prime Minister, Mrs Thatcher would see Scotland being shaped in true scale to her own individualist, pietist and triumphalist patriotic vision. Her 'Sermon on the Mound' therefore represents a three-fold challenge.

First, it provokes all Scots to ask themselves the key question for Scotland in the 1990s and beyond - Whose vision of humanity will shape our national life and our sense of national identity? The party political debate about the future government of Scotland is only one part of that question. The economic debate about the future shape of Scottish industry and commerce within the single market of the European Community is an essential context in which to consider that question. The social debate about the kind of society we want in Scotland for women, for the young and the elderly, for the poor and deprived urban communities, for those in education and health care, for the unemployed, for ethnic minorities, for Gaelic and rural communities, is a crucial part of the question, as are cultural and artistic issues.

Yet it is also a question about the very nature of human identity and the purpose of human life. That fundamental question has been central to Scottish cultural, social and intellectual life for centuries. The Thatcher vision is forcing Scots, as never before in the twentieth century, to bring this question into the forefront of public debate about the future of our society.

Second, Thatcher's address challenges Scottish Christians, especially those she was addressing in the Reformed tradition of the Church of Scotland, to consider whether or not her Christian vision is compatible with their own historic theological understanding of Christ and culture, church and nation. It is now imperative that Christians in Scotland reflect on their own vision of our nation and its future, in a critical, questioning way. If profound change is underway in Scotland, in the name of fundamental principle, then Christians should be alert to both the dangers and the opportunities inherent in such change. They have a Biblical responsibility to relate their faith to their times. During the Second World War, the Church of Scotland's General Assembly set up a *Commission for the Interpretation of God's Will in the Present Crisis* to seek 'God's Will in our Time'. The Thatcher vision presented to a later Assembly is forcing Scottish Christians to seek just that, once more.

And **third,** her address raises the challenge of nationhood and the terms in which it may properly be considered. We are confronted here with her advocacy of a triumphant secular patriotism, presumably the kind that was to the fore during the Falklands War and which reacted with such disdain to the Church service led by the Archbishop of Canterbury at the close of that conflict. But we are also concerned with the problem of what constitutes a nation. Is a nation really a mystical body to which we vow perfect love? And what constitutes such a country: its national heritage, its constitution, its cultural identity? Is the present British Parliamentary system, by which Scotland is ruled, really the best or the only form of democracy for our nation? In her Assembly address, Mrs Thatcher stated her awareness of the historic position of the Church of Scotland as a national Church recognised in constitutional law. Can there be a constitutional recognition of a national Church without some such recognition of the nation itself? Such thoughts are unavoidable. The very notion of nationhood within Britain or Europe is now in contention.

If Margaret Thatcher has unwittingly responded to MacDiarmid's call to see Scotland in true scale to the infinite, she has similarly taken up the challenge issued by another Scottish visionary, Anthony Ross. In an essay on Scotland's future, called *Resurrection*, published in 1970, he wrote, 'Before deciding what it is to be Scottish we need to re-examine our ideas as to what it is to be human, and to be Christian... '. Thatcher's Assembly address inadvertently brings home to us the force and wisdom of Ross' words. The debate about what it means to be Scottish in the late twentieth century requires us to re-examine our ideas about what it means to be human and to be Christian. In pushing for her own vision of society, Thatcher has set out her understanding of these three fundamental identities. It is for us to respond.

I for one, an inheritor of the Reformed tradition of John Knox, wish to sound a trumpet blast against her monstrous vision. Mrs Thatcher's individualist vision of human identity is a grave distortion of the Biblical view of humanity, where individual human personhood is found only in dependent relationship with God and other people. It is incompatible with the understanding of human identity found in Scottish social thought, where society is paramount. Her dualist vision of Church and State is totally alien to the Scottish Reformed and Calvinist holistic vision of reality. That Scottish Christian tradition recognises no fundamental cleavage between the secular affairs of this earthly world and the spiritual concerns of 'another country'. In the Reformed worldview all reality is under the sovereign Lordship of Christ. His Church must relate the Word of God to the secular affairs of the nation as well as to the eternal needs of the individual soul. Both are embraced within his Kingdom. Her mystical vision of nationhood sits uneasily with the Scottish preference for rational discourse on even the most abstract theological or metaphysical matters. Our approach to nationhood has characteristically been a matter of principled calculation rather than triumphal homage.

That said, Mrs Thatcher has done Scotland one great service. She has declared to us her own fundamental principles. She has committed the government she leads to seek a radical change in the Scottish identity, from paternalist corporatism to entrepreneurial individualism. In so doing, she has acted as a catalyst that will force various other elements in Scottish life to change. We are once again, in our history as a nation, in a period of profound change in our sense of national identity. We had entered upon this transitional phase in our nationhood long before the Thatcher era in British politics. We shall continue in it long after the end of that era. But like an enemy flare bursting over night-time troop manoeuvres, it has temporarily lit up the scene for us and forced us to take stock of our positions.

It is time to see Scotland in true scale to the Infinite. It is indeed time to re-examine our ideas about what it is to be human, and to be Christian, before deciding what it is to be Scottish. A new vision of first principles must emerge to guide Scotland through the rapids of change in the 1990s and beyond. If we will not listen to Mrs Thatcher's siren call, it does not mean that we do not desperately need fresh vision in Scotland. The truth is that our ideas about what it means to be human and to be Christian in Scotland, and to be Scottish within Britain, are in deep crisis.

Anthony Ross added a caveat to his call to re-examine our Scottish identity in the light of our humanity and Christian faith. He said that we must 'make at the start an act of contrition for ourselves and the community in which we live.' For me, as a Christian, that contrition must include a critical re-assessment of Christianity's past contribution to the community of Scotland. I believe that there have been three great Christian visions of Scotland in our history that have shaped the way we see ourselves as Scots and the nation we have inherited. Before going on to consider (in Part 3) what a contemporary Christian vision of Scottish identity might mean for us today, we must first turn to these earlier visions.

PART 1   HISTORICAL IDENTITY -
Understanding the Past

Chapter 2

THE CATHOLIC VISION - A Free Nation

An act of contrition must begin with an act of recollection. What was the historic Christian vision of Scottish nationhood and identity? At the Union of the Parliaments in 1707, the Earl of Seafield remarked, 'Now there's an end of an auld sang.' The song that is Scotland has been sung in many different keys. Christians have sung the Lord's song in this land of Scotland in one dominant key - the key of triumph and glory, victory and conquest. From medieval Arbroath to turn-of-the-century Glasgow, Scottish Christians have been sounding forth the trumpet that never calls defeat. Their vision of Scotland has been a powerful and persuasive picture of a triumphant Christian nation marching to Zion.

For seven hundred years, from the fourteenth to the twentieth centuries, this one theological vision of Scotland has dominated the imagination of Scottish Christians in their thinking about our nationhood. It is a vision of God as the Almighty, judge and ruler over the destiny of the nations. It is a glorious vision centred on Christ as the ascended Lord, victorious in heaven and, through the advance of his Kingdom on earth, conquering the nations in power and glory. It is a triumphant vision of the conquest of Scottish national life by the Christian Church, Faith and Ethic. Whether held by medieval churchmen, seventeenth century covenanters, or Victorian moral reformers, this vision looked at Scotland through the eyes of a triumphant Christ in glory, looking down upon the nations of the earth from the judgement throne of heaven. It assumed that any Christian vision of the nation must mean the dominant role of the Church or its Confession of Faith, or its ethics, in shaping the nationhood, national identity and national life of Scotland.

Whenever Scots today refer to their country as a Christian nation, they are drawing on the fading light of this vision and its effect on the life and culture of Scotland. Christianity was brought to this peripheral part of Europe long before the creation of the nation of Scotland out of several disparate peoples and kingdoms. The Christian religion was therefore influential in the formation and development of our Scottish nationhood and national identity from the start. That influence extended from the medieval period, through the centuries of the Scottish Reformation and Enlightenment, down to the industrial epoch of Victorian and Edwardian Scotland.

In the more secular years of the twentieth century, with declining church membership and the diminished social significance of the Churches in most areas of public and private life , that influence is seen to be waning in Scotland, as in most Western countries. Yet despite the institutional and social decline of the Churches, the glorious vision of a Christian nation continues to shape the thinking of many Scots, within and outwith the Churches. It fashions their notions of what Scottish nationhood means today as they draw on its undoubted past achievements and rich legacy in the modern Scottish identity. From the standpoint of Christian faith, that may no longer be a good thing, for the Church or for the nation. The vision may have turned into illusion if not myopia, blinding us to the realities of both modern Scotland and the Gospel.

It is this once dominant Christian vision of Scotland, in its several historic versions, that we must re-think today. We must at least be open to the possibility that it may no longer illuminate our understanding of Scotland with those Christian insights most appropriate to our time and social context. And we must recognise with honesty and rigour the often ambiguous and sometimes clearly regrettable influence of this glorious, triumphal Christian vision of Scotland on our national identity. Indeed, we must make contrition as Scottish Christians for the dark lingering failures of this glorious vision to shed light in our national life. But first we must find the source of this vision and trace its chiaroscuro effect down through our history and into the present.

Birth of a Vision - the Declaration of Arbroath

The glorious vision of Scottish nationhood was born out of the struggle for independence in the early fourteenth century. No major military and political conflict between Scotland and England could take place in the medieval era without an accompanying commentary justifying the rightness of the nation's cause. Scotland under Robert the Bruce rejected the feudal claims of the English kings to overlord the Scots, with armed resistance and with eloquent prose. Clerics such as Bernard of Linton, Abbot of Arbroath, sided with Bruce and drafted the documents that were addressed to Rome and the popes. Such propaganda argued Scotland's case against England before this international court of appeal with legal and literary skill and not a little fable-making invention. The greatest of these documents was the Declaration of Arbroath of 1320, a letter from the Scottish barons to Pope John XXII calling on him to recognise Scotland's autonomy and separate history under its own king and to reject the king of England's greedy advances north of the border under the cloak of feudal rights. We can identify several dominant theological and national themes in the Declaration of Arbroath that shaped the glorious vision of Scotland and which recurred in various forms down through the centuries.

Perhaps the key phrase in the Declaration that helps us to understand the theological perspective of the glorious vision is the one which refers to Christ calling the Scots to faith through the instrument of the apostle Andrew, 'after His Passion and Resurrection'. The Declaration imagines that the Scots were among the first to be honoured by Christ after his passion and resurrection, through the legend of Andrew bringing the Gospel to Scotland. The theological point to note here is the identity of the Christ who sends his apostle with the Gospel to Scotland. He is described in the document as 'the King of Kings, the Lord Jesus Christ, after His Passion and Resurrection'. This is Jesus of Nazareth after his crucifixion, burial and the resurrection appearances, when he still bore the marks of his death in his risen body: no longer the humiliated and suffering servant, the crucified saviour, but Christ the ascended and reigning king. In this theology of nationhood, Andrew is seen as the patron and protector of Scotland on behalf of Christ the King. The need for such a theology is made obvious in the next section of the document.

The protection of the nation by Andrew, its patron saint, was made secure on earth by the popes' recognition that Scotland was in his special care. The Scottish Church was the *filia specialis*, the special daughter of Rome and its popes, as an earlier thirteenth century papal bull had described the relationship. The nation had enjoyed freedom and peace under their protection until Edward, king of England, intervened in Scottish affairs and subjected the Scots to terrible suffering. Then Divine Providence raised up a lawful Scottish king, 'like another Joshua or Maccabeus', to deliver that other chosen little nation of Scotland from the enemy's hand. The nation needed a strong, resolute and rightful king like Robert the Bruce to ensure its survival and freedom, just as ancient Israel looked to Joshua and Maccabeus to lead and deliver it from its enemies. The theological concomitant of that was a Christ who was seen, like Bruce, to be the rightful king and lord, vindicated after the suffering and shame of his passion and now reigning in heaven. The document ends with the intention of the Scottish king and people to play their part in the relief of the Holy Land and Christian territories from the pagans, once their own country has been made secure against shameful, unbrotherly attack from the Christian prince of England. Both Scotland and Christendom are therefore seen as under threat from their enemies. A final plea is made 'to Him who is the Sovereign King and Judge', the Christ who alone can grant strength, courage and deliverance to the Scots and defend their cause.

It is not surprising theologically or historically that the Scots in the early fourteenth century should gravitate towards the identity of Christ the king in the Declaration of Arbroath. There was a good Biblical precedent which they themselves recognised. After centuries of suffering and uncertainty as to their national survival from the period of the Exile, the people of Israel looked increasingly to a regal messiah figure who would be another mighty king like David to deliver them from the hands of their enemies. Their historical experience led them to neglect that other strand in their prophetic literature which saw the messiah as a suffering servant. In the Declaration the Scots themselves draw a parallel with Israel in this period, under the rule of the Maccabees who won for Israel a short period of independence before the final onset of Roman rule. Under the hammer of invasion and oppression from England, Scotland too shaped a theology of nationhood that saw Christ as the mighty and victorious King judging the nations and vindicating his people. A small nation under external threat but with a sense of universal destiny finds in the king figure the hope for a glorious vision of national triumph. The figure of the suffering servant is too close to its own historical experience to be attractive as a source of hope for deliverance and liberation as a nation.

If the dominant theological figure in the glorious vision of nationhood is that of the triumphant Christ, the Sovereign King and Judge, then the dominant national theme is of a triumphant people motivated by high spiritual purpose and not by worldly concerns. The Christian vision of Scotland contained within the Declaration of Arbroath is of a free nation whose liberties are guaranteed by the King of Kings, providing his protection through the agency of patron saint, pope and lawful king. The key concern of the nation is to resist dominion by a foreign power and to contend, not for glory, riches or honours, but for freedom alone, 'which no honest man will lose but with his life'. This shared love of freedom and willingness to sacrifice their lives for it is seen by the barons of Scotland as the vision that unites the community of the realm in common purpose as a nation. A shared spiritual purpose undergirding the whole life of the nation is the second characteristic of the glorious vision of Scotland. The shared images of St Andrew in heaven, St Peter's successors in Rome and the biblically resonant heroic figure of King Robert in Scotland act as the carriers and guarantors of that vision. In these three centres of power - cosmic, global and local - the King of Kings offers his protection to the Scots, before the throne of God, at the heart of Christendom, and on the throne of Scotland.

Although Scotland is seen as a small nation on the edge of the world, under constant threat from its more powerful southern neighbour, it can triumph and fulfill a wider destiny within

Christendom, despite the great odds against it. This is the third characteristic of the glorious vision, a sense that Scotland's precarious existence as a nation can ultimately be made certain by sacrificial action, even if only by a faithful remnant - 'For as long as there shall but one hundred of us remain alive we will never give consent to subject ourselves to the rule of the English.' The triumph of a Christian nation is achieved through the high spiritual purpose shared by the whole nation, and ultimately the willingness of even a remnant of the nation to sacrifice itself for Christ the true King, whatever the cost.

In the creation of a free nation through their own sacrificial action, the Scots risk taking on the identity of the demiurge, becoming the subordinate agents of God in this divine creative work of nationhood. This 'demiurgic identity', which we will explore in later chapters, gave rise to the characteristic Scottish conviction that the creation and continuing existence of a free nation lay ultimately in their own hands, in great all-or-nothing, do-or-die efforts by the Scots at key moments in their history, albeit under a divine providence. The glorious vision of a triumphant nation under Christ the King, and of a nation united by a great common spiritual and moral purpose, finally seems rather fragile, in that it depends on the sacrificial efforts of the faithful few.

The theological basis for this medieval Catholic vision of Scotland as a free nation is made even more explicit in a later fourteenth century text, *The Bruce*, a poem by John Barbour, Archdeacon of St Machar's, Aberdeen. It is a narrative account of the achievements of King Robert of Scotland, written when Scotland's fortunes were at a low ebb after the reign of a weak successor, David II. Barbour wishes to remind the Scots of their past heroism as a nation and to inspire a renewed patriotism, according to the critic Kurt Wittig in a study of the poem in his book, *The Scottish Tradition in Literature*. Central to the notion of patriotism which Barbour wishes to foster are the virtues of freedom and right, the justice of any cause. To understand *The Bruce*, Wittig argues, 'It is essential to grasp the fact that the conviction on which Barbour's [moral vision] was based had itself a religious basis... "Fredome" and "recht" are here represented as things that God alone can give. This is a conception that runs like a red thread through the whole poem.'

In Scotland's struggle for independence from England, Barbour sees the kind of parallel with Israel's own fight for independence under the leadership of the Maccabees that was made in the earlier Declaration of Arbroath:

> ... Why does Barbour refer to the Maccabees? Is not the fact the he compares the Scots, especially in such a context, to a small nation defending their God-given right and God-given freedom, with God's active help, against vastly superior forces, in itself highly significant? In this connexion, it should be observed that the Declaration of Arbroath (1320), surely the most remarkable political document of the Middle Ages, expresses the same ideas of freedom and right and God's help, and also compares Bruce to Maccabeus: the crucial passage reads like a synopsis of Barbour's poem.

The vision of Scottish nationhood that emerges from these complementary fourteenth century texts is, therefore, clearly a theological one, with an emphasis on the role of heavenly and earthly kingship and a God who sustains the nation's high moral commitment to his own cause of freedom and justice. But there is one significant difference between the barons' letter and the archdeacon's poem. While the Declaration of Arbroath makes careful reference to the nation's patron saint and its special relationship with the popes in Rome to bolster its case for independence, Barbour makes no such allusions in his poem. As Wittig notes, 'He has a profound faith in God, yet nowhere does he refer to the Church as a mediator, mention its rituals, invoke its saints, or himself employ its symbolism, its allegories, its dogmas.' For Wittig, Barbour's religious outlook is remarkable for a fourteenth century churchman, in that his direct communion with God without the Church's mediating role foreshadows the approach of the Reformation a century and a half later.

More than that, I would argue that Barbour's theological approach to nationhood foreshadows the distinctively Reformed approach that we shall look at in the next chapter. He extends the triumphal Christian vision of nationhood first found in the Declaration of Arbroath earlier in the century in a way that will

allow it to be embraced by later post-medieval Christian traditions. Barbour's poetic song of triumph, in which 'God, just and
almighty, is the ruler of Destiny' for the nations of the earth, is
one that both Reformed and secular Scots could easily transpose
into their own Biblical or ethical key in later centuries, without
reference to Catholic doctrine and piety. However, before the
glorious vision could take on these later guises, it went through
its own medieval metamorphosis. If Barbour himself did not see
the Church and its religious life as essential to that theological
vision of patriotism, churchmen in the century that followed
certainly did.

The Catholic Vision - a Famous Nation

The Catholic historian Monsignor David McRoberts has
shown, in a seminal essay, *The Scottish Church and Nationalism
in the Fifteenth Century* (on which this section is based), how
Scotland was affected by the marked growth in nationalist
sentiment in later medieval Europe. The Scottish Church was
not only influenced by these new ideas from the continent, 'but,
in turn, did much to promote the new outlook among the people
of Scotland.' In the fifteenth century we see emerging in
Scotland the distinctively Catholic version of the glorious vision
of nationhood, one in which the Church identified itself even
more closely with the culture and traditions of the country, for
both religious and nationalist reasons.

The religious and political concept which gave unity to
medieval Europe was the notion of Christendom in which all the
peoples of the civilized Christian world were united in a shared
allegiance to the rule of the emperor and pope. This unity began
to break apart in the fifteenth century for a whole range of
complex reasons, not least among them the Great Schism between rival popes that lasted for forty years from 1378 and
divided the nations of Christendom according to their different
papal loyalties. As the temporal powers of the emperor and the
spiritual jurisdiction of the pope grew weaker in the period that
followed, so the kingdoms of Europe sought to strengthen their
local powers over church and state within the bounds of their
own territories. A new political and religious idea emerged in
Europe, in which each each kingdom became an autonomous

nation-state controlling its own political and ecclesiastical affairs. McRoberts shows how Scottish churchmen were very much involved in these continental disputes over the temporal and spiritual rule of Christendom:

It is not surprising therefore to find that fifteenth century Scotland was alive to the new trends in ecclesiastical and secular politics, that efforts were made to organise Scotland more effectively as a self-contained nation-state of Christendom after the contemporary fashion and that ecclesiastics apparently played a full and active part in developing that new Scotland.

According to McRoberts, the aspirations and activities of these Scots churchmen, 'who were trying to build a new and better Scotland in the fifteenth century', are to be understood in nationalist and not strictly ecclesiastical terms. McRoberts distinguishes between a negative kind of nationalism, which in fifteenth century Scotland took the form of anti-English feeling, and the kind of positive nationalism which 'sought to build up pride in the kingdom of Scotland, its traditions, life and institutions so that Scotland would be respected and take its place by right among the sovereign states of Europe.' The Catholic Church pursued this policy of nationalist identification with Scotland in a variety of religious and cultural innovations during the course of the century.

Before looking at the ways in which this happened, it is important to note that this was a continental and not just a local phenomenon. In the Declaration of Arbroath, the Scots were anxious to show that they were a famous nation with a history like that of any other famous nation within Christendom. Reference is made in the opening section to the Scots' sojourn in Spain before moving on to their present home. Had this legendary visit to Spain lasted longer the Scots would have witnessed a similar attempt by the Spanish Church to identify with the history and identity of the nation in a glorious vision of national triumph linked to the triumph of Christ the King. At the end of the fifteenth century the Catholic kings instituted the Feast of the Triumph of the Holy Cross in thanksgiving for the final recovery of Spain from the Moors and Islamic rule. The introit used in the Mass quotes Matthew chapter 25 and Christ's invitation there to the blessed ones to enter the kingdom prepared for them from the foundation of the world. As McRoberts comments:

> In this introit, Spain is assimilated to paradise and it is suggested that the Spanish people are predestined by God from the beginning to inherit this paradise. A statement like this, sung by a full choir, year by year, over the centuries, must have made Spaniards feel they were no ordinary people.

The Scots would have to wait for another century and a half, to the time of the covenants, before they began to assume in such an overt way this predestined and chosen identity as a special people. But the medieval Scottish Church was as willing to incorporate national elements into its liturgy as its Spanish sister, and for similar nationalist ends.

McRoberts has described the liturgy as a repository of the historical memories of a nation. For example, John Major, the great Scottish medieval scholar, argued for the missionary work of St Ninian in Scotland on the grounds of the collect of St Ninian's Mass. The liturgy was even more powerful in the public mind of the people as an unrivalled vehicle for propaganda, as in Spain. Behind the marked changes in the liturgical and devotional life of Scotland in the fifteenth century lay the Church's wish to instruct the Scottish people in their own glorious Christian past, exemplified in the lives of Scottish saints, and to instil in them a patriotic pride in their country's achievements. Just as later generations of Victorian and twentieth century Scots would recite a litany of great Scots, inventors, explorers and scientists, to boost national morale, so fifteenth century Scots were increasingly made conscious of their Scottish identity through the revival of devotion to national saints. Monsignor McRoberts has charted this revival after a period of general neglect in the veneration of Scottish saints in the preceding centuries.

The extent of this change can be realised by contrasting the extent of devotion to Scottish saints and their shrines before and after the revival had taken its effect. McRoberts can find only one or two limited references to Scottish saints like Ninian or Machar in devotional or liturgical books from the fourteenth century, granted the relatively few medieval works that have

survived. By the beginning of the sixteenth century there is a
marked difference. The *Aberdeen Breviary* of 1509-1510 was
published as a national liturgy intended to replace the English
Sarum Use books that had previously been in common liturgical
use in Scotland. In this work, ascribed to Bishop William
Elphinstone of Aberdeen, there are references to over seventy
Scottish saints drawn from all over Scotland. The Scottish
breviary devotes about one fifth of the liturgical year exclusively
to national saints. All of them are allocated to feast days and
provided with historical lessons so that the faithful would, with
patriotic pride in their own traditions, sense the saints' importance and know their place in the spiritual and national life of
Scotland. Important though Elphinstone's work is, McRoberts
sees it as only one outstanding example 'of a much more
widespread nationalist movement to revive the memory and cult
of Scottish saints' that existed long before the breviary was
produced and which continued to flourish in the decades following its publication and leading up to the Reformation in 1560.

Part of this strategy of liturgical and devotional patriotism, as
McRoberts terms it, was the deliberate encouragement of the
faithful to make pilgrimages to national shrines. The trend can
be seen in the records of royal pilgrimages, which must have set
a pattern for the devotional travels of all sections of Scottish
society. Prior to the mid-fifteenth century it was uncommon for
the Scottish kings to go on pilgrimage to Scottish shrines. Apart
from the occasional reference to local visits, like that of Robert
the Bruce to Whithorn, Scottish kings were as likely to venture
across the border on pilgrimage to Canterbury. They even went
abroad to Compostela or Rome, as Macbeth did in 1050. However,
all that changed in the second half of the fifteenth century.
Pilgrimages to a variety of Scottish shrines from Whithorn in the
south to Tain in the north, and including visits to the sites of
lesser shrines, became significant and regular events in the life
of the royal court from the reign of James III onwards.

Veneration of the nation's saints at their various shrines
throughout Scotland was not the only way in which the Church
sought to give the faithful powerful and persuasive visual
images of patriotic devotion. The nationalist message was also
reinforced through the impressive building programme of the

medieval Scottish Church in the fifteenth century. The particular medieval version of the glorious Christian vision of Scotland that we are concerned with here, was a vision of Scotland not only as a free nation but also as a famous one. The pre-Reformation Scottish Catholic Church wanted to show to the rest of Christendom that Scotland was a civilized nation, with a reputation for culture and learning as impressive as that of any of its larger neighbours.

Scottish churchmen pursued this aim during the course of the fifteenth century by building or by further embellishing so many of the nation's Collegiate churches and by establishing Scotland's three medieval universities. An insight into their patriotic motivation can be found in Hector Boece's account of the founding of the King's College in Aberdeen by the same Bishop Elphinstone of the patriotic breviary. According to Boece, the bishop founded the northern university 'to enhance the glory of the fatherland' and 'to promote the wellbeing and honour of Scotland', as well as the pursuit of learning in that part of the country. The reason for these church and educational foundations was in part the national pride arising out of a need to find a flattering cosmopolitan comparison between Scotland and the other nations of Christendom.

Even the international religious orders in fifteenth century Scotland seem to have been affected by this nationalist enthusiasm and sought to establish their own national independence by winning recognition for separate national provinces with oversight of their Scottish affairs. In this surge of national pride leading to demands for national autonomy, the religious orders were matched by the Scottish hierarchy itself, which secured archepiscopal and metropolitan status for the see of St Andrews. Seen cumulatively, these developments lead McRoberts to conclude:

> All of this fifteenth century activity in the provision of more elaborate churches, the foundation of universities, the compilation of new liturgical books, largely devoted to national saints, and the popularization of national pilgrimage sites, can only be sufficiently explained by accepting that there was a concerted effort, strongly supported by the Church, to organise

and equip the kingdom of Scotland so that it might qualify as one of the new type of sovereign states that were gradually taking shape in Christendom. Politicians and lawyers, soldiers and scholars all had their own contribution to make to this new Scotland: the Church's special contribution was to provide the spiritual background against which the new ideas might flourish.

In the fourteenth century the Scottish Church identified closely with the nation's struggle for independence and helped give birth to a triumphant vision of Scotland as a free nation. By identifying so closely with the national identity of the country, the Church in the fifteenth century was deliberately developing this original vision of a free nation along lines already suggested in the 1320 Declaration of Arbroath. That document asserted Scotland's fame on the grounds of a historical continuity of the Scots as a race with a (legendary) ancestry going back to classical and Biblical times. The distinctive later medieval version of that glorious vision of Scotland was also of a famous nation, but of a nation famed throughout Christendom for its contemporary and visible cultural achievements, which stood favourable comparison with those of any nation in Europe. In 1320 the other nations of Europe were assumed to have heard of Scotland's fame as an ancient nation. By 1520 they could see the evidence for that fame with their own eyes - in the churches and universities that demonstrated Scotland's national glory.

This is a point that is well made by McRoberts at the close of his essay on the nationalism of the Scottish Church in the medieval period. He illustrates what he sees as a fundamental change in political thinking about the nature of Christendom before and after the fifteenth century by comparing two surviving artistic works from medieval Europe: a fresco in a Dominican Church in Florence, painted about 1350, and the heraldic ceiling in St Machar's Cathedral in Aberdeen, erected about 1530. The fresco depicts in symbolic fashion the medieval concept of Christendom, with the twofold supreme authority of pope and emperor at the centre, and the lesser authorities in church and state below them, including the king of France and other princes. At the top of the picture sits Christ the King, enthroned and surrounded by angels and saints. The picture is designed to show that the unity of Christ's heavenly kingdom is reflected in the unity of his kingdom on earth. The slightly earlier Declaration of Arbroath articulates this medieval concept of Christendom in its own graphic parallels between the earthly and heavenly rule of Christ the King and Judge; and in its attempt to relate the authority of the kings of Scotland and England both to Christ's universal rule and to a loyalty owed to the Pope's universal jurisdiction. But it is a universal vision that is visibly losing its appeal in Scotland by the early sixteenth century.

The ceiling in Aberdeen, probably designed by a churchman, shows in heraldic terms 'how a Scotsman viewed Christendom at the end of the Middle Ages just before the final breakdown of medieval unity.' It is a significantly different picture from the fourteenth century one. In the centre of the three parallel rows of coats of arms stand the heraldic devices of the Church, beginning with the pope and followed by the Scottish archbishops and bishops. On one side lies the second row, the coats of arms of the great princes of Christendom, beginning with the Emperor Charles V and his imperial crown, and followed by the lesser monarchs. But on the other side, in the third row, runs the armorial bearings of the Scottish King, James V, and his nobles, with the king's shield also surmounted by an imperial crown, indicating that he exercises an imperial authority as a sovereign ruler within his own realm. The message of this powerful visual image of late medieval Scottish nationhood would be clear to all who saw it. While the Pope remains head of the Scottish Church, the Emperor is given only a courteous passing nod. The real power is now portrayed in coded heraldic terms to lie with the King of Scots. Fame indeed, in such august company!

With this telling visual comparison McRoberts succeeds in demonstrating how Scottish churchmen responded to the prevailing nationalist ideas of the time, 'by remodelling the liturgy, the devotional life of the people and other aspects of ecclesiastical life in order to emphasise as never before, the national character of the Scottish Church.' In this transition from the political world of the Florentine fresco, in which the clerical author of the Declaration of Arbroath would surely have felt at home, to the outlook of the St Machar ceiling, fostered by the fifteenth century Scottish Church, we can see the more universal glorious vision of 1320 - Scotland seen as a free nation - evolving into the distinctively national version of 1520 - Scotland seen as a famous nation. The figure of Christ the King is central to the original glorious vision of the nations, as in the Florentine fresco's portrayal of Christ enthroned in heaven and the Arbroath Declaration's affirmation of Christ as the King of Kings. The earthly kings, including Robert the Bruce, are seen as subject to the rule of Christ and his authorities on earth, whether in pope or the laws of the community.

In the later Catholic version of this triumphal vision that had taken firm hold by the sixteenth century, the identification of the Church with the earthly King of Scots was in danger of eclipsing the theological source of light in the glorious vision of Scotland, Christ the heavenly King. This was certainly the view of those sixteenth century voices calling for reform in church and nation.

A Subversive Vision - John the Commonweal

It is a presbyterian conceit that there were no cries for reform in the medieval Catholic Church before the work of the first Protestant martyrs and leaders like John Knox. In fact no one exposed how corrupt the glorious vision really was more effectively than the Catholic courtier, diplomat and dramatist Sir David Lyndsay. His play, *Ane Satyre of the Thrie Estaitis,* was first performed before the royal family in 1540, two decades ahead of the Protestant reformation in Scotland. As its name suggests, it is a biting satirical attack on the abuses of power, wealth and morality by the old Kirk and its clergy, at a time when the Church owned about half the national revenue and its senior churchmen were notorious for their libertine ways. The play made a telling and very popular call for social and spiritual reform without challenging the existing doctrines and structures of the Roman Church.

Kurt Wittig provides a concise summary of Lyndsay's attack on the corruption of the three estates of the realm in Scotland, the lords spiritual and temporal and the burgesses. The play begins with the king, Rex Humanitas, under the spell of the deceitful vices, while the virtues of truth and chastity are suppressed and the poor exploited in his lawless kingdom. The tide turns when Divine Correction arrives and the Parliament of the Three Estates is summoned to institute vital reforms. John the Commonweal, a figure representing the people and true Christian piety, exposes the vices of the nation's leaders; covetousness and sensuality among the clergy, public oppression among the secular lords and falsity and deceit among the burgesses. When the reform measures advocated by John the Commonweal with passionate appeal to the Gospel are put into force, his most vehement opponents are the clergy. It is their vested interests that are most threatened by the reforms.

Wittig notes one feature of the play that is very significant for our understanding of the Catholic vision of the nation on the eve of the Reformation. While Lyndsay does not challenge the dogma of the Church, 'he calls for the translation of the Bible as a source of truth. Characteristically, the Vices in the *Three Estates* quote the saints more frequently than the Virtues do.' Here we can note an important shift in Christian thinking about national identity. Unlike the movement of liturgical nationalism in the fifteenth century, devotion to saints was now seen as a cover for the spiritual corruption in the life of church and nation. In the *Three Estates* there is the recognition that a vision of the nation based on visual images can easily become an illusion based on idolatry. It is John the Commonweal who speaks out most effectively against this distorted vision and subverts it with little favourable reference to the Church and its saints and much quoting of Christ and the New Testament.

Here we see the break with the medieval Catholic version of the Glorious Vision of Scotland. That way of thinking about Scotland as a famous nation depended on a close identification between the Church and the nation. It relied on the cultivation of a strong national identity on the part of the Church. The original vision expressed in the Declaration of Arbroath and in Barbour's poem *The Bruce*, was fired by a high sense of moral and spiritual purpose. There was no uncritical alliance with the nation and its leaders, right or wrong. The Declaration stated boldy that if even Robert the Bruce himself betrayed the cause of freedom, he would be deposed and a more faithful king put in his place. Barbour's poem recognised that patriotism was a virtue only when united with the cause of freedom and justice. But that critical and prophetic note was lost to the Glorious Vision when the Church became more and more enmeshed in the structures of power and wealth in Scotland as an inevitable consequence of its policy of national identification. The free nation of the original vision became the famous nation of the later version. By the mid-sixteenth century, a vision based on projecting the national image had become increasingly unacceptable to many Scottish Christians within and outwith the old Church. Like John the Commonweal, they began to turn not to national images but to the Biblical word for a new vision of Scotland. With this move, new life was breathed into the Glorious Vision of a nation united by a common spiritual purpose under Christ the King. Out of the womb of the old Catholic vision of a free nation, the Reformed vision of a godly nation was born. As that vision grew in strength, a triumphant Christian nation was on the march to glory once more.

Chapter 3

THE REFORMED VISION - A Godly Nation

To understand the kind of national vision that replaced the old Catholic vision at the Scottish Reformation in 1560 we need to travel forward in time from then to our own day and one of the sublime ironies of recent church history.

When the Pope met the Moderator of the General Assembly in May 1982, he was welcomed under the gaze of John Knox in the courtyard of New College, Edinburgh. The press photographers and TV cameramen made sure they framed their shots of the historic meeting against the background of Knox's statue. The commentators could not resist asking what he would have made of it all. Yet the real irony did not lie in the contrast of modern ecumenism and militant Protestantism in the juxtaposition of the three churchmen. No, it lay in the fact that for most Scots today it is not John Paul, Bishop of Rome, but John Knox, Reformer from Calvin's Geneva, who offends the nation's sensibilities. How times, and Scotland, have changed!

The statue in question was erected by late Victorian Scots who were, in their own words, mindful of the benefits conferred by John Knox on their native land. It is just such claims of benign national influence that are so fiercely contested by modern Scots men and women. Until earlier in this century Knox was still revered as the key figure not only in the religious history but also the national identity of the Scots. The Rev John Ker, writing on Scottish nationality in 1887, could claim that Wallace made a nation and Knox a people, 'in which he implanted the religious principles that have since been associated with the name of Scotland wherever it is known, and that have given it a place in the world out of all proportion to its extent, or population, or material resources.' The Midlothian Journal of the 26th of November, 1909, could still express public sentiments about Knox like the following: 'The civil and religious freedom we boast of, the fairer outlook upon the world that we enjoy, and the independence of thought and action that are peculiarly Scottish were won for us largely through the instrumentality of the great man whose memory Scotsmen have determined to keep green and fresh in the minds of their countrymen.' It is precisely there, in the minds of their countrymen and women, that more recent critics of Knox have seen his malign influence. The popular memory of the Knoxian vision of Scotland seems to be not evergreen but dark and rancid.

Knox has become the scapegoat for every pathological trait in the Scottish identity. As Alan Bold, the literary critic from Markinch in Fife, observed in a recent study of the notoriously divided Scottish personality that is so familiar a subject in modern Scottish literature:

> The divided Scot needed heroes and villains. Knox is probably the best known villain and has featured as such in a play by Bridie, a meditative book by Fionn Mac Colla, the poems of Edwin Muir and Iain Crichton Smith, the stories of George Mackay Brown. In *Knox* (2) Alan Jackson put the matter succinctly:
> > O Knox he was a bad man
> > he split the Scottish mind.
> > The one half he made cruel
> > and the other half unkind.

Of course, as Bold himself goes on to comment, 'Knox did nothing of the kind, though the identification of one man with all the ills of the nation is symptomatic of national uncertainty.'

It is also a sign of the uncertain and changing relationship between Kirk and nation in the more secular world of our time. This literary Scot's trumpet blast against the monstrous regiment of Knox and his vision of Scotland is a last cultural shudder after the uncoupling of Knox's national Kirk from the main engine of national life. For most Scots today, the Kirk is relegated to a private branch line for the few spiritual steam enthusiasts who still enjoy runs with that dear old C. of S. preservation society, better renamed the National (Ecclesiastical) Trust for Scotland. It is inconceivable that John Knox himself would have tolerated such a fate. His Reformed vision for national life arrived in Edinburgh in 1560 like *The Flying*

Scotsman under full steam and changed all the timetables in our national history.

The Knoxian Vision - a Godly Paradox

1560 marks both a dramatic break and a point of continuity in the history of the relationship between Christian and national identity. The Protestant Reformation of Church and nation that came to power in that year is inseparable from two influences, the continuing legacy and geopolitics of Christendom, and the life and thought of John Knox.

In the Reformed or Calvinist vision of the nation associated with Knox and his successors, we can find all the distinctive features of the original Glorious Christian Vision of Scotland that arose in the fourteenth century. The Reformed vision continued to operate in terms of the medieval model of church and society going back to the Roman emperor Constantine, where society was seen as the *corpus Christianum* in which church and state formed the one inclusive Christian community within Christendom. The reformers did not throw out that Constantinian offspring with the bathwater of medieval corruption. Nor did they leave behind that other setting for the medieval vision of Scottish nationhood, Scotland's relationship with its more powerful English neighbour. Church-state and Anglo-Scottish relations set the common boundaries for a continuing triumphant Christian vision of national identity before and after 1560.

Yet we can also detect a marked change in Knox's version of that vison. No longer would the vision of a Christian nation come about through the identification of the Church with the past history and political triumph of the nation. Now it would be realised in Scotland through the preaching of the Word of God and through national examples drawn from Israel's history, not from the earlier Scottish struggle for independence, or Scottish traditions of saintly piety so dear to the later medieval Catholic vision. Although Knox clearly drew on certain Scottish traditions when they complemented his Biblical approach to nationhood, particularly in the parallels between the old Scottish custom of banding together in a common cause and the religious concept of covenanting together with God, his vision was primarily a theological and not a nationalist one.

Central to Knox's glorious vision of a triumphant Christian nation was the same high theology of Christ the King as Lord of the nations that we found in the Declaration of Arbroath. As he wrote in his *Letter to the Commonality of Scotland*, calling on them to carry out the work of reformation in the face of idolatrous rulers, 'Of kings and judges it is required that they kiss the Son, that is, give honour, subjection, and obedience to him, and from such reverence the subject is not exempted.' All are subject to the rule of Christ the King and Lord.

Knox also adhered to the second characteristic feature of the Glorious Vision - the conviction that the whole life of the nation should be shaped and governed by a single spiritual and moral purpose. For the fourteenth century Catholic vision, that meant commitment to a free nation and to a patriotism grounded in that noble thing Barbour called freedom and loyalty to a universal sense of justice. For Knox, the vision was of a godly common-wealth in which the whole people were to be subject to godliness in every aspect of life in church, state and society. This Re-formed vision of the godly nation permeates one of Knox's letters to the Scottish Lords in which he reminds them:

> The fear of God resides also in the hearts of all those
> inspired by God, and who with reverence receive the
> counsel and admonitions given by God's messengers
> who are determined to obey his holy will...   The
> wholesome counsel and admonition of God is given
> for the removal of iniquity, the reformation of tempo-
> ral privileges, and conservation of realms and com-
> monwealths... In order that society may be governed
> with Godly purpose, God appoints and sends to battle
> his best and most approved soldiers.

Godly preachers of God's counsel and godly rulers governing according to God's laws were both needed in the new Scotland of the Knoxian vision. True to the glorious vision of Christian nationhood, the whole life of the country was to be shot through with the moral and spiritual purpose of godliness.

Recent historical scholarship has thrown fascinating new light on Knox and his vision of Scottish nationhood. Two lines of interpretation of Knox's thought must be brought together to understand his approach to reforming church and nation in Scotland. The American author Arthur H. Williamson argues that Knox seems to have favoured a union between the two kingdoms of Scotland and England under a Protestant British Crown. Influenced by English reformers with whom he shared an exile on the continent while the two countries were under Catholic regimes, Knox may have embraced their apocalyptic vision that England had a prophesied place in the scriptural revelation of the end times - through a godly monarch who, like a second Constantine, would defeat the anti-Christ and complete the work of reforming and defending Christendom against its enemies, both Pope and Turk. The political future of a reformed Scotland lay, therefore, in a Protestant union with imperial England.

This alone would suggest that Knox was no Scottish nationalist, identifying with those earlier medieval Scottish churchmen who sided with Bruce in the fourteenth century Scottish wars of Independence against England. This thought is confirmed by the work of another American historian, Richard L. Greaves. In his study of John Knox and Scottish nationalism, Professor Greaves draws on the work of the Catholic historian referred to in the last chapter, Monsignor David McRoberts, to contrast the strongly nationalistic spirit of the fifteenth century Scottish Kirk with the singular lack of it in Knox himself. As we have seen, McRoberts demonstrated the extent to which the nationalist sentiment and ideas that accompanied the ascendancy of nation-states in late medieval Europe influenced the Scottish Church. It strongly supported Scotland's separate and national identity within Christendom by cultivating a distinctively Scottish image in its liturgy, piety and general church life. It also showed an early commitment to the political and diplomatic cause of independence. Knox's own approach to Scottish nationhood was markedly different and more complex.

Greaves argues that Knox tempered the nationalist spirit in Scottish religion. In part this was due to Knox's own personal experience. He had spent significant parts of his life in England and in exile on the continent. This left its mark not only on his spoken accent but also on his mental outlook. What Greaves draws out of Knox's thinking is the distinctive and central emphasis on the divine precepts of the Word of God as the sole motivation for carrying out the work of reform in Scotland.

In his several written appeals from exile to the different classes in Scottish society to take up the cause of reformation, Knox does not draw on patriotic sentiment, as Luther did in his appeal to the German nobility, but directs Lord and commoner alike to the Old Testament precedents for prophetic action by a godly people against idolatrous rulers. While Knox does seem to have been susceptible to the English nationalism of Protestant reformers south of the border and therefore favourable to a British union, he sought to reform the Scottish Kirk and nation on Biblical and not nationalist grounds, according to the Word of God. In his appeals to the Scots to reform church and nation, Knox did not draw on stories of Bruce and Wallace and the nation's earlier struggle for independence from an alien foreign power, or on an ancient Celtic Christian tradition free from the see of Rome, as he might well have done in rejecting French Catholic rule and Papal authority in Scotland. No, Knox drew on stories from the Bible, especially the Old Testament, stories of Israel rejecting idolatry, stories of the early Church resisting the anti-Christ, to motivate Scottish Christians. But, according to Greaves, that had a paradoxical effect on Scottish national identity, the Knoxian paradox.

The Knoxian paradox, in relation to Scottish nationalism, is that while Knox himself sought to give Scotland a Biblical and Reformed faith and Kirk, the theology, church and culture that derived from this approach was soon to take on a distinctive national character. Greaves has concluded:

> The key to Knox's actions and beliefs is thus his adherence to the divine will above all else. This principle transcended any concerns whether ecumenical or nationalist in nature. His devotion to truth as he saw it prompted him to develop in Scotland a Kirk with an eclectic foundation... It so happened that that Kirk was well suited to the growing spirit of Scottish nationalism... Knox's statements about the covenant obligations of a commonwealth to God helped lay the foundation for the later development of the notion of

Scotland as a covenanted nation. Paradoxically the
eclectic foundation of theology and polity which Knox
contributed to the Kirk of Scotland made it *sui generis*
and thus a suitable vehicle for the expression of
Scottish national consciousness.

Nowhere do we find this Knoxian vision of national reformation
better expressed than in the post-Reformation motto of Glasgow. Like that city, Scotland was to flourish through the preaching of God's Word and the praising of his name. The Reformed
vision of Knox and his successors undoubtedly sought the
transformation of national life through the application of the
gospel and laws of God. This vision was rooted in the Knoxian
and Calvinist principle that the Word of God applied to the
whole of life in both church and society - to the commoner, lord
and ruler in secular affairs as much as to the religious life of the
believer. The Knoxian and Reformed concern for popular education, the welfare of the poor, the conduct of the magistrate and
monarch in national affairs, all of these concerns reflect this
vision of the transforming effect of the Word of God in nurturing
the godly life of the nation.

However, and here is the paradoxical effect of such an
approach, this Knoxian vision of the Word of God fashioning a
godly commonwealth through godly rulers and preachers had a
distinctively Scottish result. In time, a uniquely Scottish religious and cultural ethos and identity developed, what the sociologist John Highet has called 'the Presbyterian nation.' The
Reformed Kirk, having set out to create a Reformed nation
acccording to the Word of God, became so closely identified
with its own creation that within a century and a half it became
difficult to tell them apart. Not without struggle during the
course of the seventeenth century, as Presbyterian and Episco-
palian parties fought for control of the national Kirk, Scotland
took on a new national identity, enshrined in the Westminster
Confession of Faith and set hard in the popular imagination by
strict adherence to Calvinist orthodoxy and rejection of bishops.
So successful was the transformation that by 1707 the two
identities of Presbyterian and Scottish came to be regarded as
virtually synonymous in the national mind. At the Treaty of
Union with England in that year, Scotland would only enter a

British union if a key element in its continuing national identity, the Presbyterian and Calvinist nature of its national Kirk, was guaranteed for all time. This is an ironic achievement for a Reformation that did not set out to be nationalistic. It is to that irony that we now turn.

The Godly Vision - a Covenanted Nation

The vision of transforming the whole of national life according to the Word of God was a dynamic force in Scottish society that brought many benefits in character and culture. The emphasis on the Bible, preaching and the catechising of the population in correct theological belief, and the related importance of widespread literacy and parish schools, were major factors in the growth of the democratic intellect, a Scottish educational tradition open to different social classes. This tradition stressed the importance of a general education in philosophy and facility in abstract thought for all students, giving rise to the metaphysical cast of the Scottish mind and identity which our more empiricist and utilitarian southern neighbours find so alien. The emphasis on the priesthood of all believers, the equality of all men and women before God, and the participation of laymen as elders in the government of the church, fostered a more egalitarian and democratic outlook, albeit within the constraints of the existing social order, in the life of church and nation.

The Calvinist stress on the responsibility of the local parish church for the welfare of the poor within the community, and the responsibility of the preacher to apply the Word of God to the affairs of the community and nation, meant a theological tradition in Scotland which was concerned with questions of justice in society as much as with justification by faith. The Scottish theological mind rejected any split or dualism in a proper Christian concern for the affairs of both the divinely predestined human soul and the divinely ordained state. The characteristic emphasis by Knox and his successors on the Old Testament and history of Israel as a model for national reformation led to an acute sense of God's active involvement in the affairs of people and nations. However it also led to a blurring of the distinctions between ecclesiastical and national issues. The late Professor Ian Henderson made this point well in his book, *Power without Glory*:

> There is one final and fateful consequence of the acceptance of the Old Testament as a blueprint for Scotland. The Old Testament is the story of a nation which ceased to be a nation and became a church. It is hardly surprising if Scotland, having taken the Old Testament as a political handbook, has met with a like fate. In the mid-seventeenth century the Scots followed the Old Testament to the extent of transposing political and national realities into an ecclesiastical key.

Scotland came to be seen in the 1630s and after as a nation with a special covenanted relationship with the Almighty. The National Covenant of 1638, first signed in Greyfriars Church, Edinburgh, is as important a document for understanding the Reformed vision of Scotland as a godly nation, as the Declaration of Arbroath is for grasping the earlier Catholic vision of a free nation. In the National Covenant, a protest against the Scottish church and nation policies of King Charles I, Scotland was once more declared to be a nation under the Word of God. Apart from the diplomatic wish to maintain 'the Kings Majesty, His Person and Estate', the signatories of the National Covenant declared their purpose in forming 'a general band' was:

> for defending the true Religion, as it was then reformed, and is expressed in the Confession of Faith abovewritten, and a former large Confession established by sundry acts of lawfull generall assemblies, & of Parliament, unto which it hath relation, set down in Publick Catechismes, and which had been for many years with a blessing from Heaven preached, and professed in this Kirk and Kingdome, as Gods undoubted truth, grounded only upon his written Word.

With such an exalted sense of the role of religion in national life, it became increasingly hard to distinguish between the cause of true religion and the cautious pursuit of Scotland's national interests in the complex world of politics and statecraft. This tendency to transpose national questions into an ecclesiastical key is evident no matter what kind of churchmanship dominated the Kirk at any particular period, from the seventeenth to the nineteenth centuries.

The radical Presbyterians who strongly influenced Scottish political life during the 1640s pressed for a religious settlement for the rest of the British Isles that would have brought England and Ireland into presbyterian conformity with Scotland, as a condition of Scottish military support for the English Parliamentary forces against Charles I. The resulting Solemn League and Covenant of 1643 typifies this Scottish tendency to perceive military and political questions of statecraft in religious and ecclesiastical terms. The conquest, occupation and forced union of Scotland with England by Oliver Cromwell in the 1650s shows the cost of this adherence to the notion of a covenanted nation for Scotland's independence. The later Covenanters of the Killing Times, during the reigns of Charles II and James VII, continued to adhere to the vision of Scotland as a covenanted nation at great personal cost and long after it had ceased to be a concept uniting the Scots in a common national consciousness. But the passage from the more violent years of religious conflict in the seventeenth century into the calmer waters of the eighteenth century Enlightenment did not mean the abandoning of this tendency in the Reformed vision of Scotland to conceive of national interests primarily in terms of the interests of the national church.

At the time of the Union of the Parliaments in 1707 questions of national independence were once more transposed into ecclesiastical terms by leading churchmen like William Carstares, who wrote in a letter of 1706, 'The desire I have to see our church secured makes me in love with the Union as the most probable means to preserve it...' His modern biographer Ian Dunlop has written:

> Had the Church thrown its weight and influence against the Union it is exceedingly unlikely that it would ever have passed. At this point, Carstares probably played a decisive part in persuading the ministers not to take action. Greater danger for the Church and nation lay in Scotland's being independent and soon, in all likelihood Jacobite (which proba-

bly meant being Papist and a limb of France) than in
Union with England whose Church although prelati-
cal was strongly anti-Roman.

And so in 1707 many in church and nation thought like Carstares
that the Act of Security, ensuring the Presbyterian government
and Protestant confession of the Kirk as the established national
Church of Scotland within the British Union, was a sufficient
guarantee of continuing national autonomy and the safeguard-
ing of national interests. It must be borne in mind that the Kirk
of that time played a major part in the local administration of
national life, especially in the spheres of welfare and education,
and therefore its continuing establishment and autonomy had
secular as well as religious implications.

   While acknowledging the widespread popular protest at the
Union, from burghs, presbyteries, and the city mobs, it must also
be borne in mind that the Scottish Parliament had had a rather
inglorious record as an independent force in national affairs for
most of its history and therefore did not command the level of
popular support that the Kirk did as a national institution. It is
not fanciful to see in these events the continuing legacy of both
the Knoxian paradox and the covenant nation - the tendency to
elide the interests of church and nation into purely ecclesiastical
terms under the Old Testament vision of the godly nation under
the Word of God, while recognising the attractions of a British
union for such a Protestant vision of Scotland, as Knox may well
have done himself a hundred and fifty years before.

   Similarly, during the church-state conflicts of the early nineteenth century, in the years leading up to the Disruption of the
Kirk in 1843, legitimate political questions about the treatment
of Scottish affairs by an overwhelmingly English Westminister
Parliament were transposed almost exclusively into ecclesiastical and British terms. As the historian Monica Clough has
observed about the events surrounding 1843, ' ...what might
have developed into a declaration of independence, had there
been leaders more concerned with the underlying political
implications than with religious ones, merely turned into the
Disruption of the Kirk, and not the rupture of the state.' It took
a Scottish philosopher of the time, Professor J. F. Ferrier of St

Andrews University, to recognise the constitutional nature of the Disruption controversy, in a pamphlet *Church and State* which he published in 1848. It was not until the mid-nineteenth century, perhaps as the national cost of that schism became more evident after the initial euphoria of the event itself, that some Scottish churchmen stopped perceiving the national questions bound up in the Disruption in exclusively ecclesiastical terms.

For example, in the years after 1843 a leading Evangelical minister who came out at the Disruption and was prominent in the Free Church, the Rev Dr James Begg, began to see a connection between the ecclesiastical problems of Scotland and the way in which the country was governed. This is evident from the title of one of his pamphlets, *A Violation of the Treaty of Union: the Main Origin of our Ecclesiastical Divisions and Other Evils*. Only a few years after the Disruption he advocated the devolution of executive powers to Scotland and even the establishment of a legislative body 'to dispose of purely Scottish questions' if no executive reforms were forthcoming from Westminster. In the judgement of H.J. Hanham, a historian of Scottish nationalism, when Begg published these views in 1850, this marked the first modern Scottish nationalist agitation. In the next few years it led on to the setting up of 'the first effective nationalist movement', the National Association for the Vindication of Scottish Rights, founded in 1853, of which Begg was a supporter. But this unravelling of the affairs of church and nation in the mind of one who still adhered to the Reformed vision of the godly nation came too late to save the vision itself when, as we shall see, it broke apart in 1843.

Before looking at the Disruption and its effect on the Godly vision of Scotland in greater depth, something further must be noted. It is important to recognise, within the Reformed tradition's tendency to confuse the interests of church and nation in the one godly commonwealth, three different ways in which the church was seen to relate to the nation. From the seventeenth to the nineteenth centuries, we can see different groups within the Reformed tradition: taking a strongly separatist stance in relation to the main body of the nation; strongly identifying with the established order within the nation; and earnestly seeking the transformation of national life.

(a) Separatist

The Cameronian Covenanters of the later seventeenth century became an increasingly separatist remnant in loyalty to what they saw as the binding and perpetual national covenants of 1638 and 1643 and in opposition to what they saw as an apostate nation of covenant-breakers under an uncovenanted monarch. These later Covenanters, to be distinguished from the broad social spectrum represented in the early Covenanters who signed the 1638 National Covenant, still adhered passionately to what I have termed the Glorious Vision of Christian nationhood. That is, they exalted Christ as the Lord over the nations and their rulers, and believed that the nation should find its true identity by adhering to spiritual and moral principle, enshrined for them in the Covenants of 1638 and 1643. As they declared at Sanquhar on the 22nd of June, 1680, in rejecting the rule of Charles II and his brother and heir, the Duke of York:

> ... as the representative of the true presbyterian kirk and covenanted nation of Scotland... do by thir presents disown Charles Stuart... As also, we being under the standard of our Lord Jesus Christ, Captain of salvation, do declare a war with such a tyrant and usurper and the men of his practices, as enemies to our Lord Jesus Christ... As also we disown, and by this resent the reception of the Duke of York, that professed papist, as repugnant to our principles and vows to the most high God, and as that which is the great, though not alone, just reproach of our kirk and nation.

Couched in language not dissimilar to that of the much earlier Catholic document, the Declaration of Arbroath, which also threatened to disown the Scottish King, Robert the Bruce, if he abandoned the nation's cause and principles, the Sanquhar Declaration bears all the marks of the glorious vision of nationhood shared by both Catholic and Reformed traditions alike. However, it was the work not of the great ecclesiastical servants of state, as in 1320, but of a despised minority. As they were to declare again at Sanquhar in 1685, they saw themselves as, '... the contending and suffering remnant of the true presbyterians of the church...a poor wasted, wronged, wounded, reproached,

despised and bleeding remnant...setting ourselves against all
injuries and affronts done to our Lord Jesus Christ...'

As J.D. Douglas has written, in his history of these Covenanters, they were able to continue in their increasingly desperate
resistance to a hostile state, 'heartened by their unflinching
confidence that "God... still leaned from heaven to observe the
doings of His moorland remnant".' A starker position of
separation from the nation could hardly be imagined, and yet still
these men and women adhered to the Reformed vision of a godly
nation under faithful preachers and God-fearing rulers. It is even
more impossible to imagine the established Kirk of the succeeding century seeing itself as a moorland remnant within the
nation.

(b) Identified

In total contrast with the later separatist Covenanters, although still within the bounds of the Reformed vision of Scotland as a godly nation, the Moderates, the dominant church party
in the Kirk's life from the mid-eighteenth century, identified
closely with the renascent cultural life and ruling social order of
Scotland. Rejecting the spirit of dogmatic religious conflict in
church and state which characterised the previous century, the
Moderates believed that the Church should be a source of moral
improvement in a more enlightened age. They steered clear of
any conflict with the British state, even in church matters. In
1712 (1711 depending on dating) the British Parliament passed an
act restoring the ancient system of patronage in ministerial
appointments that had been abolished by the Scottish Parliament
in 1690. The controversy over patronage became a growing root
of bitterness in eighteenth century church life, with an increasing
number of Calvinist secessions from the established Kirk as the
century progressed, despite the General Assembly's annual
protest to Parliament over the law. The Moderates accepted the
reintroduction of patronage as the law of the land with which a
creative church compromise was possible.

In their version of the Reformed vision of national life, the
fundamental Moderate principle was the integration of church
and community in the harmonious whole of civil society, through
social discipline, ecclesiastical order and moral improvement.

In a study of the Scottish Enlightenment and the Church's role in it, Anand Chitnis has written that the the Moderates, 'wished Christianity to be a crucial influence in society - especially a society that was undergoing all the economic and social change of mid-eighteenth century Scotland.' That Christian influence was to be achieved through an institutional and intellectual identification with the nation. For the Moderates,

> ... the Church was not only to interpenetrate society, but itself bore an analogy to society. Their ideal was a broad-based and undogmatic Kirk, with the Assembly being the focus for all aspects of national life. Their notions concorded well with the thoughts of the Scottish Enlightenment.

While no church party could be further removed from the later Covenanters than the Moderates, it is fascinating that we find in the latter the same conviction that the Church should play such a central role in unifying national life. They moved away from the old theocratic notion of a covenant nation but their vision of an enlightened nation was still conceived of in ecclesiastical terms. One reason why they may have been willing to tolerate patronage, apart from the practical benefit that patrons tended to choose Moderate ministers to fill their pulpits, was their concern to preserve the remaining autonomy and powers of the Kirk in Scottish civil society. They had no wish to provoke the State to further involvement in internal church affairs that were already subject to careful control by Moderate church leaders.

The Moderates were led by outstanding figures in that renaissance of learning known as the Scottish Enlightenment, such as William Robertson, historian, principal of Edinburgh University, moderator of the Kirk's General Assembly, and friend of the sceptical philosopher, David Hume. Their involvement in the philosophical and social developments of the time represents a distinguished phase in the old Reformed vision of shaping the whole life of the nation, potentially a second Reformation with as profound an influence on the life of Scotland as the first. Yet their identification with the nation was to prove a two-edged sword. The willingness of the Moderates to accept what was to many Scots the unacceptable, the intrusion of ministers by patrons on unwilling congregations, and the rise of the other

Popular or Evangelical party in opposition to both theological Moderatism and church patronage, weakened their influence and finally ended their long hegemony over Kirk affairs. By the 1830s the Evangelicals were in the majority in the General Assembly.

(c) Transforming

The Evangelical Party that supplanted the Moderates in power and influence within the Kirk as the nineteenth century unfolded, held to the Moderates' vision of an integrated Scottish society and an established national Kirk within the British Union. They rejected patronage and compromise with the British state as the means of realising it. Primarily they sought to transform the life of the nation rather than identify uncritically with its laws and social order. The Evangelicals saw the national Church continuing to shape the structures of national life in a fast- emerging urban, industrial society as it had done within the burghs and rural parishes of the old economy. This was to be achieved through the establishment by the Kirk of new parishes and centres of urban mission in the burgeoning industrial areas of central Scotland. The most able and energetic exponent of the Evangelical vision of a rejuvenated national Establishment of religion in this urban age was Thomas Chalmers.

An evangelical experience of conversion while serving as a parish minister at Kilmany in his native Fife led Chalmers away from his earlier Moderate outlook towards the Calvinist vision of a nation reformed by the Word of God. Chalmers never lost the Moderate concern for learning and intellectual enquiry but after his conversion he married it to the Evangelical and older Covenanting concern for godliness in personal and national life. In this sense Chalmers was distinct, embracing in his own life and synthesising these two different strands in the Reformed approach to nationhood within his own social vision.

Chalmers believed that the godly parish of his native Fife could be transposed into the heartland of industrial Scotland. He argued that such new urban parishes could continue to meet all the educational, welfare, spiritual and pastoral needs of the new urban masses in place of government provision of schools or poor relief. To that end, he persuaded the authorities to establish a new parish of St John's in the crowded east end of Glasgow as a model for his social vision. He mobilised the concerned Evangelical middle classes of the city to assist him in visiting and caring for the poor. Due to his own prodigious energy and organising skills, and the huge pulling power of his preaching and lecturing, it worked, after a fashion. But under the intolerable twin strains of patronage and poverty on the Kirk's life and resources, coupled with the indifference of both the British state and the working classes to his schemes for parish expansion, Chalmers' dream of the established Church adapting the rural model of the godly parish to the new industrial communities was never realised on a national scale. It lost its social dynamism and plausibility with the break-up of the established national Church, Chalmers' own chosen instrument for godly reform.

The Disruption - the Death of the Godly Vision

The Reformed vision of Scotland as a godly nation, where Kirk and people were one, died on the 18th of May 1843, at the Disruption of the Church of Scotland. When Thomas Chalmers rose to follow the Moderator and lead the Evangelicals out of the General Assembly of the Kirk, over the question of the freedom of Christ's Church from State intervention in its affairs, it was not only one of the noblest acts of sacrifice in the name of Christian principle in the history of Scotland or any other nation, as ministers left their manses and stipends, and members their parish churches, to face an uncertain future in the new Free Church of Scotland. It was also a national tragedy.

Chalmers was the last Scottish churchman to advocate a comprehensive and coherent version of the old Calvinist vision of church and nation as one Christian community that stood any chance of being realised in a modern society. Central to his vision was the national establishment of the one Kirk, supported by the State, embracing the whole community, including the poor and the urban working classes, within its local parishes. By leaving that established national Kirk at the Disruption, Chalmers was not only asserting the right of Christ as the sole King and Head of His Church, and freeing the Kirk from the shackles of state control, as he saw it. He was also destroying his own vision of the nation as a godly commonwealth united in every community through one local parish church and its provision of schools and poor relief. A divided Kirk simply could not meet the spiritual, educational and welfare needs of the whole Scottish people, as Chalmers had envisaged and striven for in his brilliant campaign for church extension over many years before 1843. Its divided members could only compete for the spiritual allegiance of the people and channel resources into duplicating churches and schools throughout the country.

By 1845 the corpse of the historic Reformed vision of the godly nation had been buried; the undertakers were, ironically, Chalmers' own Free Kirk and, not surprisingly, the British state. In that year the Free Church of Scotland abandoned its leader's social vision of comprehensive spiritual and social care for the urban poor and working class. And the State took over from the divided and now shrunken established Church responsibility for the welfare of the poor in Scottish society. The death of the Godly vision had profound implications for the national life and identity of Scotland.

The Disruption of the Kirk has been described as the most far-reaching single event of the century for Scotland. Until that point, the historic Reformed vision of the nation as a godly commonwealth gave Scotland its national ethos. Reviewing a recent book on the history of nineteenth century Scotland, Michael Fry wrote:

> In 1832 anybody could identify the Scottish ethos. It was rooted in Calvinism, and the Calvinist culture was as yet serious and fertile. Like any such culture it was also complex and full of tensions. But contradiction did not necessarily mean incoherence. On the contrary, whether people were disputing theology or affairs of state, or such mundane matters as improving the schools, looking after the poor or reforming the town councils, they still could and did refer to a set of common values, arguing from and within them even to dissimilar conclusions.

By the time of the First World War, when the Presbyterian churches of the established Kirk and the now United Free Church were still separated, 'in religion, and in intellectual life generally, there was little left that could be seriously called Scottish, and certainly no serious Calvinist culture', according to Fry. While I shall take issue with this last judgement in the next chapter, the point is well made that in the era of the Disruption the Kirk was crippled as the dynamic force in generating Scotland's national identity and ethos. Why should this have been the case?

Ecclesiastical and religious issues are, of course, central to understanding the departure of many Evangelicals from the established Kirk to form their own national church in exile, the Free Church of Scotland, in 1843. They asserted in the Claim of Right passed by the General Assembly in 1842 that they were resisting the claims of the State to intervene in internal Kirk affairs such as the creation of new parishes or the appointment of parish ministers, in the name of Christ, who alone was the the King and Head of the Church. They perceived the Disruption as a national question in as much as it concerned the national church's relations with the state. However, the Disruption can also be understood in terms of a wider nineteenth century crisis of Scottish nationhood and identity.

When Chalmers led the Evangelicals out of the Kirk on that May afternoon in 1843, it was not just the death of the Calvinist vision of Scotland and the start of almost a hundred years of Presbyterian denominational rivalry and disunity over church-state relations. It was also the end of almost three hundred years of Scottish history in which the established Kirk had been the country's 'most comprehensive institution and bulwark of its culture.' As Stewart J. Brown, a recent biographer, has argued, the Evangelical leader Thomas Chalmers embodied the Reformed vision of the role of the Kirk in the life of the nation. The vision found expression in his own social ideal of a godly commonwealth 'with well-defined programmes for the reorganisation of the nation'. Such programmes of church extension and the parochial provision of local welfare and education offered the established Kirk a way of responding creatively to the immense social and spiritual needs of rapidly expanding urban populations, without listening to what Chalmers held to be the siren calls for state intervention to solve these problems. By supporting the Disruption and adhering to his view of church-state relations, Chalmers was also caught in the tragedy of destroying his own work over many years. Without the national establishment of religion in one national church, embracing the whole community, he could not realise his own Christian vision of the nation as a godly commonwealth.

There are many flaws in Chalmers' parish model of godly reform, especially in the way he accepted some of the economic, demographic and social welfare theories of his time. As a high Tory, he was also hostile to the calls for greater democracy and workers' rights coming from the Chartist and other radical movements of the time, supported by the lone and prophetic voice within the established Church of the Rev Patrick Brewster of Paisley Abbey. Nevertheless, Chalmers' vision of the nation as a godly commonwealth even in an industrial age represents the last serious and fertile attempt to understand and transform Scotland in terms of a Christian community. There were other Christian social reformers after Chalmers who were active in national affairs, some of them radical and democratic in outlook, like Patrick Brewster, but the national rather than local or single-issue focus of their thought and action was often lacking, due to the absence of a credible and socially plausible model of church and nation in an age of massive social upheaval. This can be seen from Stewart Brown's verdict on the fate of Chalmers' vision of Scotland as a Christian nation:

> Chalmers failed to realise his vision of the godly commonwealth. His life was, in one sense, a tragic disappointment. He lived long enough to witness the collapse of the church extension campaign of 1838, the breakup of the establishment in 1843, the rejection of his social ideal by the majority of the Free Church in 1845, and the failure of his final interdenominational campaign by 1846. After his death in 1847, his godly commonwealth vision faded rapidly from the public imagination, lost amid the sectarian controversies of the later nineteenth century, and overshadowed by the new materialistic visions of capitalism and state socialism.

It is significant that Brown sees the Disruption and Chalmers' passing as the fading from the public imagination of the old

Reformed way of imagining Scotland, as a nation in the Christian style of community, a godly commonwealth under the Word of God. Although many Scots continued to think and speak of their country as a Christian nation shaped by this theological vision long after 1843, the social and intellectual reality was of a country marching to the beat of different drummers. The Church of Scotland handed over its welfare and educational work to the State, in 1845 and 1872 respectively, in part because its local parishes were no longer seen as embracing the allegiance of society as a whole. Large sections of the nineteenth century Scottish population were now to be found within the denominations of disaffected Presbyterians or in the immigrant Irish Roman Catholic community, or living outwith the influence of any church in poor urban, working class communities. The Kirk and its other major Presbyterian rivals, the Free Church and the United Presbyterians (a union of earlier secessions from the national Church), became increasingly preoccupied by denominational and doctrinal conflicts at home and missionary work abroad in the far flung corners of the British Empire. The fierce Victorian debates about whether the Kirk should be established by law or a voluntary body free of the State, and the growing alarm at the rise of critical study of the Bible among church scholars, these narrower ecclesiastical issues replaced the central concern of Chalmers and the earlier Reformed tradition, both Moderate and Evangelical, Knoxian and Covenanting, to implement a unifying national vision in church and society.

In the Victorian and Edwardian decades after Chalmers and the Disruption, there was no serious theological and national (rather than merely ecclesiastical and nostalgic) vision and model of Scotland forthcoming from the Reformed tradition. The churches were increasingly seen to be reacting to, rather than shaping the course of the nation's life and sense of national identity. Victorian Scots continued the Reformed tendency to transpose essentially secular questions about the nation's political, constitutional and cultural identity into the ecclesiastical key. Church politics continued to be a major issue in Scottish electoral and party politics after 1843. But this should not blind us to the fact that in the mid-nineteenth century the Scottish

Reformed tradition and vision of the nation underwent a historic failure of theological and intellectual nerve.

The key institution in that vision, the established Kirk within a godly commonwealth, broke apart under the conflicting pressures of trying to maintain its historic and confessional role as the national church in a changing society far removed from the homogeneous rural and burgh communities of Chalmers' youth. The new urban working class, with its large Irish Catholic and unchurched elements, the British State, governing according to alien Anglican and erastian constitutional norms, the numerically comparable Presbyterian seceders, calling for disestablishment of the Kirk, and the growing number of Scots who were slipping away from orthodox belief and worship, caught up in the Victorian and Darwinian crisis of faith: all these groups and many more were indifferent or hostile to the Church of Scotland. They rejected its spiritual responsibility for the whole nation. They ignored its historic role as the key national institution generating and guaranteeing a common sense of Scottish identity.

Subsequent Scottish Reformed contributions to Christian theological analysis of the national question lacked the rigour or comprehensiveness of the earlier vision. They tended to reduce questions of nationality and Christian faith to matters of individual conscience and preserving a national religious heritage. The intellectual challenge to refashion a Reformed theology and cultural model of nationhood in the light of modernity was abandoned for the more genteel study of 'the elements in patriotism and their general congruity with religious principle', as one Baird lecturer put it; or the more sinister and disturbing protests from the Kirk in the 1920s about the threat presented to the Scottish race and Protestant heritage by the 'Irish Menace' of the Catholic immigrant community, with its allegedly alien religion, politics and culture. This preoccupation with the moral sentiment of patriotism and the preservation of a mythical Presbyterian racial identity, rather than a proper Calvinist concern with the theological meaning of nationhood in relation to the times, reflects the scale of the crisis of the Christian intellect and loss of theological nerve which occured in Victorian Scotland.

Of course, the Church was not alone in this loss of nerve about its own Scottish traditions in mid-nineteenth century Scotland. In chapter eleven I will mention the work of George Davie and Marinell Ash in analysing the wider loss of nerve about national traditions in education and academic life. The shock waves of the Disruption swept through Scotland's other national institutions as well. The resulting Presbyterian rivalries seriously weakened the capacity of the Scottish universities, with their traditions of democratic intellectualism and national historiography, to withstand the allure of English models of education, history and culture that were by the mid-century conquering the globe on the back of British imperial expansion. Worse than that, the Calvinist loss of nerve about a modern Scottish identity also contributed to the retreat of the Victorian popular imagination into escapist fantasy about Scotland's past. Rather than face up to the harsh and conflicting realities of urban, industrial Scotland in the light of a critical intellect and Christian mind, a number of churchmen contributed to the growth of what became known as the kailyard school of popular fiction.

Ignoring the contemporary social drama of slum and factory, novels and stories in this genre were set in an illusory Brigadoon world of quaint rural parishes that provided the setting for sentimental and moralising plots 'as seen through the windows of the Free Church manse'. It was Free Church ministers like S.R. Crockett and Ian Maclaren who were among the most prominent and successful writers of such fiction, encouraged by another Free Church minister, W. Robertson Nicoll, in his popular religious newspaper *British Weekly*. It is not surprising, therefore, that the Kailyard has been described as 'a literary movement that adhered to the theological doctrines of the Free Church' as well as the public's lucrative taste for such a distorted invention of Scotland's social and religious past. Here are the roots of Tom Nairn's damning association of ministers and Sunday Post with our distorted, escapist fantasies about Scotland and uncritical retreat from the material and human realities of Scottish national identity - his conviction that Scotland will only be reborn when the last minister has been strangled with the last copy of the said newspaper!

The tragic irony is that such Free Church doctrines once

inspired Reformed Christians in Scotland to analyse and transform urban industrial reality, not escape from it. Thomas Chalmers' window looked out onto the slums and crowded streets of the east end of Glasgow, not Thrums.

The Godly Vision - Life after Death?

After the Disruption, there was one last attempt to implement an amended version of the Godly vision of Scottish nationhood. If the national Kirk was central to this vision, then the great national question after 1843 became the reunion of the divided Presbyterian parts of that historic national institution. This provides yet one more example of national questions being transposed into the ecclesiastical key. The debate developed into one over the establishment of the Church of Scotland. When Chalmers and the Evangelicals left the Auld Kirk, they still adhered to the principle of the legal establishment of the national Church, but within a few decades many in the Free Church had swung over to support for disestablishment amid the bitter denominational rivalries of the period. Free Church leaders like Rainy 'saw disestablishment as a necessary preliminary to the unity of both church and nation in Scotland, a step on the path to national greatness.' This is an astonishing reversal of Thomas Chalmers' vision and argument only a few decades before, where a dynamic Church establishment was seen as the vital step on the path to national greatness. What is even more remarkable, though, is the way in which the seventeenth century Covenanting emphasis on church questions as the key to national identity was retained, despite all the contradictory twists and turns of Victorian ecclesiastical politics.

When the Presbyterian churches were finally reunited in one national Church of Scotland in 1929, the contentious issue of establishment had been resolved through mutual compromise; and a satisfactory form of wording on church-state relations in the new Articles Declaratory of the Constitution of the Church of Scotland formed the basis of the union with the more voluntarist United Free Church. The belief that the recovery of a truly national Kirk would restore the fortunes of the nation still ran deep. As Peter Bisset put it: 'In 1929 Re-union took place. Once again the nation had a church which was recognisably Scotland's Kirk... overall it seemed that the Kirk's destiny had been restored. So much so that one commentator could aver, "The reunited Church is a national symbol. One may even doubt whether there could be a Scotland without it".'

The Kirk after 1843 and 1929 may have remained a national symbol but the Scotland of the later nineteenth and twentieth centuries could certainly get on with being a nation without it. In the words of George Davie, author of seminal studies on Scottish intellectual and cultural history in this period, '...the ten-year struggle between Church and State over the democratisation of the Church of Scotland terminated in a spectacular secession, which lost the Church its central place in Scottish society...' It is a position that the Church has never recovered, contrary to many cherished ideals about the Kirk and other triumphal memories of the Godly vision that still shape Christian thinking on Scottish identity in the late twentieth century. Peter Bisset, an expert on church growth and decline in Scotland in the years since 1929, articulates this kind of viewpoint in a recent study on that theme, significantly entitled *The Kirk and her Scotland*. Commenting on the continuing link between the Kirk and national identity after 1945, he writes:

> Part of the argument of this book has been that the Kirk in Scotland's story has been the custodian of a dream. It has been the keeper of the soul of Scotland. In some sense it has been the focus of Scottish identity. So in the aftermath of war the Kirk took its place in the rebuilding of the nation. That was certainly the vision of Church extension as it took the Kirk into the midst of new housing areas. A Scotland which did not have a Kirk in its midst was inconceivable.

Bisset faithfully describes here the way in which the Kirk has continued to think of Scotland into the post-war period. It is an honourable and historic way of conceiving our national identity, a last glimmer of the Godly vision in a secular world, a last transposition of our national song into the ecclesiastical key. But most Scottish Christians sing the Lord's song in a strange land today, with other gods in our midst.

Where now for Calvinists?

Something decisive and lasting happened in 1843. To adapt a phrase the historian Marinell Ash used to describe the fate of Scottish historical studies in the nineteenth century, it marks the strange death of the godly commonwealth, that Calvinist vision of Scotland which had helped shape our national identity since 1560. The Calvinist contribution to that identity should be neither exaggerated as in the earlier fashion of Protestant polemicists or dismissed, as in the current vogue of Knox-haters. As George Davie's studies of the 'democratic intellect' have done so much to establish, the distinctive metaphysical ethos of our national identity owes as much to the secular institutions and traditions of thought in education and law as it does to the Church and its confession. It has never been possible to reduce our national identity to religious, ecclesiastical or theological terms alone. Throughout Scotland's history, national consciousness and feeling have developed out of the complex interaction of religious and secular elements.

However, until 1843, the national Kirk remained a central player in the national drama, with an institutional and intellectual involvement in the secular as well as the spiritual life of Scotland. This cultural involvement in national life gave a social plausibility to the godly vision of Scottish nationhood. In the same way, the Calvinist theology of the sovereignty of God and the Lordship of Christ over the whole of life, and the prophetic autonomy of his Kirk in relation to the State, gave the Godly vision its intellectual appeal and credibility. By the mid-nineteenth century such plausibility and credibility were lost.

It could be argued that such a development was inevitable, given the whole movement of Western thought and culture towards a much more secular outlook in the last hundred and fifty years. How could a Calvinist culture be sustained in a modern, pluralist society in nineteenth or twentieth century Europe? Well, the little known but remarkable fact is that just such a successful Calvinist rapprochement with modernity took place in another small northern European nation with a Reformed tradition in this same period when the Scottish Calvinist programme of modernisation collapsed. In the decades when the heirs of the Godly vision were abandoning it in Scotland, their fellow Calvinist luminaries were re-casting it in appropriate modern terms in the Netherlands.

When Guillaume Groen van Prinsterer, a distinguished Dutch historian and statesman, published in 1847 a series of lectures on the philosophical origins of the French Revolution, called *Revolution and Unbelief*, he paid tribute to Thomas Chalmers as an example of a Christian who had pursued the kind of Christian social vision in the modern world which he himself was advocating. There the similarity ends. While Chalmers was caught up in the tragedy of fatally dividing the one means of realising this vision, the national Kirk, Groen van Prinsterer and his successor in the renascent Calvinist movement, Abraham Kuyper, re-thought their godly vision in the secular and pluralist terms of contemporary Dutch society and Western thought. They saw the need for Christian schools, colleges, a university, newspapers and journals, trade union movement and political party, to ensure the survival of their Calvinist worldview and social principles in a modern democracy.

Kuyper went on to become Prime Minister of the Netherlands in the opening years of this century and his movement continues to play a vital part in the nation's intellectual and social life to this day, through its distinctive Christian educational, cultural and political institutions within the mainstream of Dutch society and government.

The Netherlands, with its very different political, social and economic history, resolved the tensions of secularisation and cultural pluralism in European society in a very different way from that of Scotland. But the Dutch comparison serves to show that it was perfectly possible for Reformed Christians within the same Calvinist tradition in northern Europe to keep their theological nerve and to conceive of their faith shaping the whole of their nation's life - and not just ecclesiastical, charitable and missionary affairs, as was increasingly the case in Scotland after the strange death of the Godly vision in 1843.

Before moving on to the next chapter to consider the kind of vision that replaced Thomas Chalmers' ideal of the godly commonwealth in nineteenth century Scotland, it is important to pause and reflect on the implications of this loss of the old Calvinist vision for our contemporary Christian understanding of Scotland. The French sociologist and Reformed theologian Jacques Ellul has noted: 'What has lost its sense in the course of time cannot be recovered artificially. An obsolete institution is obsolete: it cannot be re-invigorated - that is the historic lesson of all institutions.' It is time to recognise that twentieth century attempts to maintain the Kirk as the key institution of our national identity do not take account of historical and social realities. After 1843 the Godly vision and institutions were progressively replaced by a secular vision and secular institutions as the bearers of the Scottish identity. After 1843 the Godly vision became increasingly marginal in national life. The Burning Bush had been consumed.

The task of the Kirk in the late twentieth century is not to carry the burden of an obsolete past vision by interpreting its present crisis of numerical decline as a threat to its national role and status. If, as I have argued, that national role and status changed fundamentally and irreversibly a century and a half ago, then we are only chasing ghosts not reviving visions down that path. No, the vital need today is for the Kirk to bring its thinking on nationhood more faithfully into line with Christ and contemporary Scotland. Carrying on Ian Henderson's analogy, we need to transpose false ecclesiastical questions back into a national key and true ecclesiastical questions back into a Christological key. That is, we need to do our thinking about nationhood on the basis of the identity of Jesus Christ and not the identity of the national Church. We need a new vision of Christ and nation to engage with the realities of twenty-first century Scotland. We need to recover our Christian intellect and discern new models of Scottish nationhood faithful to the style of human community and identity revealed in Jesus Christ.

The old model of the Godly vision cannot comprehend the profound changes in our national identity since 1843, through which, as Professor T.C. Smout has observed, 'Scotland is part of the modern, agnostic, consumer, capitalist society, facing problems of resource shortage, and potential nuclear extinction.' Scottish Christians must also take much more seriously in their thinking the fact that throughout this century it is this secular vision of human and national life which has been shaping our national identity, despite the parrot cries of the Scottish *literati* about the continuing blight of Calvinism on the nation's psyche. In other words, as believers exploring the question of an authentic Christian vision of Scotland for today and tomorrow, we are not dealing with the contemporary collapse of the Godly vision of a Christian nation. That happened a long time ago. We are dealing with a long-established secular alternative. If anyone's vision is in deep trouble in present-day Scotland, it is not ours. We have been off-stage for quite a few acts in the national drama; although, as I am about to argue in the next chapter, quite a few of the props and script lines have been ours in the interim.

Off stage, on the margins, is quite a good place to get a view of what is going on in Scotland today. Accepting this peripheral identity is bound to be uncomfortable for many in the Kirk, used to a more triumphal Christian view of our national identity. However, we may find this novel perspective from the borders of national life, out over the secular nation of Scotland, strangely liberating. It is the view not from Calton Hill, or even the Mound. It is the view from Calvary.

Chapter 4

THE SECULAR VISION - A Moral Nation

What vision of Scotland replaced the Godly vision that died with Thomas Chalmers and the Disruption? It had to be a dynamic vision that took account of the profound changes underway in nineteenth century Scotland:

the social and economic revolution in the large-scale movement of population away from small rural and agricultural parishes to much larger industrial and urban communities...

the assimilation of the older Scottish civic and academic culture into the ascendant English imperial order...

the move away from the old Calvinist certainties into the Victorian crisis of orthodox faith and criticism of Biblical authority...

the grim human deprivation contrasting with the scientific and technological achievements of the new industrial society...

the rise of reform, labour and socialist movements calling for greater democracy and rights from the more autocratic regimes in Parliament, workplace and community...

the small but growing nationalist call for a greater autonomy in Scottish affairs as the British State intervened in more and more areas of Scottish life...

- exactly the changes that the Calvinist vision had failed to come to terms with and which tore it apart by the mid-nineteenth century. What understanding of national life could fill the vacuum caused by the collapse of the Godly vision in the new secular age?

No one mind wrestled more earnestly with these changes or articulated the novel Victorian response to that question more clearly than that of the friend of Thomas Chalmers born in Ecclefechan in 1795 - Thomas Carlyle, writer, critic, man of letters and prophet. In 1870 a fellow Scot wrote to Thomas Carlyle, by then the revered sage of Chelsea Street. Like the famous author, the man had abandoned the orthodox religious beliefs of his father's generation. He could no longer turn to a minister for spiritual counsel, as was the custom in Scotland. Instead, he turned to Carlyle, declaring him to be 'my minister, my honoured and trusted teacher.' That declaration is as significant in its way as the Declaration of Arbroath or National Covenant for our understanding of the historical development of the Christian vision of Scottish identity. It gives us the clue as to what happened to that overarching Glorious vision after the death of its Calvinist version in the 1840s.

The Dutiful Commonwealth

During the course of the nineteenth century a growing number of Scots abandoned not only the Godly vision of Scottish nationhood but also the Christian faith and worship in which it was grounded. Thomas Carlyle was a bell-wether figure for a new kind of spiritual flock that emerged in Scotland as in so many other Western countries in this period. He was brought up in a devout Calvinist home by parents who hoped that he would enter the ministry after his studies at Edinburgh University. His childhood faith did not survive his student days. His inherited belief in the traditional Christian creed and Calvinist confession dissolved in the intellectual acids of the Scottish Enlightenment thinking he encountered at university, with its sceptical rejection of revealed religion.

However, in abandoning Christian orthodoxy, Carlyle did not embrace the sceptical rationalism that had replaced it. Like his friend Thomas Chalmers some years before, he went through a period of profound personal spiritual crisis as he struggled to find a career other than the ministry and retain a religious meaning to life apart from the new sceptical orthodoxies of empiricism and utilitarianism. Unlike Chalmers, Carlyle did not resolve this crisis through an evangelical experience of conversion and a renewed sense of vocation to preach the Gospel. Rather he met Goethe and the gospel of Idealist philosophy on his Damascus Road to German Romanticism. As he wrote to a friend on Christmas Day, 1837, Goethe 'was to me a Gospel of Gospels, and did literally, I believe, save me from destruction outward and inward.' From Goethe and other German Romantic writers and thinkers he found an affirmation of the spiritual reality denied by the rationalist, utilitarian thinkers of his day. Rejecting only what he saw as the husk of religion, the no longer tenable theological and historical doctrines of the Church, he believed that he had kept the kernel, a transcendent sense of spiritual and moral truth and purpose. He spent the rest of his life arguing for the ethical substance of the universe and human history. Duty became his watchword and work his means of salvation. In this, Carlyle retained the stamp of his Calvinist heritage. As one commentator put it:

> The whole of his life and writings can be seen as an attempt to secularise, to reclothe the Calvinist insights without mitigating them. In the effort to preserve religion while discarding its doctrines, he has affinities with several famous Victorians, particularly Matthew Arnold. But whereas Arnold, working from a moderate Anglican basis, attempted to turn Christianity into sweetness and light, Carlyle preserved to the full and even increased the fierceness, the momentous drama, the seriousness of Calvinism. The idea of the elect and the reprobate, even though turned into moral and secular terms, was an ever-present reality to him.

It is here, in the transferring of Calvinism into purely secular and moral terms, that Carlyle is such an archetypical figure in the changing landscape of Scottish identity during the nineteenth century. Carlyle's spiritual pilgrimage became a well-trodden way for many Victorian and (later) Edwardian Scots. They had an ambivalent relationship to the old Calvinist vision of their forbears. Like Carlyle, they rejected the God of its Confession but kept its high sense of moral duty. In the words of the church historian Professor Alec Cheyne:

> At the outset of the nineteenth century... only the most prescient could have foretold the coming transformation of Scotland's confessional standards. By the eighteen-thirties and forties, however, it was alto-

gether otherwise. During these decades of rapid and
far-reaching change - social, political and intellectual
- attention came to be focused not on the circumfer-
ence but on the centre of Presbyterianism's traditional
faith, and some of the basic doctrines and attitudes of
Westminster Calvinism came under serious and sustained attack... They were also the years when Thomas
Carlyle, outside the religious camp but still in commu-
nication with it, perfected his art of persisting with
much of the old phraseology while at the same time
conveying the impression that virtually nothing in
earth or heaven was exactly as it had been.

Certainly nothing in the earth or heaven of Scottish identity
would continue as it had been before these decades. Carlyle
typifies these changes. His was a secularised version of the old
Reformed vision of the Godly nation. Increasingly, this secular
vision was shared by many Scots. It thought of Scotland less in
theological terms, as in the old Godly vision, and more in ethical
and moral terms. Scotland was now conceived as a Moral
nation. Carlyle rejected the Calvinist confessional foundations
but still drew on its Biblical moral and social concepts to frame
his social vision. These secular visionaries of nineteenth century
Scotland derived their ethical vision of a Moral nation from the
Bible. They were reversing the tendency we noted in Scottish
Calvinism since the seventeenth century to transpose all national
issues into an ecclesiastical key. Carlyle transposed all theological notions into a moral key within history and human affairs.
The worship of the transcendent God of the Bible became the
awesome, immanent recognition of the total claims of moral
duty on the human soul and society. As his biographer J.A.
Froude noted:

To the Scotch people and to the Puritan part of the
English, the Jewish history contained a faithful account of the dealings of God with man in all countries
and in all ages. As long as men kept God's commandments it was well with them; when they forgot God's
commandments and followed after wealth and enjoyment, the wrath of God fell upon them... to this simple
creed Carlyle adhered as the central principle of all his

thoughts. The outward shell of it had broken. He had
ceased to believe in miracles and supernatural interpo-
sitions. But to him the natural was the supernatural...
The Jewish history was the symbol of all history. All
nations in all ages were under the same dispensation.
We did not come into the world with rights which we
were entitled to claim, but with duties which we were
ordered to do. Rights men had none, save to be
governed justly. Duties waited for them everywhere.
Their business was to find what those duties were and
faithfully to fulfill them. So and only so could the
commonweal prosper...

Here we have the Godly nation transposed into the dutiful
commonwealth. This notion of duty was a key concept in
Carlyle's thought. Commenting on a letter Carlyle wrote to his
devout friend Thomas Erskine of Linlathen in 1847, Froude
remarked, 'to Carlyle... religion was obligation, a command
which bound men to duty, as something which they were
compelled to do under tremendous penalties.' Carlyle himself
saw 'the God-appointed rulers of this world' as 'the chosen few
who do continue to believe in "the eternal nature of duty".' He
saw his own calling as that of a prophet, in itself a characteristically Calvinist role. Having abandoned any plans for the
ministry, Carlyle had worked intermittently and unhappily as a
teacher before turning to the hazardous life of an essayist,
historian and social critic. He eventually found success and
fame as a writer after his move to London in 1837. But Carlyle
continued to preach his gospel of duty and his vision of the
dutiful commonwealth, until his death in 1881.

Carlyle's devout mother got her wish. Her brilliant son did
become a minister but in a 'secular pulpit'. His writings
proclaimed to his troubled generation the dreadful, eternal
demands of duty and not the saving message of the sovereign
grace of God in Jesus Christ, crucified and risen, as believed by
her generation. He preached another gospel to that of the Godly
vision but, in Froude's words, 'Amid the controversies, the
arguments, the doubts, the crowding uncertainties of forty years
ago, Carlyle's voice was to the young generation of Englishmen
like the sound of "ten thousand trumpets" in their ears, as the

Knight of Grange said of Knox.' Froude was referring to the generation of the 1840s. In that decade, the Godly vision collapsed and Thomas Chalmers died. Another prophetic voice replaced the rich Fife tones of the great divine. It sounded the clarion call to a new ethical vision which many heard gladly, in part because it was still framed in terms of the familiar moral discourse of Calvinism, and pursued with religious zeal in the secular life of Scotland.

Carlyle spoke to the highly developed moral conscience as well as to the religious doubts of his time. The kind of moral vision to be found in Carlyle's thought and writings increasingly filled the vacuum left in the minds and hearts of many Victorian Scots by the expulsion of orthodox Christian belief and worship. The old verities were being sucked out by the drawing power of scientific discovery and critical study of the Bible and religion; the widespread and characteristically Victorian crisis of faith. Of course, the rise of this Secular vision, in which Scotland and its national life were thought of primarily in the ethical terms of the previous Calvinist vision, was in no way due solely to the influence of Carlyle. He was part swimmer and part pilot in a cultural sea-change. Nor was this shift in vision unique to Scotland, except perhaps in its note of high moral seriousness and its pervasive hold on the imagination of many of the secular reformers, public servants and activists who dominate the period. Carlyle does serve, however, as an early and influential example of how the Calvinist theological vision of Scotland was turned into a secular and moral version as the nineteenth century ran its course.

The way in which Carlyle transposed the theological terms of the godly commonwealth into a moral critique of industrial society was to prove typical of the way many Victorian and Edwardian Scots re-fashioned their sense of national identity in Christian terms. Industrial Scotland would remain a Christian nation but on the foundation of shared Christian ethics rather than one Confession of Faith. Stripped of its German Romantic metaphysical garb, Carlyle's kind of vision of the dutiful commonwealth, a secularised Calvinist vision of a moral nation, took hold of the Scottish imagination and shaped its thinking about national life for a hundred years. From the mid-nineteenth to the mid-twentieth centuries the conviction was retained that Scotland was a Christian country, not because of a common membership of one Church, as in the Catholic vision, or common adherence to one theological Confession, as in the Reformed vision, but due to a continuing consensus over shared Christian values. Here we have the third great Christian vision of Scotland in our history, the third version of the Glorious vision of Scotland as a Christian nation - a Secular vision of Scotland seen in Christian ethical terms as a Moral nation.

Transposing the Vision

It would be relatively easy to place Scotland and what I have termed the new Secular vision in this period within a broad theory of secularisation in Western societies. The main indicators of such a process, including the uncoupling of the church from the life of secular institutions, the rejection of orthodox religious belief and practice and the decline in church attendance and membership, can all be found in Scottish society in the last two hundred years. Some social theorists would argue that secularisation is a much more subtle and complex phenomenon than a simple registering of such institutional, cultural and statistical trends would suggest. Sociologists of religion have developed many different interpretations and models of the notion of religious decline in Western societies. One such theory uses a concept we have already encountered in the history and theology of the relationship between church and nation in Scotland, that of transposition.

This school of sociological thought would argue that what sometimes happens in a so-called secularised society is not the decline and extinction of religion but rather 'the transposition of beliefs and patterns of behaviour from the "religious" to the "secular" sphere.' This transposition theory of secularisation draws on Max Weber's seminal insight and historical argument that religious values with a theological origin in the Protestant work ethic were transposed into generally accepted cultural values like hard work or thrift during the rise of capitalism in the West. According to this viewpoint, Christianity has been so successful in converting Western societies and in establishing

Christian concepts and values as the self-evident common
ethical currency of Western cultures, that such transposed Christian social concepts and moral values can survive without the
recognition of their theological and religious roots or support for
the churches which generated them in the first place. The
sociologist and theologian Robin Gill, expounding this transposition theory of secularisation in these terms, raises an important
question that we must bear in mind before relating the idea of
transposition to the Secular vision of Scotland:

> ... some sociologists, otherwise quite sceptical about
> the claims of the Gospel, have begun to adopt a more
> pessimistic, Durkheimian, view about the moral sur-
> vival of Western society in the vacuum created by
> declining churches. It is still, of course, a very open
> question how long specifically Christian values can
> survive in a society in which churches are no longer
> socially significant... the possibility still remains...
> that the future of Christian values does depend, long
> term, on the survival of specifically Christian institu-
> tions in society. Values which appear to be 'platitudi-
> nous' and mere 'common sense' may not remain so
> indefinitely in a church-less society.

I wish to argue that this transposition theory of secularisation
enables us to understand the kind of national vision that replaced
the Godly vision in the century after 1843. What we have seen
in Scotland since about the mid-nineteenth century is the transposing of Reformed and Christian social values and concepts
into a secular key, in an age that increasingly rejected Calvinist
belief and worship while holding fast to its social ethos and
ethics. In Stephen Maxwell's apposite phrase, the vision came
to be preached from 'the secular pulpit'. But, as Gill's comments
make clear, a transposition theory of secularisation also raises
the question of whether or not such a Secular vision of Scotland
as a Moral nation, grounded in shared Christian ethical values,
can survive the decline of the churches and the theological
worldview which generated them. We will return to consider
that crucial question and the present-day fate of the Secular
vision after tracing its history and influence in national life since
the Victorian era.

Out of the Church, Into the World

In one sense, the Secular vision of Scotland as a Moral nation began in the mid-eighteenth century with the Moderates. These churchmen very much saw the Gospel in the civilizing ethical terms of moral enlightenment and improvement. However, what distinguishes them from the later secular Calvinist visionaries was the essential and central place the Moderates gave to the Church in realising that moral vision in national life. They did not publicly challenge the orthodox Westminster Confession of the Kirk or the importance of worship and preaching in the life of church and nation. In the later Secular vision of the nineteenth and twentieth centuries there is a rejection or abandonment of the Church as the key national or even Christian institution, sometimes explicitly, sometimes implicitly. There is a related downgrading of the contribution of Christian belief and worship in fashioning a unifying spiritual and moral vision for Scottish society, in favour of the practical Christianity of social ethics and involvement in secular affairs.

By calling this vision a secular one, it must not be forgotten that I regard it as a third form of Christian vision, a successor to the Catholic and Calvinist visions. It is secular in the sense that it removes God and the Church from the centre of the picture and focuses its vision on this world and its earthly affairs. But it remains Christian in the sense that in its concern for this secular world it still operates with Christian, and in particular, Calvinist or Presbyterian, ethical, moral and social norms.

We might take as our starting point for understanding the distinctively Christian terms of the Secular vision a book that typifies this new way of looking at Christianity in national life, called *The City without a Church*. The author was Henry Drummond (1851-1897), a scientist, Free Church professor, evangelist and devotional writer of huge popularity and influence in his day. Drummond was himself a devout Christian believer and churchman but he had both a gift and a passion to communicate the Gospel to his Victorian contemporaries in their own terms. His devotional writings were couched in evolutionary and scientific language. Christianity was presented as the highest form of man's spiritual development. In his preaching and writing Drummond was concerned to persuade his audience that Christianity should find practical expression in their everyday lives and in the life of society. Nowhere did he state this more forcibly than in this book. Though still written by a Christian believer, it is a classic manifesto of the Secular vision, its Declaration of Arbroath, its National Covenant.

The secular vision is none other than a vision of 'the city without a church'. The book is an exposition of the vision of St John in the Book of Revelation where heaven is seen as a city without a temple. Drummond sees great significance in this for a true vision of Christianity in the modern world. As an orthodox believer he does not deny the importance of the Church, its beliefs and worship for nurturing Christian faith and character in the lives of individuals. But these are now only means to a greater end. The worship, beliefs and life of the Church must no longer be the focus for a Christian vision of the nation. The life of the earthly city must be the priority for Christianity in action. Indeed, the true church is the earthly city:

> ...this vision of the City marks off in lines which no eye can mistake the true area which the religion of Christ is meant to inhabit... With actual things, with Humanity in its everyday dress, with the traffic of the streets, with gates and houses, with work and wages, with sin and poverty, with all these things, and all the things and all the relations and all the people of the City, Christianity has to do and all the more to do than anything else... In this vision of the City [St John] confronts us with a new definition of a Christian man - the perfect saint is the perfect citizen. To make Cities - that is what we are here for. To make good Cities - that is for the present hour the main work of Christianity... People do not dispute that religion is in the Church. What is now wanted is to let them see it in the City... pass out into the City... Beautify it, ventilate it, drain it... Christianize capital; dignify labour. Join Councils and Committees... so you will serve the City...to carry on the multitudinous activities of the city - social, commercial, political, philanthropic - in Christ's spirit and for His ends; that is the religion of the Son of Man... the Church with all its splendid

    equipment, the cloister with all its holy opportunity,
    are not the final instruments for fitting men for Heaven.
    The City, in many of its functions, is a greater Church
    than the Church.

I have risked quoting selections from throughout Drummond's
book at some length to illustrate and underline the Christian
nature of this secular vision. 'Do not be afraid of missing Heaven
in seeking a better earth', he wrote, 'The distinction between
secular and sacred is a confusion and not a contrast; and it is only
because the secular is so intensely sacred that so many eyes are
blind before it.'

Here is another reversal of the relationship between church
and nation in the history of the Christian vision of Scotland. In
the covenanting version of the Godly vision, the nation became
subsumed in the church and everything was transposed into the
ecclesiastical key. In the Secular vision everything is transposed
into the secular key as the church becomes the earthly nation.
That is the substance of Drummond's message and of the Secular
vision of Scotland which he expresses with such vigour. The
focus has changed from the time of the Disruption, when
everything hinged on church affairs. Now, what the Church
should aim at

    ...is not the recognition by the nation of a worshipping
    body, governed by the ministers of public worship,
    which calls itself the Church, but that the nation and all
    classes in it should act upon Christian principle, that
    laws should be made in Christ's spirit of justice, that
    the relations of the powers of the State should be
    maintained on a basis of Christian equity, that all
    public acts should be done in Christ's spirit, and with
    mutual forbearance, that the spirit of Christian charity
    should be spread through all ranks and orders of the
    people.

This Secular vision was concerned with the concrete, tangible
realisation of the Christian ethic in the life of nations on earth.
For Drummond, 'What John saw, we may fairly take it, was the
future of all cities. It was the dawn of a new social order, a
regenerate humanity, a purified city, an actual transformation of
the Cities of the world into the Cities of God.'

No city embraced this Secular vision more enthusiastically than his own adopted city of Glasgow. In the late nineteenth and early twentieth centuries Glasgow was at the height of its powers as an industrial metropolis, the 'Second City of the Empire'. It was also a city of slum housing, squalor and poverty. In tackling Glasgow's urban problems through municipal reform and practical philanthropy, its civic leaders set an example that was studied and copied by industrial cities around the world, especially by American urban reformers. The historian Brian Aspinwall has identified the ideals of 'the Social gospel' and 'Practical Christianity' as among the main motivations of municipal reformers on both sides of the Atlantic:

> ... the sacred was to be secularised and the secular sacralised - a hope which was given dramatic illustration in the Labour churches in Scotland and the socialist Sunday schools which also attracted American interest.

In the ethical socialism of the rising Labour movement and in the commitment of many businessmen to public service and municipal reform, it can be argued that Christian values were transposed into secular reform politics in turn of the century Scotland - without insistence on adherence to traditional dogma:

> Among Americans, as among Glaswegians, a theocratic strain persisted: 'The Church in reality is the society formed by those who claim fellowship with Christ, and, above all she is the still vaster society of those whom unconsciously and without knowing His blessed name, live in His Spirit and continue in his work'... in short, the new faith of the unchurched is faith in people in the coming kingdom of heaven on earth.

When the labour leader Keir Hardie stated at the turn of the century that the choice facing society was that between the Kingdoms of God and Mammon, his thrust was ethical and political, not doctrinal. As Aspinwall observes in his study of Glasgow's visionary and practical influence on America from 1820 to 1920, called appropriately *Portable Utopia*, Scotland's major city fostered a national vision shared on both sides of the Atlantic. Through improved housing and sanitation, through the provision of public education, through better public transport and municipal tramways, through improved leisure facilities for the masses, the city fathers believed they were building in stone the Christian moral ideal of a caring, socially responsible community in an urban, industrial age. Through temperance crusades, through socialist politics or trade union organisation, many working class and radical Scots believed they had found a better way of building the New Jerusalem. It was a conviction that came to be shared by many Christians active within church-based welfare work as they felt themselves increasingly swamped by the sheer scale of the social problems they sought to tackle. The moving force of practical Christianity became municipal reform or the labour movement, not the old godly parish Kirk. As Aspinwall puts it:

> In the generation before the first world war, Scottish
> national identity was found not in the church, estab-
> lished or free, but in the town hall, in an ethical
> Christian community faith rather than "churchianity".

Above all, it was a vision to be attained through a common moral education rather than divisive doctrinal preaching: 'Salvation was thus transposed from theological to social grounds and a new class of moral guardians was empowered to enforce a newly created moral code.' For many of the activists in this portable utopia, 'Morality and social order now took precedence over faith and eternal salvation.' Even Christians who had traditionally worked through voluntary agencies to tackle urban problems entered municipal politics with all the fervour of a moral crusade. Nevertheless, in developing new forms of social work, such as establishing university settlement houses in deprived areas of the city, the legacy of the Godly vision was not exhausted. According to Aspinwall, 'The settlement house movement was in most instances a more secularised version of the old fashioned Christian involvement.' We can still hear echoes of Thomas Chalmers in this Scottish ethical vision, but its preachers were increasingly secular voices speaking from secular pulpits.

In the twentieth century some of these secular preachers were to prove very influential indeed, as Stephen Maxwell has shown. In his study *The Secular Pulpit: Presbyterian Democracy in the*

Twentieth Century, Maxwell looks at the lives of three Scots: the educationalist, A.D. Lindsay; the founder of the British Broadcasting Corporation, John Reith; and the pioneering documentary film-maker, John Grierson. He argues that all three helped shape British society's response to the problems of democracy in a mass industrial age. Common to all of them was their Scottish inheritance with its distinctive themes and values:

> The dominant element in this inheritance was, of course, Presbyterian. In their different circumstances and with varying degrees of success, the three Scots translated the constitutional claims of the Scottish Church into secular terms adapted to the needs of twentieth century democracy.

Maxwell suggests that the Kirk, recognised as the national Church by the State and yet spiritually autonomous, served as a model of a public yet self-governing body for Reith's BBC, Lindsay's work with the Workers Educational Association and, to a lesser extent, Grierson's approach to the social role of the documentary film. They saw education, public broadcasting and cinema as the new secular pulpits which would offer mass society spiritual and moral leadership in the vacuum left by the churches. But the Presbyterian tradition offered more than institutional models for a mass democracy:

> The Scottish inheritance which gave Lindsay, Reith and Grierson the model of a national institution at once independent and 'established' as a source of moral leadership in society, embraced other values qualified to inspire a positive response to the problems of mass democracy. In a secular context the Presbyterian concept of an educated laity capable of playing a responsible part in Church government and of making its own judgements on theological and spiritual issues, endowed the mass public of modern society with a moral dignity...

These three influential figures in British public life held to the Calvinist sense of the higher moral purpose of all experience, echoing Carlyle's earlier vision. While they might disagree over the methods and priorities of education they '... shared... a conviction that education in a democracy had to be education in the standards and duties of political life... [they] believed that society depended on the existence of common values and that in Western democracies those standards were ultimately Christian.' This conviction was seen in their own public careers as they sought to transpose 'the Presbyterian tradition of thought about the relationship between the state and the sources of moral and spiritual leadership in society' into secular values and institutional models in the inter-war decades in Britain.

Grierson in particular pursued his convictions with all the reasoned moral indignation of the older Godly vision. Brian Aspinwall has described him as by temperament a Calvinist preacher, quoting Grierson's biographer as saying, 'He was a revolutionary, but his bombs were verbal and visual... he enraged his congregation by simply holding a mirror up so that they could see themselves.' In essence both the municipal reformers of Glasgow and these secular Presbyterian advocates of a mass democracy were pursuing the kind of Christian ethical vision set out by Drummond in *The City without a Church*, where he argued for 'a new definition of a Christian man - the perfect saint is the perfect citizen.' The godly congregation was now seen as the civic community of the machine age that still required to be transformed in line with the transposed Calvinist moral vision of an educated, public-spirited and democratic citizenry.

This emphasis on the Christian as citizen which Drummond stressed is reflected in the Christology of the Secular vision. Christology is simply the study of the way in which we understand Christ's identity and mission on earth. For Drummond, the problem was that, 'Down to the present hour almost whole nations in Europe live, worship, and die under the belief that Christ is an ecclesiastical Christ...' In the new Christian vision of the nation, 'We never think of Him in connection with a Church. We cannot picture Him in the garb of a priest... He was the Son of Man, the Citizen.' Citizen Christ was seen to be active outwith the Church and within secular affairs as He brought in the Kingdom of God on earth: 'With Christianity as the supreme actor in the world's drama, the future of its cities is even now quite clear. Project the lines of Christian and social progress to their still far-off goal, and see even now that Heaven must come to earth.' The Secular vision very much remained in the tradition of the Glorious vision of Christian nationhood. Rather than looking to the Church or the Word of Christ the King to ensure a victorious Christian nationhood, as in the Catholic and Reformed visions, it was now the Christian ethic of a progressive Christ, the First Citizen, which could be sure of an ultimate, evolutionary triumph in a nation governed by Christian principle in all its parts.

In the convergent lines of Christian and social progress, all men and women of goodwill could be brought together in the public life of the nation. For Christian believers the all important thing was putting their faith into action in the secular sphere. For those who had said their farewells to the God of Israel and Calvinist Scotland, the important thing was incarnating the Presbyterian values they retained in public life. Here was a common middleground for the national Church to occupy in modern twentieth century Scotland, as it adapted its sense of place and purpose in national life to the terms of the Secular vision.

The Common Ground

In the previous chapter I argued that there was one last attempt to re-establish a central part of the Godly vision, the necessity of a united National Church in securing Scotland's national identity, through the reunion of the Church of Scotland in 1929. That the reunion was understood in these terms is clear from the comment already quoted: 'The reunited Church is a national symbol. One may even doubt whether there could be a Scotland without it..' In reality, there was no doubt at all. Scotland was wrestling in the 1920s with the meaning and future of its national identity quite happily without the Kirk. While the Church of Scotland remained an important national institution, the serious intellectual debate about national life, once conducted on the floor of the General Assembly, now took place in secular arenas like the Scottish universities and the journals of the Scottish literary renaissance associated with Hugh MacDiarmid and Lewis Grassic Gibbon.

The triumphant ecclesiastical rhetoric of the Godly vision rang hollow after the Great War. However, the Calvinist mind continued to provide some Scottish thinkers with fundamental ideas about human nature and knowledge, albeit shorn of their theological fleece. George Davie has noted this fact in *The Crisis of the Democratic Intellect*, his history of Scottish intellectual life in this period. The debate about the direction of Scottish education in the 1920s, between the native tradition of generalist university studies and the Anglo-American specialist approach advocated by the American philosopher John Dewey, centred in part on two conflicting views of human nature.

The leading Scottish philosopher Norman Kemp Smith made a distinctive contribution to this debate through his questioning of the optimistic view of human potential and progress that undergirded contemporary educational thought. This high view of the possibilities of human achievement had theological roots in the teachings of Pelagius. Kemp Smith's own view of human nature embraced the Christian doctrine of original sin, as expounded by Augustine and Calvin, separating their lasting insights into human nature from their outdated religious thought. Like them, he stressed the limitations and frailties of human nature and knowledge. He did so without reference in his teaching to the theological origins of these ideas but, according to Davie, '... the new idea behind Kemp Smith's philosophy which made it surprising and interesting was a sort of secularised version of the doctrine of original sin.' Kemp Smith himself wrote in 1919, 'For some years I have been ambitious to write upon what I should describe as "traditional views of human nature" - meaning the Christian doctrine of original sin and the Enlightenment (or Pelagian) doctrine of human perfectibility - on the lines of a plea of a better understanding of the former view.' He was not alone in this view. It was shared by his lecturer, the Scottish philosopher John Anderson, who continued to expound it during his subsequent university teaching in Australia. In Davie's judgement:

> ... this reassertion of the limitations of human nature as opposed to the doctrine held by the apostles of progress and perfectibility has to be regarded as the chief distinguishing feature of philosophy in twentieth-century Scotland, as opposed to the form philosophy took in other Western countries.

Clearly, the Calvinist mind was not entirely dead in early twentieth century Scotland. It survived in a secularised form outwith the walls of the Church, whether at the popular level of social reform and the new institutions of mass democracy, or in the intellectual heights of academic philosophy. More thoughtful and discerning minds in the Kirk were not slow to realise this or make a response. Spurred on by the upheaval of another World War, the Church of Scotland did make one serious attempt to come to grips theologically with this dominant secularised Christian ethical and social vision of the nation.

During the Second World War the Kirk's General Assembly set up a *Commission for the Interpretation of God's Will in the present Crisis*. It was convened by a leading Scottish theologian and churchman, Professor John Baillie. The Baillie Commission, as it became known, presented annual reports to the General Assembly from 1941 to 1945. It offered fresh thinking on the shape of post-war Scottish and British society. In the judgement of Professor Duncan Forrester, the Baillie Commission, 'played no small part in swinging public opinion, not only Christian opinion, in Scotland behind a model of post-war Britain as an egalitarian welfare state'. Here, at least, is an example of the continuing impact of the national Church on the life of the nation. But how was this influence achieved? By standing on the common ethical ground of the Secular vision.

The Baillie Commission operated effectively in part because it took seriously the collapse of the godly commonwealth in Scotland and its transposition into Carlyle's dutiful commonwealth in which many Scots were no longer committed to the Church's beliefs and worship but continued to adhere to Christian social and moral values. It deliberately set out to relate the Christian Gospel to this changed social context. We can see this both in the kind of ethical method it adopted and in the mind of John Baillie, its convener, 'whose leadership left its mark on the work of the Commission.'

In the second of its annual reports, presented to the General Assembly in May 1942, the Commission set out its adoption of the concept of 'middle axioms' as its method of applying New Testament teaching to what it called 'Christian action in a mixed society'. Between Christian faith and its related ethical principles on the one hand, and concrete political, economic or social policy decisions on the other, middle axioms existed as 'middle range social goals' that were theologically and ethically grounded but practically relevant to a particular time and society. Professor Forrester has suggested that after the war one such middle axiom was the responsibility of the government to strive to maintain full employment. Middle axioms allowed Christian social thinkers to develop from their ruling theological principles what the Baillie Commission called 'certain secondary and more specialised principles which exhibit the relevance of the ruling principles to the particular field of action in which guidance is needed.' One major attraction of this middle axiom approach was that it generated social goals which could be embraced by those in society who did not accept their theological source but still adhered to Christian values. The Commission judged that such a situation prevailed in Scottish society. Their 1942 Report stated:

> In this country we can count on a much more highly instructed common conscience than that [recognised by all men]. We can count on a common conscience which, without being itself Christian, has nevertheless been profoundly affected by Christian ideas and ideals... There are many in Scotland who have themselves no part in the Church's corporate life, but who are glad to think that our public life is controlled by Christian moral standards.

Middle axioms, developed out of Christian theological conviction, offered ethical common ground with those secular Scots who retained a loyalty to Christian values. Such an ethical method took account of the changed face of Scotland, with its growing number of non-church members. By adopting this line of ethical reasoning, the Baillie Commission recognised the end of the social assumption of both Catholic and Calvinist Christendom that Church and society formed one overlapping community. Scotland was now a pluralist and secular society, with one vital qualification. The values which shaped that society remained Christian and were recognised as such even by those outwith the Church's corporate life. This was certainly the view of the Commission's convener, John Baillie, when he gave the closing address as Moderator to the General Assembly in 1943. Significantly Baillie set his remarks in the context of the one hundredth anniversary of the Disruption and 'the change which has overtaken us within these hundred years':

> A hundred years ago the principles of the Christian faith were the solid foundations of the nation's life... All the great issues of the day were joined well within the circle of commitment to Christian belief, and not yet as between Christianity and something else that was not Christian... How is it today? In the eyes of the law this is still a Christian country and our Church a national institution, but the reality of the situation has suffered a most alarming change. The life of our Scottish community has largely slipped its Christian moorings... To a large proportion of the men and women of Scotland the Church of Christ means nothing and plays no part in their life or in their thought.

Acutely aware that the Church had to read aright the true condition of Scotland, Baillie did not conclude from this profound historical change that Scots outside the Christian Church had reverted to paganism: 'What has happened between [Chalmers'] day and ours is that the public standards of conduct have been more and more divorced from the creed and worship. Diffused Christianity today means only the surviving influence of Christian moral ideals after the impulse of worship has failed and the belief grown dim and shadowy.'

He is describing what I have termed the Secular vision of Scotland, the reduction of a Christian theological vision to its ethical terms. Baillie felt that the common life of Scotland was neither Christian nor pagan but secularised:

> ... secular means 'pertaining to an age', and the age here meant is this present world - that is, the day to day round of our present transitory existence. The secularist outlook thus differs from all previous outlooks whether pagan or Christian, in being without any kind of far horizon, any ultimate background of belief, any final sanction for the routine of present behaviour.

What was significant for Baillie was that those Scots who had embraced this secular outlook did not seem to have replaced

Christian belief with any new allegiance. They had become neutral: 'Men go on living, and living decently, in observance of chivalrous and gentle manners taught them by centuries of Christian nurture and culture, but they are living in a sort of void, without any general frame of reference to give their lives a meaning.' That Baillie captured here the essence of a particular kind of secular Scot's experience in the 1940s is suggested in an autobiographical account by the late Professor John P. Mackintosh of his middle-class Edinburgh Presbyterian upbringing.

Describing his spiritual quest as a student from 1946, only three years after Baillie's observations were made, Mackintosh recounted his rejection of the materialist conception of history because of a feeling that certain human values must have a deeper basis than economic systems: 'Looking for a justification for these values, I became a Christian for a short period, but the idea of mass punishment of the ungodly and the improbability of this kind of divine intervention in history drew me back out of religion. But I still wish I could establish the values on which I operate and I still feel a great longing for the confidence and the qualities exhibited by the more progressive Christians.'

As in Baillie's analysis, Mackintosh felt himself to be without any ultimate background of belief or final sanction for the routine of his behaviour and the values he held, while retaining a certain nostalgia or longing for the benefits of Christian faith. Perhaps Mackintosh is one further name to add to those other Scots in Stephen Maxwell's secular pulpit whose Presbyterian inheritance shaped their secular contribution to public life but whose lives are indicative of the changed relationship between church and nation in twentieth century Scotland.

Baillie saw that the Godly vision of the nation operative in 1843 no longer applied a century later in a vastly changed Scotland. Just as importantly for his analysis, he also believed that the prevailing secular outlook had not thrown out Christian moral and spiritual values along with the abandonment of worship and belief. This presented the Church with its greatest challenge: 'The one supreme problem before the Church to-day is to discover the right way of bringing the Gospel to bear upon this outlook...'

Baillie's response to that challenge was twofold. In the sphere of national affairs, the Church must develop ethical judgements derived from the Gospel, middle axioms, in the confidence that many in society would be willing to follow such a moral lead in public life. His war-time Commission stated its belief that there were many in Scotland, 'even among those who adhere to other faiths, who are willing in this matter to follow an energetic Christian lead.' And second, with regard to the Church's mission to the nation, he advocated a missionary strategy that sought not conversion from paganism but the revival of lapsed Christians from their neutral secular outlook back to renewed Christian faith and worship. If the Scottish community had slipped its Christian moorings then it was a matter of sensitively pulling on the rope to return them to their true haven within the Church.

The fundamental premise of Baillie's critique of Church and culture is similar to that of the transposition theory of secularisation. The religious values and concepts of Chalmers' godly commonwealth had become transposed into the secular vision of human identity and community through which many Scots now saw their personal and national life.

The Godly vision of Scotland saw it as a Christian nation. In coming to terms with the Secular vision and reality of Scotland, the Church now saw it as a lapsed Christian nation. In its public utterances the Church could still give a welcome public lead by appealing to the ethical consensus derived from the nation's Christian heritage. In its evangelism the Church could still win a hearing by calling what it saw as its lapsed members and secular parishioners back to faith and worship. In this way the Church of Scotland could retain its national role and mission in a mixed and secular society. It could make its own accommodation with the Secular vision, recognising the decline of Christian belief and worship but claiming a unique position for the Church as the guardian of the Christian ethics which still retained their monopoly as the nation's code of private and public morality. Here was a new approach for the Kirk to try in the post-war period, as a national institution representative not so much of the Christian faith as of the Christian ethics of the Scottish people.

How successful was it? Rather embarrassingly, just as the

Kirk had developed this thoughtful approach to secular Scotland, the Secular vision was itself in the process of collapsing, after a reign of one hundred years in the national imagination.

1979 - the Death of a Vision

The ten years after the end of the Second World War in 1945 were a kind of Indian summer for Baillie's approach to church and nation in a secular Scotland. In the immediate post-war years the Labour Government created the kind of welfare provisions and the main political parties favoured the full employment policies that the wartime Baillie Commission had envisaged. Its middle axiom approach to the civil order, as he had called it, seemed to be vindicated in the broad public consensus on social and economic policy that emerged in this period. The Church of Scotland also made steady advances after the war. Peter Bisset has described the period from 1946 to 1955 as years of growth for the church, quoting the view of the Church of Scotland evangelist D.P. Thomson, 'these were days of unparalleled opportunity when the Church's ministry and mission found a new openness and readiness of response.' The Church of Scotland's membership reached a peak of 1.32 million. Bisset describes the mood in the Kirk at that time:

> These were the dream years for the Kirk. It seemed that the Gospel was unstoppable, that Scotland had found its soul, that the Kirk was leading the nation forward to a new day of glory and grace. Those involved in the Kirk's outreach over these years witnessed to a responsiveness that they had not hitherto known. Significantly it was the Kirk which was in the vanguard of advance. Other denominations did not experience growth in like measure. It seemed as though in the aftermath of the years of war a new unity had dawned, a new urgency to recreate the nation. The urgency was echoed in the prophetic cry of George Macleod, seeking renewal in church and society: 'We shall rebuild'.

The Church of Scotland engaged in widespread mission work in these years, culminating in the *Tell Scotland* movement of the early 1950s, under the inspired leadership and example of Tom

Allan, and the invitation to the American evangelist Billy Graham to lead the *All Scotland Crusade* in 1956. However, the glory years were short-lived and the Indian summer passed. After 1956 the membership of the Church of Scotland began a process of steep decline which has continued down to the present. The profound social and economic changes in the Britain of the 1950s and 1960s, with improved standards of living, more widespread educational, leisure and entertainment opportunities, the questioning of traditional authority, morality and institutions and the rise of the youth culture, altered the social climate in which the Church had been operating with such seeming success in the early years after the war. If it rose on an initial tide of social optimism to rebuild Scotland, with rapid growth in church extension congregations in the new housing schemes, it toiled in the floods of economic affluence among the more prosperous, and receded among the many areas of urban and social deprivation.

The appeals of the 1950s to return to the church and faith of their fathers fell on increasingly deaf ears as the post-war decades rolled on. The more permissive currents in personal and sexual morality flowing through the 1960s seemed to leave the Church increasingly isolated from mainstream society. It struggled with a growing indifference and even alienation from its life and message, particularly among the younger generations of Scots. By the 1970s the post-war consensus on public policy was also breaking apart and the commitment to a comprehensive welfare state and full employment could no longer be assumed in British politics, as the 1980s were to demonstrate. All this is not a tale of ecclesiastical doom so much as the charting of the social and cultural changes which have brought the assumptions of the Secular vision of Scotland, and the Kirk's modern response to it, into question.

In particular, two fundamental assumptions no longer seem to be intellectually credible or sociologically plausible. The Secular vision envisaged a moral nation in which the Church's Christian social ethics would remain the bedrock of its public life as well as its private morality long after the edifice of worship and belief had crumbled in the earthquake of modern unbelief. And the Baillie response to that model of secularisation assumed that the Church would remain an influential national institution which gave a welcome moral lead in public life. As we have already noted, the Baillie approach believed that there were many, 'even among those who adhere to other faiths, who are willing in this matter to follow an energetic Christian lead.' We must ask how these assumptions fared when this secularised Christian ethical vision of Scotland as a responsive moral nation tackled the question of the government of Scotland in the post-war period.

This is an issue that has become central to the debate about Scottish nationhood and national identity in recent decades. We shall return to it in chapter ten, when we consider in greater detail the Church of Scotland's contribution to the devolution debate of the 1960s and 1970s as that has bearing on the Kirk's sense of its own Christian identity and mission as a national church; and again in chapter eleven, where we consider the relevance of the contemporary constitutional debate for our sense of Scottish identity. Here we are concerned with what the events leading up to the 1979 devolution referendum tell us about the Secular vision that Scotland was a moral nation which still responded to a Christian ethical lead from its civic leaders or its national church. According to the Baillie Commission's approach to the role of the national Church in a post-war secular society, the Kirk's views on devolution should have been influential in shaping national opinion on the subject. If the Church appealed to a common ethical middle ground as the basis for its views on the government of Scotland, then it could be confident of giving a lead even in a mixed society.

This is of course what the Kirk set out to do, especially in the 1960s and 1970s, at the height of the devolution debate. From the later 1940s, the Church of Scotland consistently called for a greater measure of national autonomy in the government of Scottish affairs, developing that call into support for the establishment of a Scottish legislature within the framework of the United Kingdom. Up to 1979 it based that position on its deep concern as the national Church for the welfare of the Scottish nation and on a related claim to represent a consensus of Scottish national opinion in favour of devolution. Given this consistent position of support for devolution over three decades prior to the devolution referendum, and the rising public support for a Scottish Assembly in that period, it could be assumed that the Kirk gave an influential and 'energetic Christian lead' on this issue. However, the verdict of academic commentators on the Kirk's role in the devolution debate is unanimous. It was marginal. The Kirk followed rather than led national opinion, which was shaped by other, secular forces. This is the verdict of Jack Brand, a political scientist who has made a particular study of the factors that have given rise to modern Scottish nationalism and support for Home Rule or self-government for Scotland. One of the factors he has examined is the role of religion and the church in shaping Scottish identity. In his book, *The National Movement in Scotland*, Brand considers the role of the Church of Scotland:

> There can be no doubt that the Church of Scotland is unequivocally for a very considerable measure of devolution for Scotland... the Church's attitude to devolution grows out of a general concern for Scottish society... [But] we should also bear in mind the fact that the Church cannot be said to lead the Scottish people on this issue... they have reacted to events... rather than leading the country as they did in the seventeenth century. Ministers have made pronouncements from their pulpits but the fact of the matter is that the Church's opinions are important only for a tiny minority of Scots. With the drop in church attendance and general secularisation the Church of Scotland is now a peripheral organisation in Scottish life.

It seems that modern secular Scots no longer look to the Kirk even for moral judgements on pressing matters of national welfare, far less for their beliefs or worship. When it came to the referendum campaign on the then Labour Government's Scotland Act, with its proposals to set up a devolved Scottish Assembly, opinion both within the Kirk and among the Scottish electorate proved deeply divided and uncertain in the crucial weeks before the vote on March 1st. Although a majority of those voting in the referendum favoured Labour's devolution Act, the level of support did not meet the arbitrary requirement of 40% of the Scottish electorate and the Act was finally repealed by the incoming Conservative Government a few months later.

To my mind 1979 marks the death of the Secular vision - that secularised Christian ethical vision of Scotland as a moral nation. Not only did the Church fail to play a leading role in the burning question of the day, so did the government of the nation, as it tried and failed to give a public moral lead on the assumption of broad national consensus. The other assumption underpinning the Secular vision was proved false. To be effective, this vision of Scotland required generations of Scots whose involvement in public affairs and national life was undergirded by ethical judgements and social concerns explicitly or implicitly shaped by the Christian tradition, even although they had abandoned the worship and doctrine of the Church. Throughout the history of the Secular vision, from the mid-nineteenth century onwards, there had been such generations of public leaders shaping Scottish society according to Christian ethical and social norms, especially those derived from the native Calvinist tradition. With the tragically early death of John P. Mackintosh, an influential academic and political advocate of Scottish self-government who owned that presbyterian ethical inheritance, at the height of the devolution debate in 1978, that generation of 'secular visionaries' passed away. Its epitaph was the failure to create a new national political institution in 1979 to transform Scotland, a Scottish Assembly to replace the General Assembly as the catalyst for ethical reform.

Few leaders in the new generations in Scottish public life acknowledge any debt to the Christian social ethical tradition central to the Secular vision. Nor do they make an appeal to Scottish public opinion on those grounds. We must ask ourselves why this Christian ethical vision for transforming Scotland, to be realised through secular institutions and movements rather than the Church, has failed in our generation. The answer does not lie solely with the profound social changes in modern Scotland that have turned it into a more pluralist secular society, lacking the social consensus for a common religious vision of its nationhood and national identity. It lies at the heart of the Secular vision itself.

The notion that the moral and ethical aspects of Christianity could be detached from their doctrinal foundations and made the basis of a vision of national life was not new to the secular visionaries of the later nineteenth and twentieth centuries. It had been the approach of the earlier Moderate party within the Kirk from the mid-eighteenth century onwards. The Moderates had continued to pay lip-service to the old Calvinist orthodoxies of the Westminster Confession, while abandoning its theological substance in favour of a cool, rational and ethical version in its preaching and social thought. One young minister who embraced that Moderate approach to religion and society was Thomas Chalmers. However, after an evangelical experience of conversion early in his parish ministry at Kilmany in his native Fife, Chalmers abandoned the narrowly ethical approach of the Moderates. He replaced it with a concern for 'the Christian good of Scotland' grounded in a living faith in Christ. Writing to his former parishioners in Fife, after moving to Glasgow to pursue his new evangelical social vision among the urban poor, he reflected on the change of heart and mind he had undergone among them. He had begun his ministry in a typical Moderate way, attempting through moral persuasion and appeal to effect personal and social change in his parish. This had no lasting impact, until he began to preach the need for spiritual conversion to Christ:

> During the whole of that period I made no attempt against the natural enmity of the mind to God, while I was inattentive to the way in which this enmity is dissolved, even by the free offer on the one hand, and the believing acceptance on the other, of the gospel of salvation... It was not till the free offer of forgiveness through the blood of Christ was urged upon their acceptance, and the Holy Spirit given through the channel of Christ's mediatorship to all who ask Him, was set before them... that I ever heard of any of those subordinate reformations... **You have at least taught me, that to preach Christ is the only effective way of preaching morality in all its branches ...** [my emphasis]

It was exactly that theological conviction that was rejected by the secular visionaries of the Victorian and Edwardian era. They believed that you could preach Christian morality effectively without preaching Christ - through municipal reform, private philanthropy, moral crusades, public education and institutions or ethical socialism. It was exactly that ethical approach to public policy questions which the Kirk adopted in the post-war era, in the belief that it could win the support of those outside its ranks. In the Baillie Commission's work on God's will for Church and nation, the middle axiom approach to Christian social thought would enable the Church to advocate social goals that would evoke a favourable response in the common Christian values surviving the pluralism of belief and non-belief in Scottish society. The events of 1979 show that this was no longer an effective way to preach morality in all its branches, certainly not those that extended into the welfare of the Scottish nation. The Secular vision perished in the sands of the devolution referendum. It had proved a mirage.

The bankruptcy of Chalmers' own experience of the Moderate precursor to the Secular vision led him to reconsider the claims of Christ as the source of a new Christian vision of Scotland. Are there any signs of a similar change of heart in contemporary Scotland? Out of the bitter disillusionment experienced by many Scots in the 1980s, arising from the collapse of the secular hopes for radical change in state and society pinned on 1979, were there honest minds willing to think the unthinkable and reconsider the long abandoned claims of Christian belief? Strangely, there are signs of such a change in Scotland's intellectual climate, though it is only a rain cloud as small as a man's hand amid the drought of modern unbelief.

Something of that change of climate is reflected in a recent book on twentieth century Scottish thought, *The Eclipse of Scottish Culture*, written by two younger Scottish intellectuals, Ronald Turnbull and Craig Beveridge. This work is critical of a prevailing tendency in studies of Scottish history and culture to dismiss the impact of religion, especially the Calvinist tradition, as a regressive influence on Scottish society. Turnbull and Beveridge call for a recognition of the neglected theological contribution to Scottish culture, especially to Scottish thought in this century. They end their analysis with what is, after the collapse of the Secular vision, an astonishing question. Writing of the religious influences on the thought of modern Scottish intellectuals, especially the work of the radical psychiatrist R.D. Laing, the authors conclude: 'Perhaps we could say of Laing's thought...that its problematic can be defined, ultimately, by the question: "What does the religion of my fathers mean to me today?"'

One modern secular Scottish intellectual who found himself asking that question in the early 1980s was the historian Christopher Harvie. Having rejected the Kirk of his youth and embraced the sceptical rationalism of his contemporaries in adult life, he began to doubt his unbelief in the light of what he now saw as the liberating vista of a reconsidered Christian faith. In a paper on faith and Scottish identity in 1988, Harvie shared something of his journey of faith in the years after 1979:

> ... the question of faith does not simply concern the possible role of religious bodies in any political movement. It is to do with the place of religion, organised or otherwise, in our lives. In my own case I spent twenty years away from the Church, until a combination of personal circumstances and self-examination brought me back six years ago [1982]... I suppose my attitude had hitherto been that of a Voltairean sceptic, softening into... vague regret... It was then that, taking stock... I realised that scepticism was less a liberating than a constraining force, narrowing both the range of experience and, more seriously, the range of sympathy... but if one accepts Christ one accepts the challenge of what George Herbert called 'repining restlessness' - and the possibility of the uncovenanted, the unexpected... Herbert's 'rest' could simply be the quiet of death after a life well-lived, little different, perhaps, from the humanist ideal. But to believe is to hold oneself open to a greater possibility, of grace and forgiveness, of a sense of being at one with God's creation, awake to his grandeur... To know that we can tackle life with the certainties and the procedures of his science, his reason, but to know also

that there are further possibilities, further grandeurs, attainable through the broken man on the Cross, seems pure gain.

With that, we have entered a new period in Scotland's vision of itself. It is time to reconsider that broken man on the Cross.

PRISM

Chapter 5

THE OTHER SCOTTISH CHRIST

Where do we start in our search for a contemporary Christian vision of Scottish identity? There is one intriguing link between Christianity and the rise of modern Scottish nationalism that brings us to the heart of the matter, Christopher Harvie's broken man on the Cross. Hugh MacDiarmid has shaken our national identity like a bucking bronco underneath some hapless rodeo cowboy. He wrote a poem published in 1925 called *The Innumerable Christ* which bore the epigram, 'Other stars have their Bethlehem and their Calvary too.' The line was by J.Y. Simpson, professor of Natural Science at New College, a theological college of the United Free Church of Scotland. MacDiarmid was drawn to Simpson's thought because of the professor's concern to integrate the metaphysical with the scientific. Could it be that in an evolving, relative universe there were other planets with their own incarnate and crucified Christ?

> I' mony an unco warl' the nicht
> The lift gaes black as pitch at noon,
> An' sideways on their chests the heids
>   O' endless Christs roll doon.
>
> An' when the earth's as cauld's the mune
> An' a' its folk are lang syne deid,
> On coontless stars the Babe maun cry,
>   An' the Crucified maun bleed.

86

Without travelling to other planets, are there not innumerable Christs in the world today? The revolutionary Christ of Latin American liberation theology would seem to have little in common with the gentle Jesus meek and mild who hung on so many Scottish Sunday School walls. Does such a question rankle Presbyterian sensibilities? Not for us the exotic crucifixes of Latin countries, with their 'Spanish Christs' twisted in morbid pathos. Not for us the dressing of our Saviour in national garb. And yet, and yet. Can we be so sure that we have not created our own Scottish version of the innumerable Christ?

That other New College professor who has been concerned to integrate science and theology, T.F. Torrance, has written that, to interpret Jesus, 'We desperately need Jewish eyes to help us see what we cannot see because of our gentile lenses.' Torrance argues that our gentile lenses make us see Jesus in terms of our own culture rather than Christ's own world of Israel. We 'read into him the kind of observational images which have played such a dominant role in our literary culture' rather than understanding Jesus 'as he is actually presented to us in the Jewish Scriptures'. Unless the Scots are somehow immune from this gentile myopia, we must test our Christian vision in Scotland. To have a Christian vision of Scottish identity is to look at Scotland through Christ's eyes. We share our patron saint, Andrew, with the Greeks. Some Greeks once came to the disciples saying, 'Sir, we would see Jesus.' If we would see ourselves as Scots then we too would first see Jesus. But which Jesus do we see in Scotland, the Jewish Christ or the Innumerable Christ of our own Scottish culture?

It was a Scottish missionary, John Mackay, who in the 1930's analysed the way in which the Latin culture of South America had conditioned the way in which Christians there had come to see Jesus. He had become 'the Spanish Christ' hanging in every Catholic church and devout home: remote, tragic, defeated and trapped on the Cross. This Christ had become an observable image of Latin religious and social culture, embodying the fatalist vision of South American identity. If only Mackay had stayed at home and looked at his native Scotland in the same way. After four centuries of iconoclastic Protestant reformation, he would have found no crucifixes in Reformed kirks. What

other piece of our church furniture might have provided him with
the clue as to the identity of 'the Scottish Christ'? What church
furnishing dominates our traditional Scottish kirks as much as
the crucifix dominated the traditional South American chapel?

The pulpit. There, in the pulpit, we see the Scottish Christ.
The Minister in the Pulpit is our Calvinist crucifix, our Presbyterian icon. It is the powerful visual image of the minister in the
pulpit that has conditioned the way in which our reformed
Scottish eyes see Jesus. This is no fanciful parallel with
Mackay's analysis. There are sound theological and cultural
reasons for seeing the Scottish Christ in these terms. Preaching
and the preacher are central to the Scottish Reformed tradition.
When we think of John Knox, we think of the painting that shows
him preaching with arm outstretched in the High Kirk of Edinburgh to Mary and her court. When we think of a Reformed
service of worship, we think of the sermon. Indeed, the two
became synonymous in Gaelic. But, granted that the minister in
the pulpit is central to the Scottish Presbyterian experience, how
can I justify calling that image the Scottish Christ? For an
answer, we must look briefly at an ancient heresy.

A theological battle raged in the early centuries of the Christian Church over the exact identity of Christ. Was he fully God?
Was he truly man? Was he both? Was he a third kind of being?
The councils of the Church resolved these questions about Jesus
in what became the orthodox confession that he was one person
but had two natures. He was fully divine and fully human. Many
alternative ways of seeing Jesus were advocated, including one
which saw Jesus as having a human body but a divine soul. This
heresy was known as *Apollinarianism*, named after Appollinar-
ius, an early advocate of this heresy.

This is no obscure, irrelevant matter. The consequence of
holding such a view of Jesus is far-reaching and destructive of
Christian faith and worship. If Jesus has no human soul like ours,
then this diminishes his scriptural role as our high priest before
God, interceding for us before the Father. He cannot present our
whole human identity perfect to God if he has not first assumed
our whole human identity, body and soul, in his incarnation.
Christian worship means coming to God the Father through God
the Son in God the Holy Spirit. We can only fully come to God

through Jesus if he is fully human as well as God. If we hold a faulty view of Jesus' humanity, then this must affect the way in which we worship God.

T.F. Torrance has traced the way in which this Apollinarian view of Christ has shaped the patterns of worship in the Church down through the centuries, in both East and West, Catholic and Protestant traditions. As he has written, '...if the priestly agency of Jesus Christ is obscured, then inevitably a substitute priesthood arises' to mediate between us and God. The centre of gravity in worship shifts from the priestly mediating role of Jesus Christ to the mediating role of priest or minister. In the Protestant tradition which has shaped our Scottish identity, this has often meant worshipping God 'through the personality and...idiosyncracies of the officiating minister'. In this way, the minister in the pulpit, so much part of the Scottish religious experience and folklore, becomes the mediating figure between us and God. In other words, **the Scottish Christ**.

The Reformed tradition has understood the ministry of Christ in terms of his three-fold office as priest, prophet and king. It is fascinating to see the way in which the Scottish Christ-figure, the minister in the pulpit, has taken on this three-fold office. We see this nowhere more clearly than in the Scottish novel. In Lewis Grassic Gibbon's *Scots Quair* trilogy, especially in the second volume, *Cloud Howe*, we see the Scottish Christ as priest. In Fionn MacColla's novel about the Highland Clearances, *And the Cock Crew*, we find the Scottish Christ as prophet. And in Robin Jenkins' novel about the Disruption of 1843, *The Awakening of George Darroch*, the Scottish Christ appears as a kingly figure. In each of these novels, the minister is a key character. In each novel the story unfolds in part through the outworking of the conflict within the mind and personality of the minister. And in each novel a dramatic climax is reached as the minister climbs into the pulpit to address the waiting and expectant congregation. It is the Scottish Christ who speaks, as the congregation meet their God 'through the personality and idiosyncracies of the officiating minister'.

The Scottish Christ as Priest

In *Cloud Howe*, Chris Guthrie, the heroine of Gibbon's

trilogy, has married a minister, Robert Colquohoun. Chris is to her husband 'Chris Caledonia', the embodiment of Scotland itself. Colquohoun himself embodies an idealistic Christian socialism. In him, we see the struggle of the Church to relate to the Scotland of the years after the Great War of 1914-18. Colquohoun has been called to the town of Segget, to minister to a parish of small-town tradesmen and jute spinners. He had served in the trenches of the First World War and carried with him the war-wound of damaged lungs. He is aware of the economic harships and social deprivation of the Segget workers. He begins his ministry with dreams of reforming the life of the community, its foul hovels and dark workshops. Slowly, and then with gathering pace as the 1926 General Strike runs its course, Colquohoun's social idealism and public stand turn into a withdrawn private grief for both his stillborn son and his stillborn vision of a just Christian community. A spinner couple had been evicted from their home in Segget, and their baby, gnawed by a rat as they sheltered in a pig sty, had died. Dangerously ill from his own war-time injury, Colquohoun is moved by this tragedy to risk his life by preaching one last sermon in Segget kirk.

The bold, uncomfortable preaching of Colquohoun's early ministry in Segget had, by now, turned into quiet 'blethers of Jesus and Brotherhood and Love and the Sacred Heart that still bled for men.' As he reads his text, the words of the dying thief on the Cross to Jesus, his weak voice recovers its former resolute clarity. He preaches a sermon at once both mystical and materialist, as he relates the death and hoped for second coming of Christ to the death of the spinner's child, to the death of his own post-war optimism about the ending of oppression, to the death of the Christian West. At the end of the sermon, he cries out in utter hopelessness, 'Lord, remember me when Thou comest into thy Kingdom!' Then he stops, with a strange look on his face, and dies, blood flowing from his lips onto the pulpit Bible. Chris, his wife, rushes into the pulpit and finds herself speaking, 'in strange words not her own, unbidden to her lips: It is Finished.'

The symbolism is unmistakable. The pulpit has become a very Scottish crucifix, Colquohoun shedding his blood in a cry of dereliction. The imagery of his sermon is itself priestly.

Speaking of the death of the spinner's child, he says, 'In the night a rat came and fed on their child, eating its flesh in a sacrament of hunger...'. He closes with the counsel that the world must 'forget the dream of the Christ' and turn to 'a stark, sure creed that will cut like a knife, a surgeon's knife through the doubt and disease' to see 'with unclouded eyes' in some far-off future 'an earth at peace, living and joyous, the Christ come back'. In the Scottish Christ figure of Robert Colquohoun, dying in the pulpit, we see the priestly figure of the other Christ, dying helplessly on the Cross, spilling his blood and crying out in despair, and remembered in the sacrament of his body and blood on which we feed by faith.

This view of Christ is shaped by the failure of the Scottish Church in the 1920s and 1930s to perform its priestly function of reconciling the harsh social reality of Scottish society to its vision of God and Scotland as a Christian nation. Colquohoun cannot bear that children should die in such a cruel way in what he refers to as this 'Christian village' and 'Christian land'. He mounts the pulpit-cross to die in empty intercession and atonement for the sins of the nation. The Church has failed to be Scotland's effective priestly centre, integrating all sections of society around its teaching and worship. The young socialist spinners of Segget and the young reactionary mill owner have no time for Robert Colquohoun or his kirk - or his Christ. This Scottish Christ represents a dying and ineffectual Church and a dying society that is powerless to act to save itself.

The Scottish Christ as Prophet

This same note of powerlessness is struck by Fionn MacColla in his novel *And the Cock Crew*. At the start of the book the people of the Highland glen have gathered at their chief's castle to be reprimanded by his Lowland factor over some alleged illegal action. In reality, they are being intimidated and threatened with ruthless eviction from their homes and land. Two obsequious ministers in league with the factor call the people to submit to these threats as the will and judgement of God's wrath upon them. They are deaf to their flock's cries to them to have mercy upon them and be their safety and protection. One angry voice speaks out from the crowd against the factor. It is Maighstir Sachairi Wiseman, another minister and the central character in the novel. Like an Old Testament prophet, he denounces the injustice that is being carried out against the Gaelic-speaking glen folk, in a face to face confrontation with the factor. Having questioned the legality of the factor's own actions, he tells the people to disperse quietly to their own homes, safe for the present. As a true shepherd to his flock, he has acted as their protector. But it is a role that he cannot sustain. As the novel unfolds, the very Calvinism that has prompted this courageous act of defiance begins to paralyse his will and conscience.

In Maighstir Sachairi's speech against the factor he states that no one can resist the Clearances if that is the will of God, as the other two ministers had argued. At that point in the story, Maighstir Sachairi admits to uncertainty on the matter. However, he is clear that if the threatened eviction is not the judgement of God, 'then it can be nothing more nor the oppressions of men.' And, therefore, as the servant of Jesus Christ, he must act to protect his people and denounce such oppression. In the succeeding chapters, as he becomes aware of what he sees as the gross sins of his Highland parish, his Calvinist conscience becomes convinced that the clearing of the glen is, after all, the terrible and irresistable judgement of the Almighty. The people of the glen still look to him as their protector. Apart from the anti-Calvinist Gaelic poet with whom the minister has argued and bared his soul on the matter, they are unaware of Maighstir Sachairi's inner torment and ominous change of mind. Towards the end of the novel the menace of eviction once more stalks their community. The people gather in the kirk on the Sabbath to hear their minister bring God's word to them and their plight. Once more the Scottish Christ mounts the pulpit steps.

After the opening psalm, the minister reads out a bitter text that fills the congregation with dread. It is from the Book of Deuteronomy and speaks of God's judgement in sending disobedient Israel out into the wilderness to hunger there as punishment for their sin. As the people wait to hear the sermon, the minister stands transfixed and paralysed in the pulpit. He is unable to deliver the word he feels driven to preach by his stricken conscience and twisted Calvinist fatalism. He slumps down in the pulpit, sobbing and inarticulate and silent. Slowly the congregation leave the church and go out to meet their fate at the hands of the factor. Their protector has failed them. This time there has been no prophetic word from Maighstir Sachairi to condemn the oppression of men that is about to destroy their ancient way of life. By his paralysed silence, the minister has become a collaborator with the factor he so resolutely resisted at the beginning of the novel.

The way in which MacColla builds up the tension in the church as the congregation await Maighstir Sachairi's sermon is reminiscent of the scene in Luke's Gospel when Jesus returned to his hometown of Nazareth to preach in his own synagogue. Like Sachairi, Jesus has been wrestling in his own conscience about the will of God during his temptations in the wilderness. In the synagogue he takes on the mantle of the prophet by reading from the prophet Isaiah and claiming to be the personal fulfilment of the scripture. The Spirit of the Lord is on him, to preach good news to the poor and to release the oppressed. Luke records that after Jesus had finished reading this prophetic scripture, the eyes of everyone in the synagogue were fastened on him in anticipation of what he would say. In the same way, after Maighstir Sachairi has read his text, '...all over the church people were staring up at the pulpit. More and more eyes were drawn to look and became fixed.' Unlike Jesus the Prophet, the minister is unable to apply his text to his hearers with the inner confidence of the true bearer of the divine word.

Yet when Sachairi comes to after his breakdown in the pulpit he recovers his senses sufficiently to oppose the factor who is by then burning and savaging the glen, driving out his flock with brutal callousness. In his feeble attempt to stop the eviction, the minister is driven over a precipice by a herd of stampeding cattle. Similarly, when Jesus has delivered his word against Nazareth, that no prophet is accepted in his home town, this so angers the people that they drive him out of the town, to the brow of a hill, in order to throw him down the cliff. But the mob from Nazareth fail to throw Jesus over the precipice. With the kind of unassailable authority that Sachairi showed in confronting the factor in the opening scenes of the novel, Jesus walks through the crowd and goes on his way. Unlike Jesus the true prophet, Sachairi fails to proclaim good news to the poor and to release the oppressed. He has lost his prophetic authority. The blood-crazed factor refuses to listen to him in the midst of the frenzied violence of clearing the glen and Sachairi is driven over the precipice.

Whatever MacColla himself did or did not mean, the parallels with the prophetic ministry of Jesus are uncanny. Here we see Christ the Jewish Prophet through the distorting gentile lenses of our Scottish literary culture. Once more, the worshipping congregation has encountered God 'through the personality of the officiating minister', the Scottish Christ. In this novel, the Christ figure of the minister in the pulpit appears in the role of the prophet, as one called to deliver God's word of coming judgement or hope into the present situation. The inner paralysis of Maighstir Sachairi's Calvinist conscience prevents him from delivering that prophetic word and he breaks down into incoherent groaning. The apostle Paul's strictures on the limitations of speaking in tongues come to mind here. 'Again, if the trumpet does not sound a clear call, who will get ready for battle? So it is with you. Unless you speak intelligible words with your tongue, how will anyone know what you are saying? You will just be speaking into the air.'

Ever since John Knox's notorious *First Blast of the Trumpet against the Monstrous Regiment of Women*, this image has been implanted in the Scottish imagination. The minister in the pulpit has been seen to have a prophetic ministry, blasting his hearers with the divine word without fear or favour. MacColla's dramatic climax is so effective because he inverts that image and portrays a prophet who falls silent, a trumpet that will not sound. This is the novelist's indictment against the Reformation and presbyterian Kirk in Scotland. MacColla vehemently believed that what he saw as the life-denying Calvinism of the Kirk had paralysed the Scottish identity, especially its Gaelic culture, and betrayed it to alien, English destructive forces. This Scottish Christ is a false prophet who fails to speak a true word of judgement and healing of the oppression of wicked men. Once more the Scottish Christ, and therefore the Scottish Kirk, is seen as a pathetic and powerless figure that fails to defend and shape the Scottish identity.

The Scottish Christ as King

We find the Scottish Christ in his kingly role in our third novel, *The Awakening of George Darroch*, by Robin Jenkins. Once again, the key character is a minister, George Darroch. The setting is the period around the Disruption of the established Church of Scotland in 1843. As a parish minister of the established Kirk, Darroch is throughout the novel wrestling with his conscience over the stand he should take if and when the Evangelicals go out of the national Church. The key theological issue for Darroch is stated clearly in the opening lines of the novel. Darroch is found praying in his manse study, agonising over whether he could risk making his family homeless and destitute, 'in order that he could keep what he called a promise to Christ the King...', a promise to leave the established Church if the State did not protect the right of congregations to approve their own ministers.

A promise to Christ the King. Again, this theme runs deep in the Scottish religious imagination. From the time of Andrew Melville's rebuke to James VI that, secular king though he was, he was only a subject in Christ's kingdom, the call of overriding loyalty to Christ's kingship has been a recurring one in Scottish Presbyterianism. We hear it loud and clear during the religious conflicts and wars of seventeenth century Scotland, at the time of the national covenants and the later Killing Times of the Covenanters, with their cries of King Jesus and no quarter. Such cries were alien to the more moderate Scottish churchmen of the eighteenth century. They still insisted on the crown rights of Christ being recognised, as they saw it, in the legal protection of the status of the Presbyterian Church of Scotland as the established national Church, by the Treaty of Union in 1707.

Such imagery was to re-emerge in the debates between the Moderate and Evangelical parties in the later eighteenth and early nineteenth centuries. The Evangelicals asserted the right of the Church to permit congregations to veto the appointment of ministers presented to their charges by patrons. In a number of civil court cases this right was contested and rejected by the judges. The courts asserted the legal right of the patrons to impose upon a parish the minister of their choice, even when such a choice was strongly opposed by the parishioners. Increasingly the Evangelicals saw the dispute as a straight matter of asserting the crown rights of the Redeemer, Christ the King, over against what they regarded as the abuse of the State's authority. This view held that while the secular rule was called to recognise and uphold the established religion, it could not interfere in the established Church's internal government, where Christ the King was to rule alone, through the Kirk's own courts.

In the novel, George Darroch has sided with the Evangelicals in their protest to the government in 1842 over the right of the Church 'to be spiritually independent of the secular power.' The central section of the novel is taken up with an address that Darroch delivers to his congregation from the pulpit of his kirk on Sunday morning, May 7th, 1843, only days before the fateful General Assembly at which the Disruption will take place, on May 18th. The theme of his address is to be the dispute over the appointment of ministers in the Church of Scotland. Within his congregation there are those like the local laird and chief heritor of the parish who side with the Moderates and the State and there are some, like the small traders and local teacher, who support the Evangelical cause. Darroch delivers a clear and factual account of the history of legal disputes in the civil and church courts that have led up to that present moment when Disruption seems imminent. Having set the scene for this local and national church drama, Darroch sits down in the pulpit, his hands shaking, knowing that, 'Soon he would be called upon to say what part he personally intended to play in the drama.'

After Darroch's address, his hearers proceed to debate the matter in terms of the rights of church and state. Finally, when Darroch is asked to state his own view, he declines to commit himself there and then. He pleads that the grief brought on by the death of his wife only days before has clouded his mind. He would have to consult his colleagues in Edinburgh before the Assembly to decide 'what course would be best for the Church and therefore the nation.' Until then, he begs their indulgence to suspend decision. In the end, when the opening day of the General Assembly comes, Darroch is among the first of the ministers fo follow the Evangelical leaders out of the Assembly in the act of Disruption. Having wavered to assert his promise to Christ the King in his own pulpit, Darroch's Presbyterian conscience awakens in time to leave the Establishment because of 'the dishonour done to Christ's Crown, and the rejection of His sole and supreme authority as King in His Church.'

But this is not the only aspect of George Darroch's awakening to the kingship of Christ in the novel. Before setting out on his public ministry of proclaiming the good news of the Kingdom of God, Jesus faced three temptations in the wilderness. Each temptation of the devil sought to turn Jesus away from his appointed way of kingship through obedience as the suffering servant of God. He was tempted with the power of the flesh, to turn stones into bread to satisfy his hunger. He was tempted with political power, when the devil offered him the kingdoms of the world in return for homage to the evil one. And, finally he was tempted with religious power, by throwing himself from the Temple in Jerusalem in order to be caught by the angels. As George Darroch stood in his pulpit addressing his congregation on the crown rights of Christ and his kingdom in Scotland, he was inwardly wrestling with these same three temptations in the form they took in his own life.

The temptation of the flesh with which Darroch wrestled was that of sexual lust and sin. His own wife dies just before his pulpit address, her health broken by bearing and caring for too many children. Darroch himself becomes obsessed by the attractive widow of a ministerial colleague and longs to marry her. In the novel, this temptation of the flesh is linked with Christ's third temptation away from his path of Kingship, the temptation of religious power. Darroch is offered by its wealthy patron the living of a parish near Edinburgh that would make him financially secure and place him in the higher circles of polite society. With a large family to look after, and with dreams of attracting the desirable widow to marry him with these better prospects, he is tempted by the offer. It is an offer he could not accept or would lose if he sided with the Evangelicals at the Disruption. He is here being tempted to climb to the higher reaches of the Kirk rather than keep his promise to Christ the King. This leads us on to the third aspect of George Darroch's awakening.

We have seen the awakening of his fleshly desire and of his ecclesiastical ambition, but the novel is also concerned with the awakening of his social conscience. In the course of his pastoral ministry he is confronted by the appalling conditions endured by the poor of his parish and the prisoners in the local prison. On the eve of the Disruption, in a gathering of Evangelical ministers met to discuss the momentous decision before them, Darroch is moved to speak out. He is not concerned with the legal rights of the church but with the social and spiritual conditions 'of the poverty-stricken and degraded masses'. He tells of how an atheist political radical had come to his district with a message of a just and plentiful future for the poor. Darroch portrays the future as a struggle between such atheist radicals and ministers of the Gospel for the hearts and minds of the masses and the socially concerned middle class. He is heard in uncomprehending and hostile silence by his conservative colleagues. Although they are willing to quit the Establishment, they are wedded to the social *status quo* and abhor any hint of lifting the masses above their station in life. His Moderate brother-in-law and colleagues are equally dismissive of his view that the Church should concern itself with social justice. But instead of embracing a costly commitment to the cause of the poor, as the poor parish minister of his old parish and an ally of the political reformers, the temptation is held out at the end of the novel that he might salve his social conscience as a busy do-gooder in a better-paid neighbouring parish, in effect accepting a position of limited social and political influence rather than the call to work for the revolutionary Kingdom of God.

In this third version of the Scottish Christ as King, we see the Biblical temptation of kingship - the aspiration to worldly power and the temptation to use worldly power for godly ends. The question is raised as to the nature of Christ's kingship in Scotland, but the minister-Christ figure is unable to embrace a kingship that can identify with the common humanity of Scotland's poor. The internal battle over his own humanity once more paralyses the Scottish Christ, as it did the priestly Robert Colquohoun and the prophetic Sachairi Wiseman. Just as the corrupt sacramental priesthood of the medieval Kirk became the failed mediator of pre-Reformation Scottish piety, so the remote, psychologically broken humanity of the minister became the failed mediator between the post-Reformation Scot and God.

In each instance, the weak humanity of the priest and the

minister was trying to do the impossible, filling the vacuum left by the not-fully-human nature of the triumphal and divine Christ of Scottish Christianity. This triumphal Christ inspired the triumphal visions of Scotland as a Christian nation, whether Catholic, Reformed or Secular, as we have seen in the last three chapters. These three visions saw Christ as the ascended, victorious Lord and therefore saw Scotland in similar terms. If Christ is perceived primarily as a triumphant, conquering divine figure then the national vision he inspires is that of a triumphal Christian community dominated either by a divine institution, the medieval Church, or a divine contract, the national Covenant, or a divine standard, the Christian Ethic.

If there is no fully human, suffering Christ in the midst of that Church, at the heart of that Covenant, giving flesh to that Ethic, mediating the presence, word and purpose of God to frail, suffering Scots from within their own humanity and within the ambiguities of their history, then it is no wonder that two things happened to each of those visions.

Ideas remote from experience

First, the key concepts at the centre of each vision, having fundamentally a divine rather than a human identity, became remote from the human experience and needs of ordinary Scots. The medieval Church, dispensing divine grace through a divine institution, failed to meet the profound human need of the medieval Scot for pardon and communion with God through the priestly mediation of Christ's humanity. The Reformed Kirk, binding the nation to God in a divine covenant, failed to recognise the importance of secular human institutions and politics for the Christian welfare of the nation. The nineteenth and twentieth century Secular Calvinist visionaries, transforming the nation through a divinely sanctioned ethic rather than Church or covenant, failed to sustain the power of a Christian moral vision among secular Scots lacking a religious motivation.

Lacking a credible humanity, because of a failure to put a fully human as well as fully divine Christ at the centre of their national vision, the divine guarantors of each vision, Church, Covenant and Ethic, became remote from human experience in Scotland and ultimately redundant as sources of national vision -too heavenly minded to be of any earthly use. The Canadian Church historian Donald C. Smith, relating the nineteenth century Scottish Church's social views to its view of Christ, sums up the problem:

> This tragic dichotomy between the world of the 'soul' and the present life of society was a prominent feature of contemporary Christian thought. The message of the Gospel was primarily for people's 'souls', not for their bodies; for their eternal welfare, not for their circumstances and condition in this life. Without realising it, the Church preached a kind of docetic Christ, rather than the Christ of flesh and blood; a 'spiritualized', 'otherworldly' Gospel, rather than the full Gospel of the Incarnation. This failure to take the full humanity of Christ seriously inevitably meant the failure to take the real humanity of men and women - their needs and problems, their needs and degradation - seriously. It was thus destructive of any truly Christian social ethic, for such an unbiblical understanding of the Christian faith meant that the Church never attempted to bring all aspects of human life and society under the radical judgement of God. Little wonder that such 'spiritualising' robbed the Gospel of its dynamic power, and thus its searching, disturbing criticism of the corporate life of society; that the Church's prophetic voice was never raised; that for the suffering masses of the industrial population such 'otherworldly' Christianity seemed hopelessly irrelevant.

Another Mediator

Second, without a fully human Christ at the centre, each vision sought a substitute human mediator to be the instrument uniting heaven and earth and shaping the nation's life. As we have seen, in the medieval Catholic vision it was the priestly hierarchy of the Church, mediating God's purpose for Scotland as a free nation. In the Reformed vision it was the ministry of the Word in the pulpit, mediating God's will for a godly nation. In the Secular vision it was the social reformer in society, mediating the coming of God's Kingdom on earth through a moral nation. Each possessed a fallen, frail humanity incapable of bearing the weight of mediating such purposes between the Scot and the Almighty. The medieval priesthood may have helped win the nation's freedom but it fell into corruption under the weight of assuming responsibility for Scotland's guilt. The Reformed ministry may have proclaimed the Word of grace for the nation's guilt but it fell into silence under the weight of assuming responsibility for Scotland's welfare. The Secular social reformers may have advanced the nation's welfare but they fell into impotence under the weight of assumimg responsibility for Scotland's public life and institutions.

Only Christ in his humanity can bear the weight of Scotland's guilt, welfare and destiny as a human community. As the New Testament states it: 'For there is one God and one mediator between God and men, **the man** Christ Jesus, who gave himself as a ransom for all men - the testimony given in its proper time.' (1 Timothy 2:5) In as much as the three great Christian visions of Scotland have not given this full Biblical weight to **'the man Christ Jesus'**, and all that this implies in terms of his humble solidarity with suffering humanity (Philippians 2:5-11), they have sought to replace this fully human Jewish Christ with their own flawed Scottish Christ-figures, whether it be Cardinal Beaton, Thomas Chalmers or Thomas Carlyle. Without a fully human centre in Christ, holding together God and humankind, these visions of human community have inevitably fallen apart. Instead, these three visions, even the Secular one, have centred on the triumphal figure of the divine Christ, victorious and yet remote; dependent on the role of substitute human mediators to realise his rule on earth in the form of a free, godly or moral nation.

The ancient Church Fathers rightly taught that what Christ had not assumed in his incarnation, he could not heal. That is, if Jesus of Nazareth did not have a fully human nature but only a divine nature within a human body, then, as our Saviour and Lord, he cannot identify with or cleanse our fallen human nature. A less than fully human, i.e. an 'Apollinarian' Christ, cannot heal our humanity or bring us directly before God through that humanity.

The Biblical, Jewish Christ, Jesus of Nazareth did assume that fully human nature, and took on all the weakness and temptations of that nature, yet without sin (Hebrews 4:14-16). The Scottish Christ-figure has combined an all too evidently sinful humanity with the remoteness of divinity. A late-medieval churchman, remote from the people through his corrupt hypocrisy, could not bring healing to the conscience. A Calvinist preacher, remote from the people through his scholastic erudition, could not bring healing to the mind. A bourgeois social reformer, remote from the poor through his patronising condescension, could not bring healing to the oppressed. The man who called himself the Way, the Truth and the Life did, and does, bring such healing.

The Scottish Christ, however, a divine yet not fully human priest, prophet and king, has generated godly and secular visions of Scottish identity that have shaped the Scottish nation for over four centuries. In the three novels we have considered, the minister-Christ figures collapse through internal crisis and incoherence, their fallen humanity unable to bear the weight of their mediating role between God's purposes and Scotland's history. In the same way, the visions generated by the Scottish Christ have now collapsed, leaving no coherent Christian vision in their place.

It is no longer historically credible or socially plausible to envisage Scotland one day returning to the triumphal era of Christendom, even in the form of its Victorian twilight, and having its national life shaped entirely by conformity to one Church, Covenant, Confession or Ethic. Does this mean the end of a Christian vision of Scotland? No, I think not. It means the end of the old visions, certainly. It spells the death of the triumphalist Scottish Christ, thankfully. But death is never the end for the Christian. It is the eve of resurrection. It is the threshhold for a new vision of Scotland.

The other Scottish Christ

As we roll the stone over the tomb of the Scottish Christ in his latest, secular guise, we should not stand looking at the past, blinded to Christ's real presence by nostalgic tears. There is within the same history of church and nation that we have been considering another Christ. He is Jesus, the Jewish Messiah from Nazareth, born of Mary; sharing our humanity in his earthly life; healing our humanity in his incarnation, ministry, crucifixion and bodily resurrection; mediating for us in our humanity before the Father, still bearing the wounds of his cross in heaven. There is a minority tradition in Scottish Christology (the study of who Christ is) that has always known Christ in this way. This minority Scottish Christian tradition has embraced Christ in his full humanity, while confessing equally the full divinity emphasised by the dominant triumphalist tradition. We may speak of the Jesus of this minority tradition as 'the other Scottish Christ'.

But where do we find him in Scottish Christianity? The other Scottish Christ is present in many places and denominational traditions. I will only consider here the Reformed tradition of which I am a part and for which therefore I share some responsibility. I believe we find the other Scottish Christ in the Scottish Reformed tradition at the very point where its own vision of Scotland as a Godly nation is collapsing, in the period of the Disruption. We are now familiar with the Herculean labours of Thomas Chalmers and the Evangelicals to recreate the godly commonwealth of the Calvinist vision by extending the parish system of the established Church of Scotland into the expanding urban, industrial communities of early nineteenth century Scotland. I have argued that this national vision died with the split in the established Church in 1843 and the founding of the rival Free Church of Scotland by Chalmers and most of the Evangelicals. I say most of the Evangelicals deliberately. The Disruption was not the only upheaveal in the Kirk in this period. I would even go so far as to say that it was not the most important struggle for the Gospel at this momentous time in Scotland's history as a nation.

As the storm clouds of the Disruption were gathering, some Scottish Christians of evangelical conviction were wrestling with questions not about the crown rights of the Redeemer in church government but about the humanity of Christ and the scope of his rule in national affairs. Just as we identified the Apollinarian features of the Scottish Christ in the ministers found in three Scottish novels, so we encounter the other

Scottish Christ in the theological writings and sermons of three
ministers of the Kirk in this period: John Macleod Campbell,
Edward Irving and Patrick Brewster.

Each of these three men made the humanity of Christ the
centre of his thinking in three crucial areas of Christian mission
to the nations. John Macleod Campbell came to see the incarnation of Christ as fundamental to the faithful preaching of the
Gospel. Edward Irving came to see the nature of Christ's
humanity as integral to the spiritual renewal of the Church's life.
Patrick Brewster affirmed the fellow humanity of Christ as a
keynote in his call for prophetic Christian political involvement
in national life. They struggled to bring the humanity of Christ
into the centre of the national Church's life in nineteenth century
Scotland. Significantly the first two were deposed as heretics by
the Kirk, and the latter was disciplined by the church courts.
Largely forgotten by most Scottish Christians, it is time to
recover their rich insights into Christ's humanity. They are a
source of renewed vision as to what it means to be human and
Christian in Scotland today.

John MacLeod Campbell was a Gaelic-speaking minister in
Row (now Rhu), near Helensburgh, from 1825 until he was
deposed from the ministry by the Kirk's General Assembly in
1831. Charges were brought against him for preaching that
Christ died for all humanity, contrary to the Calvinist orthodoxy
of the day enshrined in the Westminster Confession of Faith.
Macleod Campbell had been led to this view through Bible study
and his experience of preaching to his own parishioners in Row.
Though he preached to them the objective good news of salvation as God's free gift to all of them through Christ, the message
was lost to his hearers. Conditioned by the doctrines of 'federal
Calvinism', that Christ died only for the Elect, they either
doubted that Christ had truly died for them or sought evidences
for this within their own subjective experience. Macleod
Campbell preached that assurance of their salvation came from
the objective fact that Christ died for all, not from personal
introspection. Many could not believe the objective good news
for all that their minister preached. Macleod Campbell's pastoral
concern for his congregation led him to a profound re-assess-

ment of the Calvinist theology of salvation, resulting in his master work, *The Nature of The Atonement*, first published in 1856.

Central to Macleod Campbell's distinctive views on salvation was the place he gave to the humanity of Christ in his preaching and theological writings. He believed that the meaning of the death of Christ, the atonement, could only be understood properly through the incarnation:

> My attempt to understand and illustrate the nature of the atonement has been made in the way of taking the subject to the light of the incarnation. Assuming the incarnation, I have sought to realise the divine mind of Christ as perfect Sonship towards God and perfect Brotherhood towards men, and, doing so, the incarnation has appeared developing itself naturally and necessarily as the atonement.

Commenting on this aspect of Macleod Campbell's thought, the Canadian theologian George M. Tuttle has written:

> When therefore it is said that Christ 'represents' God to us it can only be in the sense that in and through Christ God is present to us **as God really is**. At the same time, and this was fundamental with Campbell, the atonement was wrought out by God **in humanity** by the man Jesus Christ. The atonement is not an ethereal divine event. It is a truly secular one.

By recovering this emphasis on the humanity of Jesus as our brother man, a fully human life lived without sin in a sinful world, Macleod Campbell lifted Scottish preaching of the Gospel out of a joyless, introspective legalism, characteristic of contemporary Calvinist orthodoxy, into the robust, confident good news for all humanity, characteristic of the New Testament. Perhaps Scotland has still to hear that Gospel?

Certainly, this new wine was too much for the Kirk of his day and they banned it as heresy. But if Macleod Campbell's evangelical brew was more than they could stomach, the teaching of Edward Irving, minister of the National Scotch Church, London, was the devil's firewater. Irving had been an assistant to Thomas Chalmers in Glasgow before going to London, where he established a reputation as one of the great and fashionable preachers of his day. He was deposed from the ministry of the Church of Scotland in 1833, and died a year later.

In many ways Irving was a tragic and eccentric figure. He is remembered as a pioneer theologian of the modern pentecostal and charismatic movements, through his preaching and writings on the baptism of the Holy Spirit, and support for the phenomenon of speaking in tongues which occured in his London congregation. Our particular interest here in Irving lies in his teaching on the humanity of Christ.

Central to Irving's views on the renewing and enabling ministry of the Holy Spirit in the life of the Church, was his conviction that in his incarnation Christ had both assumed and cleansed our fallen humanity. Irving did not teach that Christ was therefore a sinner, as his critics bitterly asserted. Rather, he echoed the conviction of the Church Fathers, that what Christ had not assumed in taking our humanity, he could not heal in our humanity. As Gregory of Nazianzus put it: 'What has not been assumed cannot be restored; it is what is united with God that is saved.'

Irving did not always put it so wisely or clearly, and it may be said that he stated an important insight into Christ's humanity in a way that was open to misrepresentation. Irving believed that Christ's identification with fallen humanity was so profound that his was a fallen human nature, subject to the same pressures and temptations that we are as fallen human beings. And yet, being God incarnate in that fallen human nature, throughout his human life he never gave in to sin and lived a life of perfect obedience and holiness through the enabling power of the Holy Spirit. For Irving, Jesus was 'the Man of Sorrows' who shared our human suffering and infirmity, yet without sin:

> ... our Lord took the same nature, body and soul, as
> other men, and under the same disadvantage of every
> sort, that his flesh was mortal and corruptible, and
> passive to all our temptations... - in one word, that his
> human will had lying against it, and upon it, exactly
> the same oppressions of devil, world, and flesh, which
> lay against and upon Adam's will after he had fallen,
> and which lies upon every man's will unto this day.
> And yet, 'though tempted in all points as we are', and

'in the likeness of sinful flesh', and 'made in all things like unto his brethren', the power and holiness of incarnate Godhead was such as to sanctify his body from first to last, and sustain it holy; so that all his life long 'he presented his body a living sacrifice, holy and acceptable, and proved what was that holy and acceptable and perfect will of God'... the Holy Ghost empowering the infirmity, sanctifying the unholiness, quickening the mortality, and in all respects perfecting the human nature which he took, flesh and soul, at all times, so that he could be called the Holy One of God from his conception to his resurrection; although, between these two periods, he was flesh, enduring our conflict, our death, and all the curse, and all the law, which our sin had introduced...

For these convictions Irving was convicted of heresy and deposed. Yet, however unwisely he stated it at times, he was gripped by one of the central truths of the Christian faith, that God took flesh in Jesus of Nazareth. Irving realised the profound link between the work of the Holy Spirit in the humanity of Christ and the work of the Spirit in our fellow humanity today. Had the Church of Scotland been more open to his insights, its own humanity might have been more open to both the renewing power of the Spirit and the sorrowful, suffering humanity embraced by Christ and experienced by the people of Scotland. These insights, that renewal and such human identification remain open to the Church today which places the humanity of Christ at the centre of its preaching, worship, community, mission and service.

One minister of the same period who did take seriously the Christian responsibility for the suffering humanity of ordinary Scots was **Patrick Brewster**, minister of the second charge in Paisley Abbey from 1818 to his death in 1859. The nature of Brewster's remarkable social and political convictions can be seen from the reasons he gave for not joining Thomas Chalmers and the Evangelicals in the Free Church after the 1843 Disruption. He agreed with their principled stand against patronage and state intrusion in church affairs but deplored the conservative social and political views likely to prevail in the new Free Church. He felt he would have more freedom to preach the radical social implications of the Gospel if he remained in the established Kirk, with all its faults.

Brewster stood almost alone in the Church of Scotland as a minister who was prepared to support the contemporary working class movements for political, social and economic reform, such as the Chartists, out of a clear Christian conviction. He did not hesitate to preach against the appalling social conditions among the poor of the time or to call the privileged classes to account for unjust laws and practices. He was no political revolutionary, and called for peaceful, constitutional reform. And yet he did not hestitate to stress the social implications of the Gospel for the state and society. Accused of preaching politics, he replied:

> If to preach such doctrines be politics, then such be our politics and our preaching, for they were the politics and the preaching of the Holy Prophets and Apostles - aye and of the great Lord of the vineyard himself, who, descending from the glories and blessedness of eternity, met shame and contempt and death, that he might bring deliverance in time, and salvation through eternity, to the sinful, the suffering, and the oppressed children of men.

Again, central to his preaching and political involvement was the conviction that by his incarnation Christ had identified with suffering humanity in order to liberate it from the oppression of social as well as personal sin. The clear consequence of this for Brewster was that the preaching of Christ crucified could not be separated from the lordship of Christ over the whole of human life, including the secular affairs of the nation and the conduct of government. Brewster applied the conviction that Christ was King of Kings not only to Church affairs, as the Free Church did, but to society as a whole, in a radical criticism of social and political injustice, which the established Kirk and Free Church refused to do. This left Brewster an isolated but prophetic figure in his time.

His prophetic preaching still holds out a vision of the other Scottish Christ for the Church today, with all that this implies for

Christian social and political involvement in the contemporary life of the nation.

Who do you say that I am?

At a crucial stage in his earthly ministry, Jesus of Nazareth asked his disciples two questions. He enquired from them who people said that he was. And then he asked them, 'But what about you? Who do you say I am?' (Mark 8:29) This is the central question of the Gospels and of the Christian faith. It is the central question for a Christian vision of Scottish identity. We cannot know who we are as Christians and as Scots, without seeing clearly who Christ is in relation to our own identities. It has been the argument of this chapter that the way in which we see the humanity of Christ is central to the way in which we understand our own humanity.

The historic failure of the Reformed tradition of Scottish Christianity to give central place to the full suffering humanity of Jesus, while emphasising his triumphant divinity, has led not only to 'the Scottish Christ'. It has seriously distorted our vision of ourselves as Scottish Christians and as Scots. It has distorted the Christian vision of human identity and community and purpose which we have offered Scotland over centuries. It has led to three great triumphal visions of Scotland as a Christian nation, each of which has made a unique and lasting contribution to the way in which we see ourselves as Scots. But these three triumphal visions have taken a great toll on the humanity of the Scottish people, their psychology, culture and society. And they offer little today to a Church and nation wrestling with problems of religious and secular decline and human suffering.

By recovering a central vision of the suffering humanity of Christ, and of the transformation of all reality through his Cross and Resurrection, it is my belief that we shall recover a new, more humble Christian vision of Scotland. From the humiliated Christ, our crucified and risen Brother, comes a vision of a humbler, more human nation - a community that does justice and loves mercy through walking humbly with its God. Christians can only offer such a human vision to the nation by going the way of Jesus, suffering as servants in the midst of the nation's life. To find such a vision of Christ and nation today, we must turn now to Scripture and the Biblical understanding of nations.

PART 2 THEOLOGICAL IDENTITY -
Christ and Nation Today

Chapter 6

THE ECOLOGY OF NATIONS -
A Biblical View of Nationhood

Nations are chameleon-like communities. They change their colour according to the historical landscape in which they are to be found. From the ancient table of nations in Genesis chapter 10, through the nations listed as present at Pentecost in Acts chapter 2, to the modern roll call of nation states in the United Nations, the term nation has been used to describe an enormous variety of human communities.

The students of nations and nationalism can neither agree on nor find one all-embracing and adequate definition of the term. Theories of nationalism abound. Professor Seton-Watson has concluded that a nation is any community of people which perceives itself to be a nation. This accords with Benedict Anderson's description of nations as 'imagined communities'. He argues that nations are imagined not in the sense that they are make-believe but by the way in which their members share a common image of their national identity through time and across space. This shared image binds them together without personal contact or knowledge of one another in a way that transcends other potentially divisive identities such as class. Indeed, all communities are 'imagined' in this sense once one goes beyond intimate, face-to-face societies such as the family or the village. They differ in the style in which they are imagined. Nations are communities imagined in the style of ethnic groupings bound together by a range of social variables such as a common language, culture, history, geography, religion, or, especially in modern nationalism, a common statehood or aspiration to it.

The definition of nations as imagined communities brings us to the heart of the matter for a Christian theology of nationhood. Professor T.F. Torrance has distinguished between those concepts that are 'percepts', grasped through visual images which correspond with some observable reality; and those concepts that are 'audits', grasped though imageless images, words that refer beyond themselves to imageless realities. Nations here are clearly percepts, communities that are conceived through a shared image of common identity that can be mentally or actually visualised.

We need only think of the characteristic expressions of national identity to see that is the case: the national flag and the national capital; a distinctive feature of national geography, like the Highlands of Scotland; the anthems, songs, stories and traditions that evoke memories of a nation's past in gripping images of battle, struggle and victory, from *Scots Wha Hae* to the *Star Spangled Banner* ('O say can you see in the dawn's early light...'); and the sacred items that evoke the ethos and identity of a nation, such as a picture of the Virgin in Poland, the crown jewels in England or the sword of William Wallace in Scotland. The importance of visual objects for imagining our nationhood was well expressed in the opening text of the Exhibition *The Wealth of a Nation* in Edinburgh, during 1989. Under the title *Symbolic Wealth: Images of Nationhood* it stated:

> The kingdom of Scotland existed independently for
> hundreds of years. Despite the Union of the Crowns
> in 1603 and the Act of Union in 1707, Scotland has
> retained a distinctive identity. National identity is
> vividly represented by symbols, by objects which are
> tangible expressions of cultural and emotional forces.
> The Crown and the Church have traditionally been the
> guardians of the most valued symbols of the nation.

This dependence of the nation as an imagined community upon percepts or visual images has made it the kind of community that is open to idolatry - loyalty to created images rather than the living God: the motherland, the fatherland, the crown, the state, the people and the race, the earth and land, blood and kin, king and country. Such nationalist idolatry has seen some divine or human moral imperative immanent within the identity and community of the nation and regarded nationhood as a part of the natural and necessary order of human existence. At its most elevated it has given rise to the pure and abstract nationalist doctrine of the inalienable sovereignty of nations to exist as nation-states. At its most insidious, it has spawned the religious nationalism of the 'German Christians' who supported the Nazi Reich and the Afrikaner Christian nationalism that provided the religious ideology underpinning apartheid in South Africa. As imagined communities, shaped by powerful cultural percepts or visual images, nations are always open to the pagan temptation of adherence to natural and supernatural loyalties, like the land or the national soul.

Israel and the Nations - Imagined and Acoustic Communities

Such an analysis of nations fits well with the Biblical understanding of the nations. The *goyim*, the gentiles, are seen in the Old Testament as the pagan, unbelieving, idolatrous nations of the earth that worship the graven images forbidden to Israel. The Bible deals with nations in theological rather than sociological terms. It considers them only in relation to that other nation which is its central theme and concern - Israel, the holy nation and people of God. The cultural, political, linguistic, economic, religious and social aspects of the nations mentioned in Scripture are of interest not in themselves but only as they bear upon the story of God's dealings with humankind and with Israel. Given this way of looking at the nations, several characteristics can be noted.

First, the Old Testament sees the nations of the earth as part of God's providential ordering of human affairs, but not as part of his original creation. In the opening chapters of the Book of Genesis, there is no mention of nations until the two significant references to them in chapters 10 and 11. The first nine chapters are concerned with the creation of the cosmos, the world and the one human race by God and the subsequent distortion and marring of that good creation through the sin of Adam, that wilful act of rebellion against God and his way. Genesis deals with the common descendants of Adam down through the story of the flood and judgement of the human race and the promise made to Noah and his descendants that God would spare the earth. It is only after the creation command to Adam is repeated to Noah and his sons - to be fruitful and increase in number and fill the earth (Genesis 9:1) - that the nations are referred to, in the table of nations given in Genesis chapter 10, and in the story of the Tower of Babel in chapter 11:1-9.

As Karl Barth argues in his exposition of these passages, the nations are not part of the created order; they were given no specific command from God as to their purpose and fulfilment, unlike the natural and necessary relationships of man and woman, parent and child. Rather, the nations arose in the course of human history and culture after the Fall of Adam. Genesis 10 and 11 show two contrasting yet complementary aspects of how God orders fallen human society for good.

In Genesis chapter 10 the nations are seen as part of the creative diversity of the human race in response to God's covenant and command to Noah to be fruitful and increase in number and fill the earth. This the descendants of Noah are recorded as doing, as they spread out geographically and prolif-erated linguistically, culturally and socially in different clans and nations. Even after the rebellion of humankind and its consequent judgement with the flood, God blesses human life and its future on earth. The nations are recorded as a social fact of that historical and cultural development but not as a necessary condition of it.

However, in Genesis chapter 11:1-9, in the story of the Tower of Babel, the nations are not seen in this positive way. The story of how the one human race decides to build a tower to guarantee security without relying on divine providence shows that the diversity of nations is part of God's judgement on humanity for their presumption. God scatters the whole world with its common language in order to prevent it attempting even more grandiose acts of autonomy and rebellion against its Creator. Here the social and historical fact of division into many nations is seen in a negative way as divine judgement, with the one humanity fragmenting into mutual incomprehension. And yet, even here, it has a salutary effect in restraining the human race from acting in consort and reaching the levels of universal wickedness that brought on the global destruction in the days of Noah.

As Barth argues, it is important to hold together these two different but complementary views of the nations; the positive dimension of their cultural diversity in response to the divine command and the negative dimension of their cultural fragmentation as the punishment of divine judgement, with both the command and the judgement being given to the whole human race and not to the nations as such. The nations are the communities that arise in the course of human history, now marred by sin, but upheld by the blessing and judgement of God's providential ordering of all life on earth. So the nations can be seen in terms of both the blessing and the judgement of divine providence. It is through the creative diversity of different nations, languages and countries that the one human race now fulfils its cultural mandate to fill the earth and be fruitful. It is through the alienating differences among the many nations that God judges and restrains the sin of this one human race.

Second, the history of the nations is subordinate to the story of one particular nation, Israel. Genesis chapters 10 and 11 serve as the backdrop of world history before the main actor is introduced in chapter 12: Abram, whom God promises to make into a great nation and a blessing to all the peoples of the earth. From then on in Scripture the nations feature only in relation to the identity and destiny of Abram (who becomes Abraham, 'father of many') and his descendants, the nation of Israel. The cultural and political achievements of these surrounding nations far surpass those of the small semi-nomadic tribes of Israel, except for one short period during the kingships of David and Solomon. And yet they do not loom large in the biblical narrative. Why? Because Israel's nationhood is not based on these cultural, ethnic, territorial and military grounds, unlike the gentile nations. Israel is a people whose national identity is based on the spiritual ground of God's election covenant and law.

God chose Abraham and his descendants to be his own people out of all the nations of the earth, but not because they were a special or great nation like Egypt or Babylon. He chose them entirely for his own purposes. To that end, God made a unilateral covenant with them, an unbreakable bond of communion between them that he would be their God and they would be his own people. As the *am Yahweh*, the people of God, God revealed his will to them in the giving of the *torah*, his Word to them through Moses in the divine Law. Therefore the grounds of Israel's nationhood were very different from those of the surrounding nations of the earth. The social existence of the gentile nations was contingent upon their survival in conflict or coexistence with the other nations. In the course of history such nations could rise, fall and disappear or be absorbed by other peoples and races, all within the providential ordering of the world for good by God, the Lord of that history. Whereas, Israel's identity and survival was contingent upon the divine call and promise and word to them through Abraham and Moses.

Third, then, Israel was a paradox as a nation amid the nations of the earth. It was to be a holy nation, separated and set apart to serve a holy God amid the pagan and idolatrous nations of the earth. It was called into being through hearing the call of the unseen and living God, concerning whom it was forbidden to make any graven image. That call came to Abram at Haran and to Moses at Horeb as a voice from the unseen presence of the living God. The call was to found a family and then a nation on the basis of the word of command and promise by this unseen and imageless God. More than that, the nation of Israel was called to maintain its community life and identity without images and entirely dependent on the divine word of command and promise.

The concept of nationhood that we encounter with Israel is, therefore, entirely different from the one we have described for the surrounding gentile nations. Unlike the nations, Israel's identity is not based on **percepts**, the visual images of religion, culture, wealth, territory, military might or pagan kingship that shaped the style of imagining or imagined communities of the heathen. No, quite remarkably and uniquely, Israel's nationhood is based on **audits**, the imageless images or words of the unseen God's election, covenant and *torah*. Israel exists and prospers through the hearing of God's Word. In a real sense, if the gentile nations are imagined communities, then the holy nation of Israel is an 'acoustic community'. It exists not through a style of imagining based on images immanent within human history and culture, like the imagined communities of the nations. Israel exists through a style of hearing based on the transcendent word of the living God and Lord of human history and culture, given to a particular people in a particular place and time.

Of course, that is not to say that certain visual images were not central to Israel's sense of nationhood. God did indeed sanction the role of certain percepts or visual national images to shape Israel's sense of national identity. The act of circumcision was an early sign of Israel's covenant nationhood, established through Abraham. The blood of the sacrificial lamb and the passover meal were lasting images of a nationhood born out of the Exodus from captivity in Egypt. The Wilderness experience which forged slaves into a nation drew on the images of the Ark of the Covenant, containing the tablets of the divine law, and the Tabernacle, a focus of the sacrificial system of worship. The conquest of Caanan and its theological significance as the Promised Land were fundamental to Israel's sense of nationhood. The Temple in Jerusalem became the focus of the nation's life and sense of national purpose. It was the locus of sacrificial worship and the celebration of the festivals of faith, all rich in images of a shared national identity. The establishment of the monarchy, celebrated in the kingships of David and Solomon, and the political independence of the nation which it represented, also defined Israel's later sense of nationhood.

However, all of these images of nationhood were strictly conditional and secondary to Israel's identity as an acoustic community. They were given as tangible expressions of the covenant love and rule of the unseen God, to strengthen Israel in its calling to hear and obey his word. They had a place in Israel's life only in that acoustic context and must not be understood apart from it. They could be removed by God as a sign of judgement for failing to fulfill their true mission and be his holy nation. Israel's sacrifices could become an offence to God without a repentant heart and a just life. The Temple could be destroyed, the Kingdom divided, the land conquered and abandoned, the people scattered into exile and yet Israel did not lose its nationhood as God's people. This was an acoustic identity grounded in the promise of God and his covenant with Israel. It was the survival of a faithful remnant of true worshippers, the bond of the *torah* and the promise of the messiah which sustained Israel in exile and in the vicissitudes of its later history as a conquered nation. One classic example of Israel's acoustic identity amid the imagined identities of pagan nations can be found in the Old Testament book of Nehemiah. Here the remnant of Israel gather in a Jerusalem square to hear Ezra read the Law or *torah* to the people. This leads to the spiritual renewal of Israel as a holy nation, including a new concern for God's justice for the poor (Nehemiah 5-10, esp. ch 8).

A fundamental distinction must be made, therefore, between the nationhood of the gentiles and that of Israel. The nations of the earth are seen as the social artifacts of human history arising out of the fall of the one human race into both cultural diversity and social fragmentation. They are seen as historical and provisional human communities created by people, and not as natural and necessary human communities created by God. They are ambiguous communities bearing the marks both of divine blessing and divine judgement and manifesting the traits both of human creativity and human depravity. The holy nation of Israel is seen as the divine creation of Yahweh within human history arising out of the gracious covenant of God with the one human race made in creation, marred but not destroyed at the fall and renewed through Noah, Abraham and Moses for the sake of all the peoples of the earth. Israel is seen as a holy and elect human community created by God through the faithful hearing of his Word.

The reason for God's choice of Israel to be his people is unambiguous. It lies in the mystery of God's covenant love. Israel is to be God's faithful witness to the nations around, showing them his holy love and commands, his word of grace and judgement to all nations. Through Israel's faithful reception and response to God's Word, all nations are to come to know God and his *torah*, the command to love God and neighbour. Israel is not only to be a holy nation amid the nations; it is to be a light to the nations. Through this one people, God wills to bring all the divided nations of Babel back into the one people of God in the city of Zion. As the gentile nations hear and see the word of God through Israel, they too will cease to be imagined communities, bound together by pagan images or idols, and become acoustic communities like the holy nation.

Fourth, as its name in Hebrew implies, Israel struggled with God to get out of this national identity as an acoustic community based on the words of election, covenant and *torah*. Time and again it wanted to be an imagined community like the other nations and base its national life on the images of gentile nationhood, especially kingship and the idols of pagan worship. It wanted a king like other nations. It turned to the gods of other nations. It made alliances with foreign powers to ensure its security. And, perhaps worst of all, it adopted the oppressive and exploitative social practices of the surrounding nations, neglecting the poor, the widow, the orphan and the stranger contrary to the *torah* of God's justice and shalom. Against such deafness to his word, God raised up the prophets to proclaim his message of judgement and hope to Israel and the nations. In his sovereignty, God also used other nations to chastise Israel and be the rod of divine judgement against his people. Even in its wilful deafness, God dealt with Israel as an acoustic community, warning them and pleading with them through his speaking prophets and dumb pagan instruments. It became the growing conviction and witness of these prophets that in the fulness of time God would send to faithless Israel his chosen servant and annointed one. This messiah would hear and fulfil God's word of election, covenant and *torah* not only for Israel but for all the nations of the earth.

The Church - the New Acoustic Community of All Nations

It is significant that when the New Testament describes Jesus of Nazareth it often does so in terms of the nationhood of Israel as an acoustic community. We see this clearly in that most Jewish of New Testament letters, the letter to the Hebrews, (1:1,2): 'In the past God spoke to our forefathers through the prophets at many times and through various ways, but in these last days he has spoken to us by his Son, whom he appointed heir of all things, and through whom he made the universe.'

And in the prologue to John's Gospel, there is revealed to us the most profound mystery of Israel's existence as an acoustic community, a holy nation created to receive and respond to the word of God. God not only speaks to Israel. He is himself the

Word spoken to Israel: 'In the beginning was the Word, and the Word was with God, and the Word was God. He was with God in the beginning' (John 1:1,2). The imagined communities of the earth, the gentile nations of the one humanity created by the Word, they could not recognise him (John 1:10) - he had no form or beauty to attract him and he refused to base his community on their images of kingly power, of bread and magic. Jesus was not to be known through percepts. His coming could not be recognised by those who dealt in visual images alone, like the Romans. He was the Word, to be received by the people that the word of the law and prophets had shaped into an acoustic community capable of receiving his word of good news: Israel, the people of God.

John records the tragedy of his coming, that his own nation of Israel did not receive him (John 1:11): 'Yet to all who received him, who believed in his name, he gave the right to become children of God - children born not of human descent, nor of human decision or a husband's will, but born of God (John 1:11,12). In that last statement we see God creating a renewed holy nation, a new acoustic community which John deliberately contrasts with the imagined human communities of natural birth or human construction. The people of God here are those who believed in his name, who received him as the Word of God made flesh among them, as the one who reveals the unseen God to them (John 1:18). John is describing a community based on the audit of the incarnate Word who reveals the unseen God to us, both Jew and Gentile.

Those who are in this community, described in 1 Peter 2:9 as the holy nation, are all those who have heard the Word and who have accepted it and bear witness to it. They have not disobeyed the message and so they too now share in the holy nationhood of Israel: 'But you are a chosen people, a royal priesthood, a holy nation, a people belonging to God, that you may declare the praises of him who called you out of darkness into his wonderful light. Once you were not a people, but now you are the people of God; once you had not received mercy, but now you have received mercy' (1 Peter 2:9,10).

Jesus came as the Word to the acoustic community of Israel. He was always astounded both by the stubborn deafness of his own nation to his word and by the receptiveness of Gentiles to his word of authority. After his resurrection he called on his disciples to see his death and rising again as the fulfilment of the Jewish Scriptures. But he also called on them to see the preaching of his Gospel to all nations as the fulfilment of the scriptures (Luke 24:45-47). As the messianic Word, Jesus saw himself as the fulfilment of God's purposes for both the holy nation of Israel and the gentile nations of the earth. His Church was to be the new acoustic community of all those who hear his Gospel preached through the witness of his apostles.

On the day of Pentecost in Jerusalem, as God poured out his Spirit upon the Church, this new acoustic community became a reality; every nationality gathered in the city heard the Gospel in its own language (Acts 2). Then Peter preached the Word who is the incarnate, crucified and risen Lord, Jesus Christ, whom the Jews reduced to silence in his crucifixion but whom God raised to life and voice again.

In the story of the early Church in the Book of Acts we see the Jewish disciples of Jesus wrestling with the implications of the Gospel, that it is a word of forgiveness and new life in the Spirit for Gentiles as well as Jews. Supremely, we see Paul as the Apostle to the Gentiles, under the conviction that the whole earth has now become the acoustic community where he is called to preach the Gospel. As he wrote in his letter to the Romans: 'I am bound both to Greeks and non-Greeks, both to the wise and the foolish. That is why I am so eager to preach the Gospel also to you who are at Rome' (i.e. while on the way to Spain, the uttermost ends of the Western world, Romans 15:24,28). 'I am not ashamed of the Gospel, because it is the power of God for the salvation of everyone who believes: first for the Jew, then for the Gentile' (Romans 1:14-16).

In the New Testament we see the acoustic community of the holy nation of Israel expanded to include all those Gentiles who faithfully hear the word of the Gospel. Although there was some glimpse of this gentile response in the Old Testament (Isaiah chapter 2), it was only with the coming of the messiah and his commission to go to all nations preaching good news, and with the carrying out of that command by the early Church in the power of the Holy Spirit, that the gentile nations became the direct focus and central theme of the Biblical narrative. Not since Genesis chapters 10 and 11 had they received such attention in Scripture. What we see is the mighty act of Pentecost recreating what was lost at Babel. Through the hearing of the Gospel and the receiving of the Spirit, the nations of the world can become one people once more, through the Word coming forth from the acoustic community of Israel (Ephesians 2:11-22). Through the coming of the Word, incarnate, crucified, risen, ascended and reigning through the Spirit poured out on the expanded acoustic community of Jew and Gentile, Greek and Barbarian, through the coming of that Word there is a fundamental shift in the nature of both gentile nationhood and the holy nationhood of Israel.

Response to Jesus who is the Word of God has now become the key to understanding the concept of nationhood both for Israel and for the nations. The nation of Israel did not receive the Word as the messiah promised by its prophets. But this rejection by Israel is, in God's sovereign purpose, the opportunity for the gentile nations to hear the Word and to be brought into the holy nation of God's people, as the Gospel is preached everywhere. Only then, when the gentile nations have responded to the Word and been brought in to the people of God, will 'all Israel' be saved (Romans chapter 9 to 11).

The final mention in Scripture concerning the nations is in the Book of Revelation chapters 21 and 22, where John's vision of the new heaven and the new earth includes three enigmatic references to the nations: in the new Jerusalem, symbol of God's new creation, the nations will walk by the light of Christ (Revelation 21:24); the glory and honour of the nations will be brought into it (Revelation 21:26); and, finally, the tree of life within the city will have leaves for the healing of the nations (Revelation 22:2). Here in the immediate presence of the living God in all his glory, there will be no more need for acoustic communities, the nations of the earth living by the Word of the unseen God, because they shall see him face to face. Nationhood is now described in terms of images, images for all time and every place.

In Scripture, then, we see two kinds of nationhood. There is the imagined community of the Gentile nations, the *goyim* and *ethne* of the Jewish and Greek worlds. And there is the acoustic community of holy nation, the *am* and *laos* of Israel and the Church. The teaching of Scripture could be summed up thus:

(a)   The human race rebels against its gracious Creator, consequently falls from its purpose and fragments into the nations of the earth, who vainly imagine their own identity without God and illustrate both his providence and judgement in their diversity and divisions.

(b)   Out of all the nations of the earth God chooses one people, the descendents of Abraham, to be his holy nation amid the nations; to hear his Word and make it known to the nations, first through the faithful keeping of the *torah* and then, after their rebellion against this acoustic identity, through the incarnation of God's own Word among them.

(c)   When the representatives of Israel and the Gentile world power together silenced that Word by crucifying Jesus, God by his Spirit vindicated his Word when Jesus rose again to life and speech.

(d)   Through the Word of the Risen Christ the Church was commissioned, in the power of the same Holy Spirit, to be the new acoustic community bringing the Word within the hearing of all the nations. And through this Word of the crucified Jesus, all the barriers of Babel among the nations are broken down, as the Word makes all nations, Jew and Gentile, into one people of God.

From Imagined to Acoustic Communities

The Bible sees nations not primarily as **imagined** communities, in sociological terms of human culture and history, although it recognises the social fact of their historical existence within the providence of God. It sees them primarily as **acoustic** communities, in theological terms of hearing the divine Word and obeying it where they are. On reflection, and in the light of the Gospel, we must call gentile nations acoustic communities as well. For ultimately Scripture sees all nations, both Jewish and Gentile, as communities that are open to the Word that came through the chosen people of Israel, through the prophets and, finally, through the Prophet, Jesus, the Word made flesh (salvation is from the Jews - John 4:22). The Word came through Israel but now is addressed to all the nations of the earth. Therefore all nations must be acoustic communities, called by God to hear and understand and obey this Word and declare his praises. The holy nation of God's people, including all nationalities in the one new humanity, is called to broadcast the Word to the nations, while the historic nations of the earth are called to receive it in the obedience of faith.

As the members of the different nations hear this Word, repent and are baptized for the forgiveness of their sins, they are called into this new humanity, the holy nation of God's people. They take on a new national identity, an acoustic identity through the Word. But these gentile Christians do not lose their particular local ethnic or national identity. That is the social context in which they hear and respond to the Word of the Gospel. It is the social setting in which they are called by God to obey the Gospel, to worship God, to love one another and to witness to Christ in mission and service. Their nation becomes the acoustic community in which they must live out the Word they have heard within the worship, community and mission of the holy nation, the Church.

As Professor Alan Lewis puts it, the Church exists as a community through the hearing of the Word, *ecclesia ex auditu*. That is the Reformed theological understanding of the Church. In our terms, it is an acoustic community; its holy nationhood exists through the faithful hearing and proclaiming of the Word. But can we not say that the nations are also called to exist *ex auditu* by the Gospel? To exist through the hearing of the Word, *nationes ex auditu*? It is the Church alone that is called by God to proclaim the Word to the nations. That is its identity as an acoustic community, grounded in its divine existence as the people of God for all eternity. But the nations are called to hear and obey this Word proclaimed by the holy nation in its midst; Israel amid the nations being a light to the Gentiles. That is their identity as acoustic communities, grounded in their human existence as provisional, providential communities for time only. Like Glasgow, they flourish through the preaching of the Word and the praising of his Name - a perfect description of what it means for a nation to be an acoustic community.·

On the Day of Judgement, according to Matthew chapter 25,

when Jesus comes to inaugurate his Kingdom, he will gather all the nations before him. **All** nations will be judged together as acoustic communities. The parting of the ways will occur between those who heard the Word of the king and obeyed it and those who heard it and ignored it. Once again, it is the Word of the king who comes unseen in the needy of God's world that determines who is in the Kingdom of God. The Kingdom of God is the acoustic community of all those who hear the Word of Jesus and who obey it (Matthew 7:21-23).

A Biblical theology of nationhood is now emerging. The Scriptures of the Old and New Testaments recognise no natural or necessary existence for nations. They are not part of God's original creation and God gives no specific command or word to them. They arise in the course of human history under the providence and judgement of God as temporal and conditional communities that share a common style of imagining their nationhood. As gentile nations their biblical significance lies in whether or not they are open to the Word of God that comes to them through that other, holy nation of Israel and the Church.

In the history of salvation, the provisional communities of nations must never be confused with the saving community of God's people. But neither must they be shut off from the Word that comes from the holy nation. Indeed, God's people are called to a dual nationality in which they live out their eternal Christian identity within the provisional community and identity of their nationhood, seeking to sanctify and transform it according to the command and promise of God in the Gospel of the Kingdom. And both nationhoods only operate within the overarching environment of the Kingdom of God, the eschatological community of those who obey God's Word in Jesus Christ.

This brings us to the third kind of community which has a bearing on a Biblical understanding of nationhood, the Kingdom of God.

The Kingdom Of God - the Tangible Community

We cannot complete a Biblical understanding of nationhood without reflecting further on the nature and significance of the Kingdom of God and of the nations in relation to it. For Scripture not only draws a clear distinction between the acoustic community of Israel's holy nationhood and the imagined communities of the gentile nations. In certain prophetic and apocalyptic passages of the Old and New Testaments it holds out the hope and promise of another future community where God reigns: within which Israel, the Church and the nations will find their ultimate identity and destiny. That community is the holy City of God envisioned in such passages as Isaiah chapter 60 and Revelation chapter 21 and 22. As the American Christian philosopher Richard Mouw has pointed out, in his study of these passages *When the Kings come Marching in*, the vision of the new Jerusalem includes the entry of the kings of the earth and the wealth of the nations into its community, life and worship. Mouw argues that this should be read to mean not only that the nations will be converted to the God of Israel but that the life of God's Kingdom, envisioned as the holy city of the new Jerusalem, will be a multi-national community enriched by the multicultural achievements of the nations:

> In short, ancient kings served as the primary authorities over the broad patterns of the cultural lives of their nations. And when they stood over against other nations, they were the **bearers**, the **representatives**, of their respective cultures. To assemble kings together, then, was in an important sense to assemble their national cultures together... This is why Isaiah and John could link the entrance of the kings into the City with the gathering in of the 'wealth of the nations'.

At the end of fallen human history, Mouw suggests, when God reigns over the new earth symbolized in the vision of the City, the tangible achievements of the nations, their history and culture, may contribute to the life of the new humanity in the new creation. Perhaps the references to the wealth and healing of the nations in Revelation chapters 21 and 22, mean the bringing of the sanctified aspects of national identity into the new Jerusalem to enrich the multi-cultural life and diversity of the new humanity. The description of the relationship between the Kingdom of God and the nations in the tangible terms of wealth and healing is not without significance.

In Scripture the Kingdom of God is described in very tangible ways. In the Old Testament prophecies the future reign of God is envisioned in terms of the restoration of right relationships in the Kingdom of God's peace, where 'Calves and lion cubs will feed together, and little children will look after them' (Isaiah 11:6). In the New Testament, with the coming of the King himself, the Kingdom is described in the tangible signs of an annointed deliverer who proclaims freedom for the prisoners, recovery of sight for the blind and release for the oppressed (Luke 4:18-19). So often it is with a touch that Jesus brings his healing power to sick and broken lives. It is in his invitation to Thomas to touch the wounds of his risen body that his Kingdom is displayed after his crucifixion and bodily resurrection. It is in the breaking of bread that he was made known to the Emmaus road disciples, and in the tangible signs of water, bread and wine that his disciples are to enter his Kingdom and share its life. It is through the tangible acts of feeding the hungry, quenching the thirsty, welcoming the stranger, clothing the naked and visiting the sick and imprisoned, that the nations will enter the eternal Kingdom of God on the Day of Judgement (Matthew 25:31-46).

In this sense, therefore, we may think of the Kingdom of God as a tangible community, shaped not so much by images or words but by the tangible acts of God's grace and power restoring a broken creation to wholeness again in peace and justice. The tangible community and identity of the coming Kingdom of God was foretold in Old Testament prophecy, inaugurated in the coming of the King and the spread of his reign on earth through his Church, and will only be realised fully with Christ's coming again in judgement, to reign in the new heaven and the new earth. The tangible nature of the Kingdom is found supremely in the incarnation, when the Word took flesh in the womb of Mary. It is through the tangible human nature of Jesus of Nazareth that God's image is restored to humanity, God's word is heard and God's acts are fulfilled. As the 1st Letter of John puts it in the opening chapter: 'That which was from the beginning, which we have heard, which we have seen with our eyes, which we have looked at **and our hands have touched** - this we proclaim concerning the Word of life.' It is this tangible community of the Kingdom of God which touches on the nations and finally defines their nationhood and identity.

As those who would display for touch and sight the life of God's Son, Christians are called to have two national identities, or a dual nationality. They are called to be in the church, hearing and proclaiming God's word in that community, and they are called to be in the nation, obedient to God's word in that community. Both callings are part of their life in Christ and his Kingdom, where his redemption and rule are tangible in restored relationships with God, humanity and creation.

In relation to the Kingdom of God, it is important to remember that the holy nation is also a provisional community like the gentile nations. However, there is this profound difference between their provisional identities; the **church** is the prototype and corporate sign of the coming rule of God on earth, and will give way to that everlasting kingdom in the new heaven and the new earth. The **nations** have no such calling or ultimate reference. Yet the case can be made that all aspects of their existence that are good, fulfilling the cultural mandate given to all humanity to be fruitful in ways that honour the Creator, may be brought into the eternal Kingdom. God has provided for this in creation, and where goodness falls short he has provided for this too in redemption; it is in union with Christ that 'all things have their proper place'. (Colossians 1:17)

The Biblical Ecology of Nationhood

What emerges is an ecology of nationhood in which nations are understood fundamentally as acoustic communities through which the lifegiving Word of God is proclaimed, heard and obeyed among the nations. Some theologies of religious nationalism see nations in fixed static ways, as natural communities to be observed, measured, preserved and protected as part of the created order of things, and as historic communities with a national destiny to be pursued in its own terms. The biblical theology of nationhood is different: it is dynamic and relational. It sees the gentile nations and the holy nation existing in a profound relationship to one another shaped by the audits of the Word of the unseen God and the tangible acts of his coming Kingdom.

The Biblical model of nationhood may be thought of as an ecological one in which the three communities of Church, Nation and Kingdom exist as three living systems within the divine economy revealed in Scripture. They function in a complex set of relationships with one another. The pattern of these relationships is determined by the identity of each community within the biblical drama of creation and fall, redemption and restoration. The nations exist within fallen human history as provisional, providential communities, divided through God's judgement in mutual rivalry and incomprehension but continuing to express something of God's original creative, cultural purposes for humanity in their national diversity. They are communities that share an imagined identity through common images of ethnic and national identity which unite them in distinction from other nations and social identities. They function within the divine economy as both a sign of God's judgement and a blessing of God's providence.

The holy nation of God's people, the church drawn from all nations, tribes and tongues, is God's missionary community for the redemption of the nations. It shares a common acoustic identity through faith in the Word of God, incarnate in Jesus Christ. Its function is to bring that Word to the nations and to anticipate in its holy life among them the tangible community of the coming Kingdom of God. That tangible community of the Kingdom exists wherever the fallen creation and its history have been restored by God's rule in Christ into the right relationships and purpose of the Gospel. This restoration of all things in Christ will always be partial and often hidden within human history but complete at its consummation in final judgement and the new creation. The nations find their biblical meaning and purpose as they function within this drama and in relation to the acoustic community of the holy nation and tangible community of the coming Kingdom.

Nowhere do we see this ecology of nationhood more clearly than in two incidents in Mark's Gospel: the encounter in the gentile region of Tyre between Jesus and the Greek woman, born in Syrian Phoenicia (Mark 7:24-30); and the encounter between Jesus and the chief priests and teachers of the law in Israel when he cleared the Temple following his triumphal entry into the city

(Mark 11:12-19).

In the story of the Syro-Phoenician gentile woman, she came to Jesus begging him to drive the demon out of her daughter. Jesus had come to a house in this gentile area in secret, not wanting anyone to know he was present. The woman receives a stern and what at first seems to be a strangely ungracious reply from Jesus to her request: 'First let all the children eat what they want, for it is not right to take the children's bread and toss it to their dogs.' Not daunted by this, the gentile woman gives a spirited and persistent reply: 'Yes Lord, but even the dogs under the table eat the children's crumbs.' In response to her persistent faith, Jesus tells her: 'For such a reply, you may go; the demon has left your daughter.'

For such a reply, you may go. Here we see not Christ's aloofness but the Biblical ecology of nationhood in operation. The children at the table are the people of Israel. To them has been given the living bread of the Word. But, like the household pets that run around the feet of the children at the family meal table, so the Gentiles are also part of the household of God, the whole created world. And for every Gentile who is humble enough to come to Israel for even a crumb of this life-giving bread, a simple word of command by the Word to cast out the demon, there is salvation too. Both the nation of Israel and the gentile nations live within the one life-giving environment of the coming Kingdom of God. Sometimes it is the Gentiles who hear the Word that comes from Israel but which Israel itself increasingly closes its ears to receiving. And so healing comes to the nations that abandon their imagined identity for an acoustic one but judgement comes to the acoustic community that has adopted an imagined identity, as the story of the clearing of the Temple powerfully shows.

After his triumphal entry into Jerusalem, redolent with the prophetic signs of his messiahship, Jesus went to the Temple late in the evening. Mark records that Jesus looked around at everything. What did he see? As is clear from his actions in clearing the Temple the next day, Jesus saw a nation that had abandoned its acoustic identity as the holy nation that faithfully heard and obeyed the word of the Lord and replaced it with the imagined identity of the pagan nations. After clearing out the traders from the courts of the Gentiles, Jesus taught them, quoting two of the Old Testament Prophets, Isaiah and Jeremiah: 'Is it not written: "My house will be called a house of prayer for all nations"? But you have made it "a den of robbers".'

The reference to Isaiah chapter 56 indicates how Jesus understood the nationhood of Israel, as an acoustic community of true prayer and worship, a house of prayer for all nations, through which the gentile nations would hear the Word of God, repent of their pagan identities and be welcomed into the people of God. But the reference to Jeremiah's description of Israel, as a den of robbers (Jeremiah 7:11), indicates how Jesus saw the kind of nationhood that Israel actually practised in his own day. He applied Jeremiah's critique of Judah's apostate nationhood to Israel in his own day.

Judah had maintained the pretence of being a faithful acoustic community when in reality it was a faithless nation that had adopted the imagined identity of the pagan nations, worshipping false gods, oppressing the weak and breaking the law (Jeremiah 7:1-11). With this comparison, Jesus was declaring the moral and spiritual bankruptcy of the holy nation in its transcendent identity to hear and manifest the word of the Lord on earth. He was declaring in the Temple, the heart of the nation's identity and community, that Israel was no longer an acoustic community of the living God, a house of prayer for all nations, but had become a den of robbers, a community full of images and practices stolen from the pagan nations. Just as Jeremiah records the Lord as declaring, 'But I have been watching!', so Mark records that Jesus, the Lord incarnate, looked around at everything - he too had been watching.

Once more, in this incident in the Temple we see, not the harshness of Jesus, but the Biblical ecology of nations in operation. The dynamic word of God offers life to the pagan nations if they will but hear that word while that same Word brings judgement on the holy nation for abandoning its true identity as an acoustic community, being deaf to that word and embracing pagan images.

While the nations are a species of imagined community the holy nation is a unique kind of acoustic community. Salvation is from the Jews. They alone have been tuned in to hear and receive the word of God as he spoke to them through the prophets at many times and in various ways. In the fulness of time, when he becomes flesh among them and lives as the incarnate audit of the unseen God within the acoustic community of Israel, only the frontier Jews of Galilee and the exiled Jews of the foreign Diaspora receive his Gospel on the Day of Pentecost in Jerusalem. Those at the centre of power in the nation of Israel are deaf to his word. Their rejection of him means the fulfilment of the prophetic vision that in the last days God would bring the nations to worship him at the Temple in Jerusalem, Mount Zion, the city of God,and include them in the people of God. Then the Temple would become a house of prayer for all nations (Isaiah 56:1-8). Through the coming of the incarnate messianic Word to Israel, the nations of the earth become acoustic communities in two distinct but related senses: they are called to enter the one renewed acoustic community of God's people and they are called to hear his word and obey it within their own imagined communities. Both developments are to be understood in terms of the spread of the tangible community of God's Kingdom through the Church and among the nations.

This Biblical model of nationhood operates with three assumptions. First, it has what may be termed its pluralist assumption that the church, nations and Kingdom of God operate as three distinct but related communities in a set of relationships determined by the Biblical drama of salvation. These communities and relationships cannot be confused or replaced without a breakdown in the spiritual ecology of nations and injury to the health of church, nation and Kingdom. Secondly, this Biblical model makes what may be termed an incarnational or **Christocentric** assumption that it is only through Jesus Christ that the holy nation of the Church finds its identity. It cannot reduce that identity to the terms of the nationhood of the communities among which it lives, reducing the Church to a national rather than a Christian institution. And, thirdly, this Biblical model makes what may be called the evangelical or **missionary** assumption that church and nation will always be two separate communities with an evangelical relationship, rather than exist as one community with an inclusive ecclesiastical identity that excludes the need for mission to the nation. If these three assumptions are missing then there is a crisis in the relationship between a particular church and nation.

The Ecological Crisis of Scottish Nationhood

To illustrate how controversial these three assumptions of the Biblical model of nationhood are for us in Scotland, let us contrast them with those that have prevailed in the Reformed understanding of Church and Nation. From what we have already seen of the once dominant Reformed vision of Scotland, in chapters three and four, the Scottish Calvinist model of nationhood might be characterised as monistic rather than pluralist, cultic rather than Christocentric, and ecclesiastical rather than evangelical. It is valid and illuminating to make such a comparison between Biblical and Reformed models because both operate with the notion of the church and nation as acoustic communities, due in the latter case to the centrality of the Word in the Scottish Reformed tradition since Knox.

Traditionally the Scottish Reformed vision of church and nation is to see them as interchangeable and almost indistinguishable communities - the Kirk and her Scotland. This is in part a legacy from the Christendom model of church and society that the reformers inherited and did not abandon when they sought to reform the medieval Scottish Church. The whole nation was seen within the membership of the Kirk, part of one godly commonwealth, one all-embracing social reality of the church-nation. In that sense it was a monistic model, seeing church and nation as only two aspects of the one absolute system. This monistic model is a definite distortion of the pluralist ecological model of church and nation we have found in Scripture. There, while the nations and the people of God exist only in relationship to one another, they exist as separate and distinct social entities within the one environment of the Kingdom of God. Each has its own function: the nation as a provisional and providential community enriching yet checking the wider community of fallen humanity; the church as a provisional and redemptive community expressing yet only anticipating the new humanity and Kingdom in Jesus Christ.

It was suggested in chapter five that at the heart of the Reformed vision of what it means to be Christian and human there lay a defective view of Christ, a wrong Christology. The Scottish Christ is Apollinarian, that is, he has been seen in Reformed piety to be fully divine but only human in body, lacking a human soul. In an essay on the way in which this Apollinarian heresy has affected the worship of the Christian Church, Professor Torrance has shown how, for the worshipping community, the lack of a fully human Jesus to act as mediator has led to various substitute intermediaries between the people and God. In the Protestant tradition it has led to what Torrance has called 'psychological sacerdotalism', the worshipping of God through the idiosyncratic personality of the minister.

This Apollinarian tendency has also affected the relationship between Church and nation in Scotland. It has led the Kirk to see itself as a representative intermediary in the life of the nation; representing the Christian faith of the Scottish people and representing the Scottish people as a national institution. In this way the Kirk has seen itself as the nation at prayer, expressing the cultic or religious life of Scotland through the idiosyncracies of its own institutional life. Again, the Biblical model of church and nation is very different. In its relationship with the surrounding culture of the nations the holy nation has only one way of relating to it, in and through Jesus Christ. The Church functions not as a representative national institution but as the Body of Christ, relating to the nation in the dynamic way in which Christ did in his incarnation and continues to do in the Holy Spirit. In the cultic model the Church finds its identity through identification with the nation in a static, cultural and institutional way. In the Christocentric incarnational model revealed in Scripture the Church finds its identity in relation to the nation through the incarnate life of Jesus.

Finally, the Biblical model of the relationship between the holy nation and the nations is fundamentally evangelical and missionary. The Church exists only because Christ has reconciled and brought the Gentiles into the community of God's people through the Cross. It came into existence as a community only by drawing the gentile nations into faith in Jesus Christ through the preaching of the gospel to all nations. It exists only to proclaim this gospel to the nations and so hasten the coming day of the Kingdom. On the basis of a pluralist relationship with the nations and a Christocentric incarnational model of its own national identity, the Church exists apart from the nation, having been called out of the nation, but only in order to move back towards it in mission. As we have seen in chapters three and four, in the Reformed model of church and nation there is no such separation and thus possibility of movement in mission. The Church is seen as an all-encompassing national ecclesiastical community, existing to bring the ordinances of religion to the whole nation, on the assumption that they are either practising or lapsed Christians who belong to the Church through virtue of its national status and their nationality.

In the missionary evangelical model, the nations are seen as gentile, pagan communities in need of conversion, whereas in the ecclesiastical model they are seen as Christian communities in need of discipline and instruction. In the Reformed model there is also the tendency which we noted in chapter three, the habit of turning national and societal issues into ecclesiastical issues dealt with by church committees and ministers. This has inhibited autonomous lay Christian involvement in national life as part of the mission of the whole people of God in society; and, just as seriously, inhibited the development of other autonomous national institutions as a legitimate forum for dealing with national affairs, such as a Scottish parliament.

The lack of these three pluralist, Christocentric and mission-ary assumptions in the Reformed model of Church and nation constitute a deep crisis for a national church like the Church of Scotland. It has hung on to a view of its identity which looks increasingly shipwrecked in the secular tides of the late twenti-eth century. We shall explore that crisis in chapter ten and suggest that the recovery of these three assumptions might transform its identity and even turn the crisis into a new vision of church and nation.

Singing the Lord's Song in a Foreign Land

This chapter has sought to argue that, biblically and theologi-cally, nations are to be understood as acoustic communities. Scripture is concerned with the nations in as much as they are open to the hearing of the Word of God and the praising of his Name. The Biblical drama of creation, fall, redemption and restoration recognises nations as existing on the stage of fallen human history as provisional and providential communities with a precarious existence apart from their significance in the history of the holy nation of Israel and the Church. We have seen that the nations do not have an insignificant role in that drama as the coming of the Kingdom of God welcomes them into the one new humanity of Jesus Christ without effacing their cultural diversity and distinctiveness.

The setting of the nations within the drama of Church and Kingdom of God suggests, finally, a liturgical framework as a fruitful context in which Christians may explore the meaning and purpose of nationhood. As Wolfhart Pannenberg has written, commenting on the relationship between the Church and the Kingdom of God:

There is no reason for the existence of the church except to symbolize the future of the divine kingdom that Jesus came to proclaim. This explains in what specific sense worship is in the centre of the life of the church: the worship of the Christian community anticipates and symbolically celebrates the praise of God's glory that will be consummated in the [final] renewal of all creation in the new Jerusalem.

Worship that anticipates the restoration of all creation in the Kingdom speaks to the nations as part of that drama. It is within worship that both the holy nation and the nations of the earth are opened up to the claims of the tangible community of God's Kingdom. Worship is the spiritual context within which a Biblical model of the ecology of nations exists. The story of Christ clearing the Temple suggests a link between the Biblical meaning of nations and worship that is applicable to our own time and nationhood. 'My house will be called a house of prayer for all nations', said Jesus. It is within worship that the holy nation and the historic nations find their identity and purpose exposed, either as houses of prayer or as dens of robbers. In worship that anticipates the tangible community of God's Kingdom in the new Jerusalem, all nationhood, whether acoustic or imagined, is opened to God, judged and transformed.

The place of worship in a Christian approach to nationhood will be taken further at the end of chapter eight. Before leaving the theme of the nations in Scripture, however, we must consider one last Biblical passage which shows the context of worship for wrestling with the meaning of nationhood.   Psalm 137 is a lament by devout Jews in exile in Babylon: 'By the rivers of Babylon we sat and wept when we remembered Zion.' Tormented by their Babylonian captors to sing their songs of home, they cry: 'How can we sing the songs of the Lord while in a foreign land?' Defiantly, the psalmist affirms that he will never forget his identity in Israel: 'May my tongue cling to the roof of my mouth if I do not remember you, if I do not consider Jerusalem my highest joy.'

That remembrance of Jerusalem brings back painful memories of the city's ruthless destruction. The psalmist cries out to God for judgement against the nation of Edom for supporting Jerusalem's downfall. Then he gives in to a bitter cry for revenge against Babylon: 'O Daughter of Babylon, doomed to destruction, happy is he who repays you for what you have done to us - he who seizes your infants and dashes them against rocks.' The Babylonian conquerors murdered Jewish children in that way and their bitter memory makes the psalmist wish for repayment in kind. Here worship brings out the painful relationship between the holy nation of Israel and the gentile nations. It exposes the cruel heart of Israel and the nations before God. It reminds us that conflict among nations and empires has led to untold death and destruction.

How can we sing the Lord's songs in the foreign lands of our time? The lack of justice and peace seems to mock our faith in God's Kingdom. That psalm is a bridge from the nations of the Bible to the twentieth century world of nations which demonstrates the same violence, the same contrast. The faith of the psalmist passes on the same Word by which churches and nations both live, in response to which the people of God worship and look forward in hope.

Chapter 7

NATIONALISM: The Modern Judas?

Where have we come so far in our understanding of nationhood? To an acoustic community, called to hear, obey and proclaim the Word of God. To the Church as a holy nation, set apart from the gentile nations. The latter are **imagined** communities under God's providence and judgement. They may yet become **acoustic** communities, shaped by God's word as they respond faithfully to the life and witness of the holy nation in their midst. Both holy nation and gentile nations, as faithful acoustic communities hearing and doing God's word, may be transformed into that other, tangible community which is the coming Kingdom of God on earth. The Biblical hope is that one new multi-national humanity will be restored into unity through Jesus Christ, enjoying God's presence in a new heaven and a new earth, enriched by the cultural wealth of nations and purged of their idolatry and division.

If the Bible does offer this distinctive theological understanding of nationhood, an important question follows on from this Biblical viewpoint: what possible relationship can there be between the nations of ancient Israel and Rome, and the modern nation-states of Europe or the Third World, that would allow for a contemporary theology of nationhood from such Scriptural sources? Certain nationalists would wish to argue that the continuity lies in the intrinsic and natural division of humanity into nations and ethnic groupings over millennia. But Biblical scholars and modern students of nationalism alike would insist that there was nothing 'natural' about national identity to encourage such a comparison; nations are simply the product of human cultural development and history. Nor would many scholars see any connection between the loyalties of older ethnic communities and those of contemporary nation-states.

137

Nevertheless, not all academic experts on nationalism and ethnicity would see such a gulf between the ethnic communities of the ancient world, the tribes and peoples of the Bible, and the nations of the modern world, the member states of the United Nations or the nationalities contained within them. Anthony D. Smith is a scholar who has made extensive study of both the phenomenon and the theories of ethnicity and nationalism. Smith recognises that nations are not natural human communities but culturally constructed within human history. He defines ethnic communities as groups which share a sense of common origins and history and some distinctive and shared cultural attributes. Nations are more complex and developed political communities and so he accepts the point that there are important differences between such ethnic and national phenomena. Yet he sees an important element of continuity between them as well, arguing that 'Nations are closely related to ethnic communities, often "growing out" of the latter, or being "constructed" from ethnic materials.' This leads Smith to make a further point, in his book *The Ethnic Revival*, a study of the survival of ethnic identity in the modern world:

> Now, if a clearcut distinction between ethnicity and nationality and between ethnic sentiment and nationalism cannot be established, then there is more continuity between nationalism and its ethnic forbears than many modern scholars admit. Nationalism, though still an eighteenth or nineteenth century ideology and movement, has deeper and firmer roots in the distant past; and nations are not simply the inventions of a modern breed of intellectual. National loyalty and national character may not be inborn, and they are certainly historical phenomena; but their modernity, their embeddedness in a specific recent history, is anchored in an antiquity, a prehistory, of ethnic ties and sentiments, going back to the Sumerians and ancient Egyptians.

While there are clearly profound differences between the ethnic communities, the tribes and peoples and ancient Egyptians of the Biblical world, and the national identities shaped by modern nationalism, there is sufficient connection to allow for the possibility that Biblical insights into nations **then** may help in a Christian understanding of nationhood **now**. Smith suggests that the nation is a recent political phenomenon which has used and transformed the style and content of much older ethnic ties. If so, then we may legitimately use the ancient Biblical insights into the ethnic groups of antiquity to construct a practical theological understanding of their successor communities today. Before proceeding to do that, however, one further barrier to a contemporary theology of nationhood must be considered - nationalism itself.

From Arbroath to Auschwitz?

Nationalism has been a shunned loyalty for many Western Christians in the postwar period. Amid the indescribable horror of the Holocaust and the nightmare of Nazi Germany with its neo-pagan worship of race and power, there was a particular shame for Christians. Among Hitler's most fervid supporters were those who called themselves 'German Christians'. These religious nationalists sought to accommodate the Christian faith and Church to Nazi ideology and interests, especially its anti-semitic elements, by denying the Jewish roots of Christianity and replacing them with the myth of a divinely ordained German Aryan destiny. So called German Christians welcomed Nazi state control of the Church and offered their supreme loyalty to the Fuhrer and Fatherland rather than the God and Father of our Lord Jesus Christ. It was against this nationalist captivity of the Church in Germany that Christians like Dietrich Bonhoeffer and Karl Barth signed the Barmen Declaration confessing the Church's supreme loyalty to Jesus Christ, and set up the Confessing Church outwith state control. Here at least nationalism was seen as the deadly enemy of the Gospel.

This German experience of religious nationalism, both pagan and pseudo-Christian, cast a long shadow over any postwar European attempts to re-evaluate nationhood and national identity in the light of the Gospel. Even in the 1980s it darkened an attempt by the Church of Scotland Church and Nation Committee to reflect on the Christian significance of Scottish identity. A 1982 report on that theme was denounced by the distinguished theologian Professor T.F. Torrance as 'a dark whirlpool of

error'. For Torrance, someone profoundly influenced by the
theologies of Barth and Bonhoeffer and the lesson of their
resistance to Hitler, the report's affirmation of a religious dimension to national identity showed 'the same subtle twist to biblical
ideas given by "German Christians"... who provided a "religious
dimension" for the racist ideology of National Socialist Germany.' Despite strong denials to the contrary by the Church and
Nation Committee at his reading of their report, Torrance saw it
as infected with the same racist and nationalist poison spread by
the German Christian movement: 'It is sad to learn that pagan
ideas such as these are now finding currency in the membership
of the Church.' Seen in this light, the road from Arbroath, scene
of the Scottish nationalist Declaration of Independence in 1320,
to Auschwitz, scene of the worst German National Socialist
atrocities, would seem to be short and direct.

However, even the worst of human tragedies and evils must
not cloud our critical faculties and lead us to compare like with
unlike in sweeping judgements that do not bear close scrutiny.
Nationalism is a complex and diverse historical and political
phenomenon. The corporate Fascist racism of German nationalism under the National Socialist regime makes an odious comparison with the humanitarian and liberal nationalism of some
movements for national liberation, not least those which resisted
Nazi occupation during the Second World War. The marxist
intellectual Tom Nairn has called nationalism 'the modern
Janus', with two faces, one progressive and one regressive.
Nationalist movements have been described as bourgeois and
proletarian, reactionary and revolutionary, left-wing and right-
wing, empire-building and anti-colonial, depending on the
country and context.

In these distinctions, secular critics of nationalism are echoing
the Biblical perception that all human reality is fallen, distorted
by sin, and contains within it both the marks of God's good
creation and our own wilful breaking of the divine image. And
so we noted in the last chapter that Scripture sees the nations of
the earth as manifesting in human history both the judgement
and the providence of God in the one cultural phenomenon. In
reply to Nairn's concept of nationalism as the modern Janus,
looking both ways and manifesting progressive and regressive

elements, scripturally we may think of it as the modern Judas. The same nations that express the human creativity given in creation, enjoy the divine providence, and which are called to order their common life in response to God's Word in Jesus Christ, so often betray him in pursuit of their own loyalties - not least, in the modern period, nationalist ones.

There is as much scholarly disagreement about the definition of nationalism as there is about the identity of nations; academic theories and ideological versions of both abound. Many scholars of nationalism would say that its birth as a modern political movement dates from the period of the French Revolution in 1789, when the nation replaced the monarchy as the repository of sovereignty and loyalty, as well as from the rise of the German philosophical doctrine that each nation possesses a unique culture and understanding of life. Others would see it as a much older movement going back to the rise of the nation state in renaissance and reformation Europe, if not earlier, in the medieval period. It is certainly hard for Scots to think of nationalist sentiment as a modern phenomenon when a medieval version of it can be so clearly identified as part of the country's struggle for independence from England as early as in the fourteenth century and the 1320 Declaration of Independence.

We have already drawn on Professor Seton-Watson's conclusion that it is impossible to devise any 'scientific definition' of a nation apart from saying that one exists 'when a significant number of people in a community consider themselves to be one, or behave as if they formed one.' Seton-Watson was more forthcoming with his definition of nationalism, in his enquiry into the origins of nations and the politics of nationalism, *Nations and States*. He saw it as having two basic meanings. It was 'a doctrine about the character, interests, rights and duties of nations' and it also meant 'an organised political movement, designed to further the alleged aims and interests of nations'. He went further and wrote:

> The two most generally sought aims of such movements have been independence (the creation of a sovereign state in which the nation is dominant), and national unity (the incorporation within the frontiers of this state of all groups which are considered by

themselves, or by those who claim to speak for them, to belong to the nation). In the case of many, though not all, nations there has been a further task for nationalists: to build a nation within an independent state, by extending down to the population as a whole the belief in the existence of the nation, which, before independence was won, was held only by a minority. Defined in these terms we may see Scottish nationalism as both a very old phenomenon and a more recent movement in this country. The struggle for national independence took place from the thirteenth and fourteenth century onwards until incorporation into a British state in 1707. Efforts towards national unity ranged from the earlier period of Celtic-Pictish assimilation to the relatively recent eighteenth and nineteenth century assimilation of the Gaelic Highland culture within the Scottish Lowland sense of national identity. Even in the twentieth century the immigrant Irish Catholic and Asian communities have developed a sense of Scottish identity to varying degrees.

That the Scots thought of themselves as one nation is clear by the early fourteenth century. This idea of Scottish nationhood survived the end of independent statehood in 1707. The union with England was only possible through the retention of key national institutions like a separate established Church, education and Scots law, which ensured the continuing sense of a distinct Scottish identity and an autonomous civil society within the new British state. The existence of a separate and distinct Scottish nationhood within the United Kingdom has never been in doubt, at least north of the border. Despite Enlightenment and Victorian genuflection to 'North Britain' and recurring fears of Anglo-American assimilation, Scotland can claim its place as one of the ancient nations of Europe which has retained its identity over many centuries down to the present-day.

The emergence of nationalism as an organised political movement, committed to Scottish self-government and the extension of Scottish national consciousness throughout all levels of Scottish society, is a more recent development. Professor Hanham dates the rise of modern Scottish Nationalism to the founding in 1853 of the National Association for the Vindication of Scottish Rights, the first proper though short-lived nationalist body. The Scottish Home Rule Association was set up in 1886 as an all-party body campaigning for Scottish self-government, after the creation of the government post of Secretary for Scotland in 1885, one of the demands of the 1853 National Association. Growing frustration with the failure of the main political parties to establish Scottish home rule before the outbreak of the First World War led to the formation of two nationalist parties in the 1920s. The National Party of Scotland was founded in 1928 out of a fusion of smaller nationalist groups; the more right wing Scottish Party was set up by dissident Tories and moderates in 1932 in favour of home rule; they united to form the Scottish National Party in 1934. The SNP was set up with the object of Self-Government for Scotland and contained within its ranks both outright nationalist separatists and Home Rulers open to cross-party alliances.

This party continued into the 1950s as a small movement on the fringe of mainstream Scottish politics. The failure of John MacCormick's all-party Covenant movement to translate millions of signatures in favour of self-government within the UK into political change in the early 1950s, led the nationalist movement in a more separatist direction, with the SNP favouring complete independence from England. It pursued this line with little political impact until electoral successes in the late 1960s and mid-1970s led on to its standing in 1989 as the second party in popular support at the European parliamentary elections, committed to a revised policy of 'Independence in Europe'. Throughout the rise of political nationalism in Scotland there has been a tension between those favouring home rule or self-government within the framework of the United Kingdom and those supporting complete independence. This is typified by the refusal of the SNP to take part in the all-party Campaign for a Scottish Assembly's Constitutional Convention, which was set up in March 1989 to draw up an agreed form of self-government for Scotland and supported by the Scottish home rule parties. That tension will continue to run through the politics of nationalism in the 1990s and beyond, until a new constitutional settlement for Scotland is agreed and established.

What are the factors which have led to this rise of modern Scottish nationalism? Various cultural, political and socio-economic interpretations have been offered. As we have seen, there is **first** the existence of a strong sense of nationhood and national identity going back over seven centuries and more. Modern political nationalism has been able to draw on that historic and continuing national consciousness as a motivation for political change. Dr Jack Brand has identified a growing sense of Scottish identity and culture in the twentieth century which has formed the essential cultural basis for a strong nationalist political movement. The late Professor John P. Mackintosh explained the rise of nationalism in the 1970s in terms of a continuing sense of Scottish identity, based on the experience of distinct national institutions. This offered an attractive alternative political option when the other side of the Scots' dual sense of national identity, their Britishness, waned in attractiveness, with the economic and political decline of Britain as an imperial and world power. The other element in this cultural basis for nationalism has been an anti-English feeling. This has often arisen in reaction to perceived English insensitivity to Scottish interests within the Union and its own potent if denied English nationalism.

A **second**, political factor that led to political nationalism in Scotland was the rise of the modern state and its growing intervention in industrial society. This led, from the mid-nineteenth century onwards, to a growing demand for a stronger Scottish dimension to the UK government's increasing   involvement in Scottish social and economic affairs. There was little call for such a political development in the period between about 1750 and 1850. The survival of a Scottish civil society which retained a large degree of national autonomy after 1707 and the relative lack of direct involvement by the British state in the lives of most Scots, together with Scotland's improving economic position within the Empire, dampened the hostility to government from Westminster evident at the time of the Union. However, as that autonomous civil society began to break apart under the impact of the 1843 Disruption of the national Church and the spread of a more urban, mass industrial society, many Scots saw the need for a greater devolution of administrative and even legislative powers to Scotland. In part, the legitimacy of that political claim to nationhood has been recognised in the last hundred years with the establishment of the Scottish Office as a territorial department of the British government and the office of Secretary of State for Scotland as a cabinet post.

A **third** factor identified by some theorists to explain the rise of Scottish nationalism concerns the effects of socio-economic changes on national life. From his materialist interpretation of history, in a seminal study of nationalism entitled *The Break-up of Britain*, the marxist scholar Tom Nairn put forward a theory of uneven economic development within capitalism in Britain and the West to explain the growth of political nationalism in the 1970s in areas like Scotland, where it had failed to develop during the classic age of European nationalism in the late eighteenth and early nineteenth centuries. During the latter period the Scottish middle class enjoyed sufficient of the economic and social benefits of British Imperial prosperity and power without losing their own local institutional autonomy, to prevent them from seeing their class interests in nationalist terms. In the 1960s and 1970s, however, the poorer economic performance of Scotland in comparison with England, and the potential of North Sea oil wealth for the Scottish economy, led sections of the middle class to see their future prospects in neo-nationalist terms. While the Scottish National Party would continue to be a vehicle for such bourgeois nationalism, Nairn believed that the association between nationhood and the uneven development of advanced capitalist economies could be harnessed to progressive change towards a socialist and self-governing Scotland.

Such an aim has certainly been the distinctively new clarion call of Scottish nationalism in the 1980s. Out of the upheaval of the devolution debate in the 1970s, with its 1979 referendum on Labour's proposals for a Scottish Assembly, the Labour MP Jim Sillars led a new breakaway Scottish Labour Party pressing for much more radical self-government proposals, an independent socialist Scotland within the European Community. The SLP did not survive but Sillars took his political vision for Scotland into the Scottish National Party, which he joined in 1980. Initially his brand of left-wing nationalism, shared by some of the younger and more radical party members, caused deep division within the SNP and led to the expulsion of the socialist

'79 Group from the party. By the end of the decade he was SNP Member of Parliament for Glasgow Govan, after a stunning 1988 by-election victory in a formerly solid urban Labour seat, and the SNP had embraced the policy of independence in Europe. With four MPs, a strong presence in local government, and second place in the European elections, the Scottish Nationalists faced the 1990s as a major force in Scottish politics. In the late 1980s its 'Independence in Europe' policy had stolen the intellectual initiative in the debate about Scotland's future.

But what kind of nationalism is Scotland being offered in the late twentieth century? And is it in any sense compatible with a Christian understanding of human community, identity and purpose? Or is it an insuperable obstacle to any Christian appreciation of Scottish nationhood and identity?

The answer to these questions lies in part within Scottish nationalism itself. In what terms do nationalists perceive their own nationalist commitment? If they are terms inimical to the Christian Gospel then any new attempt to develop a theology of Scottish nationhood would indeed be dangerous and Professor Torrance's warning about 'a dark whirlpool of error' would be well heeded. The literature on Scottish nationalism and by Scottish nationalists is a relatively large one and space does not permit a comprehensive review of nationalist thought here. If a movement should be judged by its best minds then three recent nationalist analyses of their position, one philosophical, one political and one cultural, will offer sufficient insight into the essential nature of modern Scottish nationalism to allow us to make a critical Christian assessment of it.

Professor Neil MacCormick, Regius Professor of Public Law at Edinburgh University, is a Scottish nationalist with a distinguished pedigree, his father John being a founding figure in the SNP and the leading Home Rule coalition advocate within and outwith its ranks in the 1940s and 1950s. Professor Mac-Cormick has brought all the clarity and eloquence of his legal philosophical mind to his own reflections on Scottish nationalism, in two essays on nationalism published in 1970 and 1979 respectively, at the beginning and the end of the devolution decade. In both essays MacCormick draws a fundamental distinction between two different conceptions of nationalism.

'Pure nationalism' makes a number of metaphysical assumptions about the nature of nations about which rational discussion is hardly possible: 'Simply because Scotland is a nation, she ought to become a separate state.' Here independence is seen as an end in itself, rather than a means to an end. Associated with that kind of nationalism is often the claim that the nation is the highest form of human community, conferring moral significance on its members and properly demanding an absolute loyalty from them. MacCormick describes this as a morally intolerable claim: 'If nationalism implies ascribing that sort of absolutist, overriding force to the claims of "the nation", then it is indeed a morally intolerable philosophy', with which he himself would have nothing to do: 'But what is morally intolerable is the assertion of the *overriding* force of the claim, not the suggestion that some such claims are morally valid and politically justifiable.' Therefore, he believes there to be another conception of nationalism which is morally and rationally acceptable. MacCormick calls this form of nationalism utilitarian, because it is open to rational argument about its claims in a way that a metaphysical 'pure nationalism' is not. His own preferred 'utilitarian nationalism' sees national independence only as a means to an end: 'the best means to the well-being of the Scottish people.' That can be discussed, disputed and disproved or accepted through rational discourse.

The key question arising from MacCormick's analysis must therefore be: what kind of nationalism prevails in Scotland today? As I shall argue, it is a question that Christians in particular should ask. But first we must listen to a nationalist reply. The fullest political reflection from a Scottish Nationalist in the 1980s came from Jim Sillars in his 1986 book, *Scotland - the Case for Optimism*. Analysing the current state of political philosophy within the SNP in the 1980s, Sillars draws his own distinction between what he terms the old 'traditionalist' nationalism, which dominated the party's thinking in the 1970s, and the new 'progressive' nationalism typified by the exponents of a left wing political analysis of the SNP in the 1980s. Sillars draws on Tom Nairn's argument that all nationalist ideologies are both clean and dirty, progressive and regressive. It is important, therefore, for him to distinguish between these two tendencies in Scottish nationalism:

> ...when nationalism is based upon assertions of inherent racial or cultural superiority, the people turn in on themselves and develop a diabolical insensitivity to other nations. That kind of nationalism can lead people to evil and that cannot be denied. On the other hand there is evidence that when a nation does no more than assert the economic, social and cultural integrity of a distinctive group of people, insists that while they are no better than anyone else, they are no worse; insists upon a full entitlement to exercise freedom of judgement in both internal and external policies and contributes constructively to the world's life, it presents dangers to none.

He links the traditionalist nationalist wing in the party with regressive elements such as chauvinistic and anti-English feeling, a hostility to political theory and any class analysis of Scottish society, and a dependence on the memory of medieval struggles alone to inspire Scottish unity and independence - back to Bruce and Bannockburn! In its place, Sillars would assert the progressive nationalism of his own position, firmly democratic and internationalist and firmly rooted in contemporary political, social and economic analysis of the case for independence in Europe. The debate between the traditionalist and progressive wings within the SNP, to use Sillars' analysis, will continue in the 1990s - a debate between those traditional nationalists who believe in independence as the SNP's sole aim and Scotland's national destiny and right, and those who would argue for independence as the best means of achieving the party's left of centre social and economic policies. There are echoes here of MacCormick's distinction between pure and utilitarian nationalism. While his political style is combative and jugular, Sillars' reflections on nationalism show the utilitarian nationalist's preference for rational discourse about means and ends. At the end of the 1980s, the SNP claimed that it was taking its stand on the intellectually irrefutable case for independence in Europe, based on careful economic and political analysis of Scotland's interests and social well-being. This was a significant shift away from the earlier emphasis on the rights of nationhood, an argument that owed more to the metaphysical claims of pure nationalism.

Not that metaphysics have been ignored in modern Scottish nationalism. One of the most significant developments in the nationalism of the 1980s has been the development of sophisticated analyses of Scottish culture by a new generation of younger Scottish intellectuals who may best be described as cultural as well as political nationalists. Typical of this kind of new nationalist cultural critique is the work of Ronald Turnbull and Craig Beveridge, in a collection of essays published in 1989 under the title, *The Eclipse of Scottish Culture*. For Turnbull and Beveridge our present understanding of Scottish culture and history has been blighted by the phenomenon of what they call 'inferiorism'. This is a concept they have adapted from the work of the African writer Franz Fanon who used it to describe the way in which a colonised people internalise the imperial power's judgement on them that they are an inferior culture in comparison with the dominant metropolitan one. Scotland, a small nation under the hegemony of a once major world power, has internalised that sense of inferiority about its own past and culture when compared with those of England.

Scottish inferiorism can be found in a range of historical studies and cultural interpretations, in which certain periods and aspects of Scottish life, such as seventeenth century Scottish intellectual life, or Calvinism, are automatically labelled dark, barbaric and regressive. Inferiorism also leads to the virtual ignoring of whole other areas of Scottish cultural achievement, such as the rich contribution of twentieth century Scottish philosophical thought to modern culture.

What is striking about Turnbull and Beveridge's analysis is its willingness to reconsider and affirm the positive contributions of Scotland's religious and especially Calvinist traditions of thought and culture, not least and perhaps most surprisingly in twentieth century Scottish thought, when they are so vigorously denied by many cultural critics and historians in and beyond Scotland. They identify a historic and proper Scottish metaphysical concern not with some mystical notion of nationhood but with the moral pursuit of God or the Good as the foundation for national life and any rational discourse about the true ends of

F

human life. And they root that concern in a longstanding and sympathetic Scottish intellectual dialogue with continental and Western thought and culture.

What do we find, then, among these three representative examples of modern Scottish nationalist thought that would allow us to judge whether we are dealing with something intrinsically and irredeemably evil or something bearing both the sinful and the righteous aspects of fallen social reality? We find, first, a consistent discrimination between different kinds of nationalism, pure and utilitarian, metaphysical and rational, regressive and progressive, inferiorist and cosmopolitan. Such discrimination is accompanied by a moral judgement of abhorrence against forms of nationalism which would give to the nation any absolute or overriding loyalty against all other forms of human community or moral principle. It is matched by a consistent wish to engage in rational argument and moral discourse about nationalist claims, such as the case for Scottish independence, on the grounds of a greater good and end, the well-being of the Scottish people and wider community of nations within a common humanity. This is encased in the SNP's commitment to human rights, internationalism and a view of Scottish citizenship based on residence rather than ethnicity or country of origin. Among some younger nationalist intellectuals at least, there would seem also to be a new willingness to reconsider the truth and relevance of the theological and cultural insights of the Christian tradition in Scotland, within its catholic context, in the shaping of any new post-Enlightenment Scottish culture and identity.

All this must be put alongside the painful recognition of the chauvinist, regressive, inferiorist, metaphysically idolatrous elements within the complex phenomenon and ambiguous fallen reality of modern Scottish nationalism. These may well represent the 'dark whirlpool of error'. But clearly this would be the judgement of many nationalists as well as many Christians. The discovery of categories of moral discrimination, rational discourse and openness to the claims of Christian truth in contemporary nationalist thought in Scotland must not be dismissed by Christians concerned to evaluate Scottish nationalism in the light of Christian categories of morality and meaning. There is the recognition here, welcomed and even required by nationalists themselves, that nationalist claims and the phemomena of nationhood and national identity are open to critical assessment according to principles, loyalties and communities of human thought and identity which transcend nationalism and nations. Scottish Nationalist claims and national loyalties would be seen in this light as provisional and limited, never absolute and incontrovertible. At the very least, a Christian case against Scottish nationalism in any form is not proven, to use a good Scottish legal category.

There are evil forms of nationalism that no principled person, whether Christian or not, could ever embrace. Scottish Nationalists like Jim Sillars and Neil MacCormick have been as categorical in their denunciation of such nationalist ideologies as any Christian theologian reacting to the pro-Nazi German Christian betrayal of the Gospel with a blanket rejection of all nationalism. Nationalism needs a discriminating analysis not a total anathema. But what are the proper Christian categories with which to evaluate nations and nationalism? Before any final verdict can be delivered on Scottish nationhood and nationalism, we must return to the question of what form a practical theological approach to national identity should take, according to the Biblical witness to Jesus Christ, the light of the nations.

Chapter 8

INCARNATIONALISM -
A Practical Theology of Nationhood

As we wrestle with the meaning of the relationship between identity in Christ as Christians, and identity in Scotland as Scots, we need to remember that this dual identity is nothing new. Christians in the New Testament letters faced a continuing tension between two identities - their identity in Christ and their identity in Rome, or Corinth or whatever local community to which they belonged. As new men and women in Christ, their first loyalty was to God. Their primary identity was as Christians. And yet they remained members of their local community, sharing its culture and way of life. An early second century Christian apologist put it this way, in the Epistle to Diognetus:

> The difference between Christians and the rest of mankind is not a matter of nationality, or language, or customs. Christians do not live apart in separate cities of their own, speak any special dialect, nor practise any eccentric way of life... They pass their lives in whatever township - Greek or foreign - each man's lot has determined; and conform to ordinary local usage in their clothing, diet and other habits. Nevertheless, the organisation of their community does exhibit some features that are remarkable, and even surprising. For instance, though they are residents at home in their own countries, their behaviour there is more like that of transients; they take their full part as citizens, but they also submit to anything and everything as if they were aliens. For them, any foreign country is a motherland, and any motherland is a foreign country.

Christians share the nationality, language and customs of their motherland, their own country, and yet their ultimate loyalty and longing is directed towards another country, the Kingdom of God: 'For here we do not have an enduring city, but we are looking for the city that is to come.' (Hebrews 13:14) The tension between these two identities is evident throughout the New Testament, as Jewish and Gentile Christians alike work out the relationship between their own cultural identities and their new spiritual identity in Christ. Questions of Roman citizenship, the conflict of loyalty between God and state, the degree of involvement or abstention for the Christian in their local culture, these are recurring concerns in the New Testament writings. They remain the concern of Christians today, because we never cease to be in Christ and in our own local community, culture or nation.

Therefore, for Scottish Christians. a practical theology of nationhood must be found in that place of tension between identity in Christ and identity in Scotland. An authentically Christ-centred and Biblical understanding of nations can never resolve that tension by falling back into either a religious nationalism that identifies exclusively with the nation or an escapist pietism which denies the human context for our relationship with God amid the nations. Rather, Christ and the Scriptures call on us to live with that tension as a proper context for our discipleship.

That tension was never better expressed than in an essay written by the Swiss theologian Karl Barth early in 1945, entitled *The Germans and Ourselves*. Here Barth reflects on the proper relationship that the Swiss should adopt as a Christian people, with a defeated and formerly Nazi Germany. For him it was an urgent and unavoidable concern which was central to the Swiss's own sense of national identity. His stance against German religious nationalism has already been referred to. But in this essay he also argues that we cannot escape this particular national question. Though they may not have answers, he saw the Swiss as called in humility to tackle the question of the future of German and thus Swiss nationhood: 'That we find we are not equal to the task does not release us.' Everything depended on seeing these national concerns in the light of Christ, however dimly. Barth sums up the tension inherent in that task by linking it to what he calls the mightiest of all prayers: 'Lord I believe: help thou mine unbelief.'

Only one person has ever held that tension in a true balance, Jesus of Nazareth, the Messiah of Israel, the Light to the Gentiles, God incarnate. The only way in which Christians can maintain that creative tension between their two identities, in Christ and in the nation, is through sharing in Christ's own dynamic and relational approach to nationhood. In the incarnation we have a model of how we should relate to nationhood as Christians.

The vision of Christ emerging from the previous three chapters is of one who cannot be reduced to a divine figure with only the appearance of our humanity, the Scottish Christ of our heretical Apollinarian religious and cultural tradition. The Jesus of the Scriptures is fully human as well as fully divine, the other Scottish Christ we encounter in the preaching and theological writings of such as Edward Irving and John Macleod Campbell. In his full humanity Christ enters into a threefold relationship with Israel and, through Israel, with the nations. As our human priest, he intercedes for the nations in a profound identification with our humanity. As our human **prophet**, he is God's Word to the nations, separating himself from them in judgement and yet bringing to them the word of salvation which comes from that separate nation, the Jews. And as our human **king**, he brings in God's rule over the nations, transforming the kingdoms of this world into the Kingdom of God.

In our union with Christ, Christians share that same threefold relationship with the nation. As priests to God we are called to intercede for the nations and identify with their common humanity and culture. As the holy nation of God's people, the acoustic community who hear, obey and proclaim God's Word, we are called to incarnate a prophetic life separate from the nations in their idolatry. As servants of the King of Kings, we are called to transform the life of the nations according to the rule of God, the coming Kingdom that is the tangible community within which both church and nation find their destiny and purpose. This would suggest a dynamic and variable relationship with the nation, a flexible rather than a fixed response to the question of national identity. That would be nothing new.

Models of Church and Nation

Throughout the history of the Christian church different models of the relationship of church and nation have been developed. From the earliest days of the Church in the Book of Acts and the New Testament writings the position of the Gentiles, the nations, in relation to the believing community, the holy nation of God's people, has been debated and discussed. Indeed the debate goes much further back into the Old Testament itself. Down through the centuries Christians have responded to the ethnic communities of which they have been members in different ways, in the light of Scripture, their Church traditions and their own historical situation. This has been part of the much wider question of the Gospel's relationship to all cultural activity and identity.

The American theologian Richard Niebuhr wrote a pioneering study of that relationship between Christianity and human culture called *Christ and Culture*. He offered there five different models of the way in which Christians down through the centuries have related faith in Christ to the cultures of which they have been a part. In varying degrees and in different ways Christ was seen as against culture, identified with culture or transforming culture.

Indeed a more recent American Christian writer, Robert Webber, has suggested such a threefold simplification of Niebuhr's five types of the relationship between Christ and culture. The way in which Christians relate to human culture may fit broadly within these three distinct models. First there are identifying models of Christ and culture: 'These advocate participation in the structures of life either by compromising with culture or by recognising the tension with culture.' Then, secondly, there are separating models: 'These include all attempts to withdraw from the world, either by refusing to participate in the structures of society or by actively creating a counter culture.' And finally there are transforming models: 'According to these, the structures of life can be changed either now, through the application of the gospel, or in the future, as the ultimate goal of history.' These three models of identification, separation and transformation are not dissimilar to Niebuhr's relationships of opposition, synthesis and conversion between Christ and culture.

Together they offer us a helpful theological analysis of that other, more particular kind of cultural community and identity we associate with nations. We can speak of different types of relationship between 'Christ and Nation' as well as 'Christ and Culture'.

Drawing on different aspects of the Biblical narrative, different Christian theological traditions and different local historical experiences, Christians have made three broad responses to national identity which may fit in with the typology Niebuhr and Webber developed to describe a wider response to culture in general. Three 'ideal types' of Christian response to nations and nationalism may be set up, even if no actual Christian response fits any one of these types exactly and without qualification.

First, there are **identifying models** of Christ and nation. These embrace a synthesis between loyalty to Christ and loyalty to the nation in a common community of Christian nationhood, or find aspects of the nation and nationalism fully compatible with loyalty to Christ. Second, there are **separating models** of Christ and nation. These envisage a fundamental opposition between loyalty to the nation and loyalty to Christ, and view his Church as a supra-national community which rejects nationalism in any form. And, thirdly, there are **transforming models** of Christ and nation. According to this type, the nation can undergo cultural as well as personal conversion by the transforming of all aspects of national life according to Biblical norms; this approach may be open to the critical and conditional affirmation of the constructive role of nationalism in that process of transformation. While these models may seem abstract and simplistic, they do shed light on the often complex interaction between Christianity and nationality by highlighting certain significant features of that relationship which might otherwise be missed.

For example, the three historic Christian visions of Scotland which we have already considered can be understood in terms of these three models of Christ and nation in a way that illuminates the strengths and weaknesses of each vision.

(a) The medieval Catholic vision of Scotland as a free nation is
a clear-cut example of an identifying relationship between
Christ and nation. We saw the extent to which the medieval
Scottish Church sought to identify with the nation of Scotland,
first in its support for the nation's struggle for independence
from England and, second in its deliberate cultivation of a
Scottish national identity in its liturgy, piety and institutional
life.

This close identification with the nation was a source of great
strength both to the church and to the country. It added legitimacy to Scotland's claim to political autonomy within the
international community. It enhanced the culture and social life
of Scotland through the establishment of universities and substantial churches. It helped shape the shared images of national
consciousness which bound the Scots together into one community. But ultimately it may be said that its identification with the
structures of political power and economic wealth led to the
corruption of its own spiritual autonomy and integrity as a
Christian church. In turn this led to the failure of its mission to
sustain the moral, spiritual and social welfare of Scottish society,
as Sir David Lyndsay's attack on the Church in his *Satire of the
Three Estates* amply illustrates.

(b)   The Reformed vision of Scotland as a godly nation is
much more ambiguous in the way it related Christ to nationhood.
We have already explored some of these ambiguities in considering the 'Knoxian paradox', with its vision of reforming church
and nation according to the Word of God and not the nationalist
images and precedents so dear to the earlier Catholic vision. In
this sense the Reformed approach to nationhood may be said to
be a separating one, at least in its relationship to the earlier
medieval nationalism and in its initial impetus to reform the life
of the nation. Yet, paradoxically, this vision gave rise to a new
sense of Scottish national identity, as the Reformed vision
generated its own distinctive ethos, with its central and dominant
role in national life over several centuries. However, that identifying strand in the Reformed vision was largely restricted to
those aspects of Scottish life which could clearly be identified
with the interests of the Reformed religion and Kirk. As we saw

when we looked at the Godly vision, it tended to transpose all national questions into an ecclesiastical key and see Scottish national interests reduced to narrowly religious terms, as in the seventeenth century national covenants and 1707 Treaty of Union.

In certain of its Calvinist forms, it did not so readily identify with other aspects of Scottish national life, such as the country's secular linguistic, cultural and intellectual traditions, which could be dismissed as worldly. That should not blind us to the rich and strong strand within Scottish Calvinism of identification with aspects of Scottish culture, such as the sixteenth century literary brilliance of the Reformed humanist George Buchanan or the eighteenth century Moderates' involvement with the intellectual world of the Scottish Enlightenment. The tendency of many commentators to reduce that diverse Reformed tradition to a culturally oppressive and intellectually stultifying caricature says more about their own 'inferiorist' bias against Scottish culture than it does about Scottish Calvinism.

Internationally, the Reformed and Calvinist approach to culture has been recognised as a transforming one. The Scottish Reformed approach to Scotland bears many of the marks of that social vision of Christ transforming culture, particularly in the Kirk's involvement with education, social welfare and public life. But I would still suggest that at the heart of the historic Scottish Reformed vision of the nation lies a separating model of Christ and nation. This was both the secret of its strength as a reforming force in national life and its Achilles heel, once it became the dominant vision of Scotland. Its emphasis on the authority of the Word of God and the call to be a godly community shaped by that Word proved a powerful antidote to the spiritual inertia of a medieval polity in Scotland where the Church had become compromised through its uncritical identification with the established regime. Separation from that Scotland and that national identity and the call to godly reformation according to Biblical rather than nationalist norms was immensely attractive and persuasive to many Scots disillusioned with the old medieval order in church and nation.

But this separating model led to a lack of Christian concern for secular as distinct from ecclesiastical issues in national life, such as the survival of an ancient Gaelic culture, the Lowland Scots language or an autonomous Scottish state.

The Reformed vision sought to identify with and to transform the life of Scotland only to the extent that it had already re-made it in its own image of a separate and godly church-nation. The elements of identification and transformation which are so evident in the Scottish Calvinist relationship to Scotland are all contained within what is fundamentally a separating model, in which Christ is seen as separate from any notion of a secular and autonomous nation. Only in as much as the Church absorbs the nation within the Biblical notion of the covenant nation, where the Church becomes the key national institution, does the Reformed vision easily identify with Scotland or have a strategy for transforming its life; as in the social vision of the early Reformed Kirk's Books of Discipline or Thomas Chalmers' schemes to tackle the problems of an urban, industrial Scotland through the national establishment of religion. The preoccupation with ecclesiastical issues and their confusion with national interests so typical of the Reformed vision of Scotland arises out of the separating model of Christ and nation at its heart. The failure of the Reformed vision to come to terms with the secular realities of modern Scotland, and ultimately to transform them in the light of its Calvinist confession of the sovereignty of God over that secular life, was really a failure to recognise the proper autonomy and identity of the Scottish nation apart from the Kirk but still under Christ's Lordship: a failure made inevitable by its separating model of Christ and nation.

(c) The Secular vision of Scotland may be described as operating with a transforming model of Christ and nation. It certainly took seriously the challenge of transforming the secular life of Scotland according to the Christian ethic which was its inspiration. And it also took seriously the proper autonomy and value of the secular society it sought to transform. The secular visionaries are to be credited with taking seriously the immense human problems of poverty, injustice and deprivation generated by the industrial revolution in Scotland, seeing them as central to an authentically Christian vision of the nation's life, and recognising the role of non-ecclesiastical institutions and move-

ments in tackling these problems. It is no coincidence that the
rise of modern Scottish nationalism in the mid-nineteenth century coincided with the rise of the Secular vision, as it filled the
vacuum left in the national imagination by the collapse of the
Reformed vision after the 1843 Disruption. The secular visionaries recognised and reflected upon the increasing role of the
British state in Scottish life and the importance of the political
dimension of Scottish nationhood within the Union. They did
not make the mistake of reducing Scotland's national interests to
purely ecclesiastical issues, as the Reformed visionaries did
before and after 1843.

Indeed, in its most radical form, the Secular vision argued that
a Christian transformation of the nation's life could come about
without reference to the Church's role in national life, something
unthinkable in the older Catholic and Reformed visions. Again,
this was both a source of initial strength and ultimate weakness
and failure for the Secular vision. The detachment of the Christian ethic from Christian belief and worship was attractive for
post-Christian Scots searching for a moral basis for their vision
of a socially and politically transformed nation. However, as we
have seen, the Secular vision assumed the survival of a universally shared Christian ethic as the common and persuasive bond
of public life, even after the decline of the faith and church which
generated that ethic.

Later generations of secular Scots have not found this formula
so intellectually credible or socially plausible. What in fact has
come about is a pluralist society which is deeply divided about
its contemporary social ethic, with a minority of Scots giving
uncertain loyalty to the historic Christian ethic, and others no
longer certain about any values. This secularised Christian
ethical vision of transforming Scottish society has largely run
into the sands by the late twentieth century. Where does that
leave a Christian vision of Scottish nationhood for the 1990s and
beyond?

An Incarnational Model

If we have already experienced the possibilities and the
limitations of all three approaches to Christ and nation in

Scotland - the identifying approach of the Catholic vision, the separating approach of the Reformed tradition and the transforming approach of the Secular vision - what is left for Christians seeking to relate their faith to their national identity and the life of their nation? I have already argued that we cannot go back to any one of these historic Christian visions of Scotland. Each in turn has made a unique contribution to Scottish nationhood and to the way we see ourselves as Scots. Each vision had unique insights and strengths in its Christian approach to questions of nationhood. Each vision has left a practical theological legacy from which any new Christian vision of Scotland can learn much of lasting value.

The medieval Catholic vision shows the power of an identifying approach to shape a country's culture, its sense of national identity and freedom. The Reformed approach grasped the potential of the vision of a separate godly community to challenge and reform a corrupt Church and nation. The Secular vision realised the importance of Christian social ethics in transforming the social, economic and political fabric of a nation's life. Yet each vision was rooted not only in Christ but in a particular era of Scottish history, which cannot be repeated in what is now a post-Christendom, indeed a post-modern and post-industrial society. And each vision failed Scotland at a crucial juncture in its history.

The medieval Catholic vision failed to sustain its image of a free nation by its failure to reform the corruptions flowing from its identifying approach. The Reformed vision failed to adapt its call for a godly nation to the changing secular world of modernity because of the ecclesiastical preoccupations of its separating approach. The Secular vision failed to sustain its crusade for a moral nation because it rejected the necessity for any theological foundation for its exclusively ethical transforming approach. Do these three failures mean the end of a Christian vision of Scotland? I think not. They mean the kind of contrition which Anthony Ross called for in 1970, a contrition for the failure of the Christian Church to re-shape Scottish society in the light of the Gospel. And contrition can bring not only forgiveness but a new clarity of thought after the removal of old visions now turned into deceptive illusions.

Our commitment to re-examine our Christian traditions in Scotland in that contrite spirit has led us in this book to see the strengths and weaknesses of these earlier visions and to a frank recognition of their fate. It has led us to what I have seen as the most important act of contrition for a renewed Christian understanding of Scottish identity - contrition for our false, heretical Apollinarian understanding of Christ as not fully human, the Scottish Christ; and to a fresh perception of the other Scottish Christ, who has assumed and therefore healed our full humanity in a saving solidarity with us. It has led us to a clearer understanding of the source of our vision in the Biblical narratives, with their theological understanding of nations as an ecology of imagined, acoustic and tangible communities under God. Out of that contrition for our past, that greater clarity about the theological and Biblical resources still available to us in the present, it may yet be possible to construct what the American theologian Robert Schreiter has called a 'local theology' for Scotland, a new vision for the future of our identity as a nation.

I believe that we cannot have a Christian vision of Scotland without looking at Scotland through Christ's eyes. That means not only a more authentically Biblical vision of Christ himself in Scotland, in his full humanity and divinity. It means developing an approach to Scottish identity modelled on Christ himself. If we take Christ, his identity and relationship with the nations as the centre of our vision then it will be possible to hold together the lasting insights of earlier Christian visions of Scotland in a new and dynamic way. This new vision of Christ and nation could generate different, liberating perceptions of Scottish identity from those we have inherited.

We can take a lead here from current theological reflection on the wider question of Christ and culture. When Robert Webber reduced Richard Niebuhr's five types of relationship between Christianity and human society to three models of identification, separation and transformation, he went further and suggested that it was time to integrate these three approaches into one model of Christ and culture. He has called this model an 'incarnational paradigm', developed out of Christ's own relationship to culture expressed in his incarnate life on earth.

Christ himself did not limit the way he related to his own

Jewish culture to any one of the approaches followed by later Christian traditions. In the incarnate life of Jesus of Nazareth we see a profound identification with the Jewish people, religion and way of life, combined with a radical separation from aspects of that culture which he rejected, especially the Pharisees' distortion of the law and religion of Israel. These elements of identification and separation were combined with a unique mission to transform Israel through his suffering messiahship and triumphant resurrection, the new wine in the new wineskins. In his own person and human life, Christ showed a flexible and differential approach to his culture, determined by a sense of his own divine identity and mission, and the wisdom he was able to bring to bear on Israel.

Webber argues persuasively for the adoption of this incarnational model, offering a variable and threefold Christian approach to culture, in faithfulness to Christ's own example and in response to changing cultural contexts. Depending on that cultural context, different Christian responses may be more or less appropriate and faithful to Christ. In some situations the Christian may be able to identify with and even affirm the life of a particular culture, as Christ himself did. In a different situation, Christians may be called to separate themselves from aspects of a particular culture out of a greater loyalty to Christ. And in many situations, the Christian approach must be to seek to transform a culture in the light of the Gospel. The response in any particular cultural situation, whether in identifying with it, separating from it or working for its transformation, will be determined in a dialogue between what is going on here, and what God commands here; between discerning the nature of the cultural context, and interpreting the particular demands of faithful obedience to Christ within that culture.

If this incarnational paradigm offers us a more constructive and coherent model of Christ and culture, overcoming many of the inadequacies of any single approach, then I believe it also provides us with a more adequate model of Christ and nation. For we can also think of Christ's relationship to the nations in this threefold and differential way. Christ has a complex and variable relationship with both the holy nation of Israel and the gentile nations of the New Testament world. He identifies with Israel as the acoustic community through which God speaks in judgement and mercy to the nations. As he says to the foreign woman at Jacob's well in the gentile land of Samaria, 'You Samaritans worship what you do not know; we worship what we know, for salvation is from the Jews.' (John 4:22) Here as so often in the Gospels, Jesus is separating himself from the surrounding nations, from the idolatry of their imagined communities and wayward culture, as when he condemns their piety and their politics (Matthew 6:7; 20:25).

And yet he separates himself also from Israel in its apostasy, as when he warns Jerusalem about its rejection of God's word (Matthew 23:37-39); and weeps over its failure to recognise in his own person God's coming to bring it peace (John 19:41-44). This sense of separation from Israel is sometimes combined with an astonished sense of identification with those from gentile nations who hear and believe his message. When the Roman centurion expressed his faith in Jesus as the healer of his servant, Christ said to his Jewish followers: 'I tell you the truth, I have not found anyone in Israel with such great faith. I say to you that many will come from the east and the west, and will take their places at the feast with Abraham, Isaac and Jacob in the kingdom of heaven. But the subjects of the kingdom will be thrown outside...' (Matthew 8:10-12) It is possible for the gentile nations to become acoustic communities as they respond to the universal vocation of Israel and its messiah, hearing and obeying God's Word through the Jews and being welcomed into the tangible community of the kingdom of God; while members of the holy nation may be cast out of that tangible community along with the imagined communities of the pagans.

Christ's variable approach of identification with and separation from both the holy nation of Israel and the gentile nations is determined by the criteria of a third community. The coming Kingdom of God, that tangible community incarnate in his own person, will transform the life of Israel and the nations into one new multi-national humanity. In his parable of the sheep and the goats in Matthew chapter 25, a parable of the Final Judgement, it is the nations which come before God to see if they will enter his Kingdom. The criterion of judgement is whether or not they have lived out the life of the Kingdom already in compassion and service to those in need.

And how is that new life of the Kingdom to spread among the nations before the Final Judgement? Jesus calls his apostles to go and make disciples of all nations, welcoming them into the holy nation through baptism and sharing with them his commands for God's rule over the nations (Matthew 28:16-20). Israel and the nations are transformed through the rule of God on earth inaugurated by his own coming and extended through the mission of his followers to all nations. Until Christ's final appearing and the Day of Judgement, the transformation of Israel and the nations will be only partial and often hidden. But in the Revelation and vision of John, the life of the nations will be completely transformed in the new earth and heaven (Revelation 21:26; 22:2). Christ approaches the transformation of the nations through the coming of the Kingdom, which also determines the extent to which he will identify with or separate himself from these communities.

In the incarnation of God in the womb of Israel amid the nations, we have a model of how we should relate to the nations of which we are part. As those who find their true identity in Christ, our approach to our own national identity will always involve his threefold response of affirmation, opposition and conversion: identification, separation and transformation. In Christ we can identify with all those aspects of our national identity which are a wholesome expression of the divine mandate in creation to develop a human culture worthy of our Creator, mediated through the imagined community of historic nations. In Christ we can identify with our nation in as much as it responds to the Gospel in every sphere of its life and aspect of its national identity as an acoustic community. In Christ we must separate ourselves from any part of our national life and identity as an imagined community which breaks God's image in our common humanity or denies our stewardship of his creation. In Christ we must work and pray for the transformation of every aspect of our nationhood through the coming of the Kingdom of God; knowing that the whole life of a nation is subject to the scrutiny of divine judgement, especially its nationalism, and yet also subject to the hope of redemption into the multi-cultural richness of the new humanity in Christ.

God's reign comes in the midst of the nation's frail historical existence as a provisional and partial community within the wider circle of humanity. Its national history is an uncertain part of the the tragi-comedy of a wider human history whose course and end yet lie with a sovereign God.

The Nations and the Biblical Drama

The three dimensions of an incarnational model of Christ and nation can be understood in terms of the place of the nations in the threefold Biblical drama of creation, fall and redemption, and final restoration of all things in Christ.

(a)   According to this perspective, there can be a proper Christian identification with the nation to the extent that its life reflects within a particular community and identity that which constitutes our common humanity - the image and calling of God, given to us in creation and restored for us in Jesus Christ. As we saw in chapter six, nations are not regarded in Scripture as part of God's original creation. They are not divinely instituted, natural human communities, like marriage, the family or the state.

In that sense there can be no natural theology of nationhood, as the German Christians and Dutch Reformed Afrikaners read into Scripture from their prior nationalist and racialist commitments. Nations arise after the fall of humanity, as a sign of God's judgement on the one proud, rebellious human race, as a providential restraint on its imperial idolatries. And yet it is within the diverse nations, peoples and tribes of the earth that the one humanity continues to work out its universal cultural mandate from God to develop life on earth. They are humanly instituted communities, a historical response to both the God-given creative diversity and God-sanctioned cultural and political divisions of the one humanity, within a creation and history now marred and disrupted by human sin.

Christians can identify with the nations of which they are part and affirm their national identity in as much as they are diverse and particular expressions of a God-given universal humanity. If a nation affirms in its life as an imagined community, for example its culture, language, traditions, institutions, politics or relations with other nations, something of the created image and revealed purpose of God for humanity, then a Christian can share in that life and affirm its value. Under certain conditions, that may involve the Christian identifying with a nationalism that would affirm and establish the nation's life in these terms. However, that identification is always conditional and never absolute. It is an identification with a community that has a provisional, conditional and passing existence within human history; a partial and incomplete community within the one human race which can never escape its mortality, live in isolation from other nations or claim an absolute loyalty from its members.

Identification with the nation also means identifying with God's providential ordering of human life in and through the life of nations. Such an identification must never confuse national self-interest with God's purposes, as has so often happened in time of war when nations have confidently claimed that God was on their side. Rather, Christians have rightly seen, on Biblical grounds, that God rules over the affairs of nations, as the many divine judgements brought by the Old Testament prophets of Israel on the surrounding gentile nations make clear. This kind of identification always stems from a repentant humility and intercession for the life of the nation in full awareness and confession before God of its sin and yet also of its possibilities through grace.

This kind of Christian identification was expressed by the French Christian Simone Weil during the Second World War, after the collapse and occupation of France by the Nazis. The Free French government in exile asked her to write a spiritual manifesto for post-war France and the restoration of its national independence. Sharing that exile in England, but identifying with the wartime hardships of her fellow citizens in occupied France to the extent of living on a starvation diet that contributed to her early death, Simone Weil created a Christian vision for France in her book, *The Need for Roots*. At the heart of that vision for the re-building of the nation after the Liberation was the need to come to terms with the fact that France was not eternal, as French patriotism had asserted since the 1789 Revolution, but frail and temporal, as the Nazi occupation and conquest had cruelly shown.

In that vulnerable historical condition, where its nationhood could be so easily corrupted or destroyed, what France needed was not the idolatrous love of a patriotism that was blind to the nation's mortality and failings, but the unconditional love of Christian charity, *agape*, which alone had the power to contemplate the beloved country in all its shame, and yet love it still with an undiminished clarity and compassion: 'When a Christian represents to himself Christ on the Cross', Simone Weil wrote, '... such a love can keep its eye open on injustices, cruelties, mistakes, falsehoods, crimes and scandals contained in the country's past, its present and in its ambitions in general, quite openly and fearlessly, and without being thereby diminished; the love being only rendered thereby more painful.' That is what is meant by a Christian identification or affirmation of the nation and its national identity. Such an identification is possible because the nation is seen with the love of God revealed in the death of his Son, Jesus Christ. But it is obvious also from this definition that identification is inseparable from the Christian calling to separate from and oppose in a nation's life all that denies the image and purpose of God for humanity as revealed in Christ crucified.

(b)   This leads on to the place of the nations within the second act in the Biblical drama, fall and redemption. In as much as the nations and nationalism express the idolatry and oppression of human sin, and reject God's image and purpose, then the Christian is called to a two-fold separation from national identity. First, it is the Christian's calling to live as a loyal member of the holy nation of God's people, set apart to incarnate God's image and obey God's purpose in the midst of the nations. That separate, holy nationhood has the first place in the Christian's identity. It means that Christians belong first and foremost to the holy nation of God's people, embracing all nations in one new humanity in Christ, and only in a secondary and conditional way do they belong to the historic nations of which each may be a member through birth or choice or circumstance.

In this sense Christians are a separate nation within the nations to which they belong or among whom they live. Their nationhood is defined by the saving activity of God in Jesus Christ, to redeem humanity from its sin and restore it to God's image and purpose. The holy nation of God's people has been set apart, called out from among all nations, for a specific purpose in human history: to make known God's redeeming love to those same nations. This was the missionary identity of Israel in the Old Testament: '... I will also make you a light to the nations - so that all the world may be saved' (Isaiah 49:6); and the reason for the separate identity of the Church among the nations in the New Testament: 'But you are the chosen race, the King's priests, the holy nation, God's own people, chosen to proclaim the wonderful acts of God, who called you out of darkness into his own marvellous light.' (1 Peter 2:9) It is precisely because of that missionary calling to bring the light of the Gospel to the nations that Christians must be separate from the nation in a second sense. They must be set apart from all the darkness in the life of the nations or the cause of nationalism exposed by that same light and their own confession of Christ's salvation and lordship.

The nature of this twin calling to separation **from** the nation's idolatry and **for** God's purpose was set out by those Christians like Bonhoeffer and Barth in Nazi Germany who supported what became known as the Barmen Declaration of 1934. In opposition to what they called the errors of the 'German Christians' who tried to bring the Christian Gospel and Church under the control of Nazi nationalist and racist ideology, they confessed the evangelical truths of Christ, his Gospel and Church, and declared: 'We reject the false doctrine that there could be areas of our life in which we would not belong to Jesus Christ but to other lords, areas in which we would need no justification and sanctification through him... We reject the false doctrine that the Church could have permission to hand over the form of its message and of its order to whatever it itself might wish or to the vicissitudes of the prevailing ideological and political convictions of the day.' The Christian approach to nations and nationalism must always involve a similar rejection of the idea that there could be sinful areas of the nation's life or ideology outwith Christ's lordship, or that the Christian Church and its Gospel should be reduced to the form and content of religious nationalism.

(c)   If the second act of the Biblical drama, the redemption of fallen humanity in Jesus Christ, defines the nature of the Christian's separation from the nation, the third act, the restoration of all things in Christ, is the setting for the transformation of the nations. As we have seen, the nations have their place in the coming of God's Kingdom on earth. Christ calls his Church to share the Gospel of his Kingdom with the nations and the Revelation of John sees the wealth and healing of the nations as part of the life of the new humanity. As the Gospel makes its impact on the life of the nations, for time and for eternity, it transforms those nations and every aspect of their nationhood and identity. It is the call to share the Gospel of the Kingdom of God with the nations and the prayer for that Kingdom to come which motivate Christians to work for the transforming of their national life according to Kingdom norms of justice and peace.

The conviction that Jesus is Lord moves Christians to see his lordship transforming our nationhood and national identity. This vision was expressed by the Christian Gaelic poet Fearghas MacFhionnlaigh in his poem *A' Mheanbhchuileag* (The Midge), in which the sight of a midge struggling in a spider's web reminds him of his nation's plight:

> We need a Messiah
> who will bear the weight of our torment,
> plucking us from the dust of our thralldom,
> and raising us on high...
>
> And when he comes
> the government will be on his shoulder...
>
> And I noticed with a smile
> that shoes were out of fashion;
> for all Creation was holy ground.
>
> And I knew
> that Pharaoh was no more.

The Christian criterion for deciding which approach to take to the imagined communities of nationhood in any particular context must be determined by the concerns and values of that coming Kingdom of God. That Kingdom is the tangible community of Christ's reign - the holy ground where shoes are out of fashion and Pharaoh is no more - which the acoustic community of God's people, his holy nation amid the nations, is called to manifest and the nations are called to embrace. Through loyalty to that Kingdom Christians living in Nazi Germany or under South African *apartheid* have rejected an identification between church and nation which they held to be incompatible with their confession of the Lordship of Christ, and separated themselves from such a nationalist synthesis. Through loyalty to that Kingdom Christians in many Third World and European countries have identified with the struggles for justice and peace or the work of economic and social development that would seek to transform their nations in the light of the Gospel; knowing that all human schemes of transformation are sinful and will never be more than ambiguous signs of the Kingdom which God alone gives as a gift.

This brings us back to our initial observation about the inescapable and continuing tension for Christians between their identity in Christ and their national identity. All three Christian approaches to nationhood already experienced in Scotland have either abandoned that creative tension or snapped apart under the force of it. The medieval approach of identification with the nation failed to hold its national identity in proper tension with loyalty to Christ and his Kingdom by making the Church subservient to secular interests. The vision of the Reformation failed to recognise that there was a proper tension between the nation's identity and the interests of the Kirk which could not be resolved by turning the secular nation into the ecclesiastical model of a covenant nation. The Secular vision abandoned that tension altogether as it reduced loyalty to Christ to acceptance of a national identity which was assumed to guarantee loyalty to Christian ethics. Why the collapse of each of these models of Christ and nation? Because the adoption of any one approach leads first to the dangerous assumption and finally to the illusion that the form of national life created by that one vision is the final settlement and form of a Christian nation.

And so the sixteenth century Catholic visionaries failed to see the need for radical separation from much in the life of church and nation that had become corrupt; indeed they lacked the power to carry that through even when they recognised the need for reform. The nineteenth century Reformed visionaries like Chalmers failed to identify with the profound economic, social and political changes that secular Victorian Scotland was undergoing. They separated themselves from these changes and any possibility of transforming them by holding on to a no-longer-plausible ecclesiastical model of the nation as a godly commonwealth of self-contained parishes. The twentieth century Secular visionaries saw the nation as 'the city without a Church' yet imagined that it would somehow retain its Christian ethical consensus on the direction of social change as the Church became a more marginal institution in private and public life. When that public social consensus on the national question fell apart in the 1970s, secular Scots had long ago let go of any slack rope that once might have pulled the Scottish community back, tense and taut, to its Christian moorings, to use John Baillie's phrase. All that was left to the Secular vision was an increasingly empty public moralising on the issues of the moment, knowing full well that they were totally beyond its control or power to transform in the 1980s.

The incarnational model of Christ and nation restores the creative tension within the Christian's dual nationality, her or his two identities in Christ and in Scotland. It holds out the possibility of creating a new Christian understanding of the meaning and significance of our Scottish identity into the twenty-first century. By recognising the validity of identifying with the nation in its authentic human existence within its present history, this model offers a more realistic perception of Scotland as it actually exists and not as it was perceived to be in past Christian visions. By requiring an unremitting opposition to the sinful aspects of the nation's life which diminish our common humanity or institutionalise injustice, this model affirms the need for the Christian community to maintain a critical solidarity with the nation that can only come out of a prophetic separation from its claims to any ultimate loyalty. This holding together of separating and identifying elements in the one model may offer the Church of Scotland a way forward as a minority community which would yet retain its sense of national mission and social responsibility, a prospect I shall consider in chapter ten.

And, finally, the incarnational model holds out the call to work for the transformation of the nation's life through establishing tangible signs of the coming Kingdom of God within its culture and intellectual life, its economy and social institutions, its politics and international relations, This third dimension of transformation offers the motivation for Christian involvement in national life even when such a course of action is costly or seen as deviant by those within or outwith the Church who would relegate such involvement to the past, or choose to focus on the concerns of personal piety. The presence of both separating and transforming dimensions in an incarnational model of Christ and nation suggests the tension of the Church's particular calling in the world. The Church must stand apart from all that will not own Christ's touch in national life. Too close an identification with the nation would make it blind or numb to his suffering presence among those who suffer injustice or break his commands. But it must stand apart in the true separation of its calling to be a holy nation, as a people set apart for God and his mission to transform the nations, not as those who stand aside from involvement in their human struggles and concerns. When these tensions are lost, the Church slides into the pit of narrow religious nationalism or pietism.

A Biblical Ecology of Nationhood Modelled on Christ

This incarnational model, or paradigm, for a Christian approach to nationhood is thus based on Christ's own threefold relationship with Israel and the nations of affirmation, opposition and conversion. It also requires to be modelled on the identity of Christ himself, as I argued in chapter five, and on the Biblical understanding of nationhood, considered in chapter six. It is the Son of Man, Jesus our sympathetic priest, kinsman prophet and suffering king who must shape our critical approach to our national identity, not the unsympathetic, unrelated and triumphalist figure of the Scottish Christ. It is the Biblical ecology of nationhood which must determine our understanding of the relationship between church and nation, not any Parliamentary Act securing church establishment. Too often it has been our inherited cultural vision of Christ or captivitity within a particular church-nation relationship that has determined our thinking on such questions. While we can never fully escape such a blinkered vision or such a mental captivity, and while our understanding is flawed, we can at least recognise their dark existence and continually hold them up to the light of Christ and Scripture.

At the heart of the incarnational approach to national identity lies our relationship with Christ and our identity in him as a holy nation amid the nations, called to be a living demonstration of his coming Kingdom among them. His rule is to be tangible in all our relationships with the nations. Through our union with Christ we are called to minister to the nations, sharing in his threefold ministry as priest, prophet and king.

As our sympathetic high Priest, from his birth and baptism, through his life and teaching, to his passion and ascension, Christ identified with suffering and sinful humanity, bearing the marks of his cross in his risen body. Christ now calls us to identify with the nation in a ministry of priestly intercession on its behalf; offering prayers of thanks for its blessings, confession for its sins, and supplication for its life. As our kinsman Prophet, God's Word born from the womb of Mary, Christ shared our humanity and cleansed its depravity from within our life by his birth, holy life and healing ministry among us. Christ now calls us to be holy and set apart for God, hearing and proclaiming his Word in the midst of the nation's fallen life. As our suffering King, Christ brought in God's rule over the nations through the Cross, refusing the option of his wilderness temptations to worldly power. Christ now calls us to dethrone the powerful idolatries of nationalism and serve the coming of his Kingdom among the nations.

An incarnational vision of Scotland requires us to share in Christ's ministry to the nations in Christ's way, through sharing in his profound identification with their humanity, separation from their sin and transformation of the powers that rule their life.

The incarnational model also seeks to sustain the ecological balance in the Biblical understanding of nations between the three kinds of national community found in Scripture. First, the holy nation of God's people exists as a supra-national acoustic community to hear, incarnate and proclaim God's Word among the nations. This was done, first through the nation of Israel and then through the renewed Israel of Jew and Gentile in the Church, an anticipation of the new humanity in Christ. Second, the gentile nations exist as imagined communities, provisional human creations, expressing in history both the sinful divisions and the creative diversity of a common humanity under God's providence. And finally there is the tangible community of the new heaven and the new earth, the multi-national community of God's Kingdom which restores humanity's unity while redeeming its diversity.

Nations function according to the Biblical pattern or ecology when the holy nation's mission to the nations transforms the imagined communities of God's providence which rise and fall in history, into acoustic communities of God's redemption which hear and obey God's Word. That Word, Christ himself 'clothed in his Gospel', transforms both holy nation and the nations into the tangible community of God's Kingdom. Where any one of these relationships among church, nation and Kingdom is missing, then the Biblical ecology of nations may be said to have broken down. Where the nations fail to receive God's Word and refuse their dual identity as imagined and acoustic communities; where the Church refuses its dual identity as acoustic community and sign of the tangible community of the Kingdom; where both church and nation fail to manifest the tangible life of the Kingdom, then both holy and earthly nations come under God's judgement.

The Church's worship of God, life together and mission to the nations as the faithful acoustic community, makes tangible among them the life of the Kingdom. It must both share in Christ's ministry to the nations and maintain the Biblical ecology of nationhood. In these two movements of worship and mission, Christ-centred and Scriptural, the holy nation will discover what its approach to the nations among whom it lives should be, whether in priestly identification, prophetic separation or regal transformation as priests and kings to God; bearing his Word as the prophetic acoustic community and giving it flesh as a foretaste of the tangible community of his coming Kingdom.

In our earthly discipleship, the Church will never escape the tension between its identity in Christ as God's holy nation and its identity as a community of those who belong to particular nations and are called to minister to them. Neither Church nor nation can escape the tension of conforming their respective national identities to the citizenship of God's Kingdom. That means that no model of Christ and nation can ever be a blueprint for Christian nationhood or the coming of the Kingdom of God within a particular nation's bit of the earth. It can only be a frail, provisional guide to those who would take seriously God's call to love our 'near and distant neighbours', to use Barth's title for a theology of nationhood.

The frailty of this particular theological exercise was poignantly expressed by the Afrikaner critic of apartheid, Willem de Klerk, in the concluding words of his study of Afrikaner Christian nationalism, *The Puritans in Africa*. Quoting the words of Jesus in Luke's Gospel when he wept over Jerusalem because it failed to recognise God's moment when it came, he wrote:

> Knowledge of our true condition must be attained before it is too late (for South Africa), and no new synthesis can grow. This is very much the concern of the philosopher, theologian, statesman and creative artist. But for a lasting renewal to take place, wider sensibilities will be needed. Grace is no prerogative of the 'creative minority'. Their task is best fulfilled along the dusty roads of life, beside the wells and springs of a thirsty land, among the hungry people on a hillside in the veld. To be immersed in the human situation is to assume without illusion, in the mood of playful irony, all that life requires from us. It means accepting, with the prospect of humour, conflict, struggle, disaster, death, never surrendering to depression or guilt, but rather to the knowledge of human frailty...

De Klerk's words on nationalism from South Africa bring us back to the thoughts of Anthony Ross on the renewal of the Scottish nation, expressed in his essay, *Resurrection*: 'Before deciding what it is to be Scottish we need to re-examine our ideas about what it means to be human and to be Christian, and make at the start an act of contrition for ourselves and the community in which we live.' Ross suggested that this re-examination and contrition would be helped by setting aside the glossy media image of Scotland and looking instead on the suffering human face of vulnerable Scots broken by our so-called great Scottish institutions, social morality and religious traditions.

We have re-examined what it has meant to be Christian and human in our history, in the three great Christian visions of Scottish identity which we have inherited from our past. We have returned to the sources of Christian vision, in Christ, Scripture and theological tradition, in a spirit of contrition for past visions that have wandered far from these sources. Now it is time to re-think our ideas about the human, Christian and national dimensions of our contemporary Scottish identity, in terms of the incarnational model sketched out above. However, de Klerk and Ross serve a timely reminder that Christian vision will not be found from a theological map but from the vulnerable, broken faces of human frailty.

A Liturgy for Scotland

Before we re-think our Scottish identity through that model and vision, there is one last question to ask. What would breathe life into this incarnational model? Where would we catch such a vision for Scotland today? There is one neglected catalyst for the renewal of our vision for the nations - worship. It was in worship that Isaiah received his vision that Israel would be a light to the nations. It was in the place of worship in the Temple that Christ called Israel back to its mission as a house of prayer for all nations. It was in worship on the Lord's day that John had his vision of the defeat of the pagan Roman empire, the vindication of God's holy nation and the healing of the nations in the new earth. It is in the worship of God that we may work out a new understanding of our Scottish identity as Christians, in the light of the incarnational model of Christ and nation developed above. It is in our worship of God that we can receive the wisdom and power to re-establish a Biblical ecology of nationhood for Scotland in the 1990s and beyond.

In the liturgy of Reformed worship in the national Church of Scotland, there is a threefold movement of approach, listening and response to God. We approach God as those created in his image, the priests of creation who utter his praise and offer thanksgiving not only on behalf of the Church but also of the nation. We approach God as those who have marred his image, confessing and seeking his forgiveness not only for our own sins but also for those of the nation of which we are part. We make this approach in the Spirit through Jesus Christ, our sympathetic high priest who identifies with us in our humanity. Then we hear his Word, incarnate in Jesus Christ our kinsman prophet, revealed in Scripture and proclaimed in the preaching of the Gospel to church and nation alike. And finally we make our tangible response to Christ our suffering king in the sacraments of his death and resurrection; and in intercession for his healing touch among the nations, the coming of his Kingdom.

In worship we are the true imagined community. We approach God as those who understand our common humanity in the style of one shared image, the image of God. We are all fellow sinners approaching God only through the mediation of the man Jesus Christ. In worship we are the acoustic community, set apart to hear and obey God's Word, Jesus Christ, and to discern his will for church and nation. In worship we share in the tangible community of Christ's reign around the Lord's table, touching his risen presence in bread and wine, before going back out into the world to share his healing touch with the nations. We approach God in the imagined identity of humanity. We listen to God in our acoustic identity as hearers of his Word. We respond to his Word in the tangible identity of obedience.

Such worship lies at the heart of the Church's life - and it shakes our Scottish identity to its roots. But already our identity is being shaken by other gods.

The Scottish Identity Crisis: a Shaker Triptych

I began this book by suggesting that Scotland was being shaken to its spiritual roots by three long-term crises concerning our human, Christian and national identities. I used the then Prime Minister, Mrs Margaret Thatcher's 1988 Sermon on the Mound to illustrate this three-fold Scottish identity crisis, though of itself the speech is only of passing significance for Scotland. (It has been suggested that Mrs Thatcher had already decided to preach a sermon in defence of her policies long before she alighted on the hapless Kirk as her pulpit!)

It is our historic Scottish philosophical and theological conviction that to be human means to have a social identity as persons in community. This is being shaken by the counter-conviction that, in Mrs Thatcher's tell-tale phrase, there is no such thing as society, only competitive, property-owning indi-viduals regulated by an amoral market and an absolute state. But what picture of our humanity would emerge if our Scottish identity were to be shaken by Christ's humanity?

It is the historic conviction of the Reformed religious tradi-tion that to be Christian means to confess that Jesus is Lord of every aspect of reality, in heaven and earth. This is being shaken by the contrary view that Jesus is Lord only of the interior life of the soul and the superior life of heaven. But what picture of our Christianity would emerge if our Scottish identity were to be shaken by Christ's authority?

It is the democratic intellectual and moral conviction of the Scots that our nationhood should be grounded on first principles, rationally discerned and debated by conflicting viewpoints within one community of discourse. This is being shaken by another mentality, at once pragmatic and mystical, which coun-sels irrational devotion to country - and no questions asked! But what picture of our nationality would emerge if our Scottish identity were to be shaken by Christ's wisdom?

We now turn to these three pictures of Scotland - Christ the Shaker's triptych of our three crises - to re-think what it means for us to be human, Christian and Scottish today.

PART 3 CONTEMPORARY IDENTITY -
Seeing the Future

Chapter 9

THE HUMAN IDENTITY CRISIS -
A Common Humanity

One of the ablest minds to reflect on Scottish identity in our time has been that of Tom Nairn, the marxist philosopher. In an essay on Scottish nationalism he coined a memorable paraphrase of a French Revolutionary slogan. Scotland will only be free, he wrote, when the last minister has been strangled with the last copy of The Sunday Post. The original quotation required the strangulation of kings in priestly entrails! But the paraphrase makes the same point with comic effect. Only the death of the old Christian religion in Scotland will bring about the new humanity that every revolutionary movement since 1789 has longed for and promised. For over a hundred years the leading Scottish minds have been engaged in Nairn's murder plot, seeking to establish our humanity in Scotland without reference to the Christian God or Gospel. Despite continuing adherence to Christian belief and worship by a significant number of Scots, albeit within a declining church membership, an explicitly theological understanding of human identity has long ceased to grip the imagination of Scottish intellectuals and national leaders.

As we have seen in chapter four, this does not mean that there has been no kind of Christian vision of Scotland operative in the last hundred years. Many Victorian Scots believed that you could abandon faith in the old Christian orthodox beliefs while retaining a loyalty to Christian ethics. But a much bolder project has been under way in Scotland since then, part of a wider movement in Western thought and culture. We have been living for a long time with the nineteenth century German philosopher Friedrich Nietzsche's pronouncement of the 'death of God' and its implications for our sense of human identity, not least in Scotland. No one saw this more clearly than Hugh MacDiarmid.

Nietzsche's thought was an early and profound influence on Christopher Murray Grieve, MacDiarmid's own name before he adopted his better known literary pseudonym. The brilliant if disturbed mind of Nietzsche would have nothing to do with the nineteenth century endeavour to hang on to Christian morality after letting go of its God. Ridiculing the attempt to do so by English novelists like George Elliot, Neitzsche wrote in 1888, in *Twilight of the Gods*:

> They have got rid of the Christian God, and now feel obliged to cling all the more firmly to Christian morality... In England, in response to every little emancipation from theology one has to reassert one's position in a fear-inspiring manner as a moral fanatic... With us it is different. When one gives up Christian belief one thereby deprives oneself of the right to Christian morality... Christianity is a system, a consistently thought out and complete view of things. If one breaks out of it a fundamental idea, the belief in God, one thereby breaks the whole thing to pieces: one has nothing of any consequence left in one's hands.

While many of his contemporaries in early twentieth century Scotland believed with Thomas Carlyle that they had thrown away only the husk of Biblical religion, belief in Jehovah, while keeping its kernal, belief in its high moral view of human life, Chris Grieve would have none of it. As Alan Bold, MacDiarmid's biographer, has noted, quoting the poet, 'What Grieve valued in Nietzsche was, "...his devastating attack on the social philosophers who thought that you could destroy the whole basis of the Christian religion and yet retain a few of its ethical principles."' Hugh MacDiarmid's creative work and vision of Scotland must be understood, in part at least, as an outworking of this Nietzschean conviction that the Christian understanding of human identity dies with the death of the Christian God. What was to be put in its place, as a vision of human identity? For MacDiarmid, humans must become as gods themselves; like Neitzsche's Superman, creating their own beliefs, values and order through their 'Will to Power'.

The literary critic Raymond Ross has described MacDiarmid as a 'God-builder', a phrase coined by the Russian writer Maxim Gorky. God-builders are to be distinguished from 'God-seekers', those who acknowledge a transcendent deity. God-builders are those who aim to construct a new humanity possessing God-like powers and consciousness. MacDiarmid put it this way, in a poem published in 1926:

It's time to try God's way
When we've his poo'er tae.

MacDiarmid sought God-building Superman figures and found them first in the Russian writer Dostoevsky and later in the Russian revolutionary Lenin. According to Ross, the poet's adulation of them was an expression 'of a Nietzschean cult which MacDiarmid never entirely outgrew.' It was MacDiarmid's hope that through the genius and will power of a Man-God, none other than himself, Scotland and all the world could be transformed. We must be ourselves, that is, create ourselves, through 'the Nietzschean Will to Power':

By what immense exercise of will,
Inconceivable discipline, courage, and endurance,
Self-purification and anti-humanity,
Be ourselves without interruption
Adamantine and inexorable?

These lines from his poem *On a Raised Beach*, find a strange echo in the rhetoric of one contemporary politician. The Scottish historian Christopher Harvie has pointed out the bitter irony that MacDiarmid's iron-willed Superman figure finally appeared on the political scene in the form of Mrs Thatcher, a revolutionary of the Right and not the Left, as he had envisaged! MacDiarmid's vision represents the major cultural and intellectual attempt in the twentieth century to re-cast the Scottish identity in thoroughly post-Christian, Nietzschean and marxist terms - although his work is steeped in Christian and Biblical references and imagery, reflecting his upbringing by devout Christian parents in his native Langholm.

In the Scotland of the 1920s and '30s, faced with economic depression at home and the rise of fascism abroad, MacDiarmid saw Christianity as fatally compromised with an oppressive if dying social order. He believed that his own sure scientific and revolutionary creed of materialism would sweep all that away and bring in the dawn of a new humanity in Scotland and throughout the world. Such is the vision of MacDiarmid's drunk man. The years since then cannot take away the poet's monumental contribution to Scottish life and literature, especially in the renaissance of Scots as a creative medium for the highest order of human thought and poetry. Yet the passage of time since MacDiarmid's cosmic vision in the 1920s has only served to mock its dreams for Scotland. The revolutionary Will to Power which MacDiarmid saw as the saviour of the Scottish identity, embodied in some 'greater Christ' yet to come to Scotland, has turned out too often to be the false messiahship of a Stalin or a Pol Pot. The threat to a distinctively Scottish yet thoroughly international vision of humanity, posed by the cultural dominance of a larger, imperial neighbour, which MacDiarmid resisted with every sinew of his being, continues unabated. But the solution which he offered, whether at the hands of a super-man of iron will or, unexpectedly, an iron lady, has been stripped of its attractions by the subsequent history of our time.

Our traditional Scottish sense of human identity is in crisis for two reasons, therefore. **First**, our institutions and social life are currently being re-shaped according to an alien English social philosophy. For centuries our religious and secular social traditions have emphasised the solidarity of human beings one with another in the common life of society. Whether in the community of the realm of the medieval Catholic tradition, the godly commonwealth of the Calvinist tradition, the civil society of the Scottish Enlightenment or the municipal and socialist commonwealths of Victorian philanthropists and the Labour movement, the Scots have seen human identity primarily as a social identity, found only in society. The notion of the 'common weal', the public good, has been dominant in Scottish social thought and institutional life. And the notion of the common good, worked out through a range of Scottish institutions, including the Kirk, the law and education, has been firmly based on the notion of fundamental principles 'with an authority independent of the social order', as the philosopher Alasdair MacIntyre has put it. These fundamental principles sit in judgement on that social order, determining the common good. We see this most vividly in Sir David Lyndsay's late medieval *Satire of the Three Estates*, in which both the king and the three estates of the realm are subject to the judgement of Divine Correction and John the Commonweal, a figure representing the people; their authoritative judgement is inspired by divine law and the social principles of the Gospel. In the Scottish social tradition, principle and society are prior to the individual, be he King or commoner, whose human identity is dependent upon self-evident truth and a pre-existing society and social history. We are now faced with a British government that declares its own fundamental convictions, an appealing move guaranteed to beguile some Scots, but in the context of a view of society that appalls far more Scots in an intuitive gut-reaction of dismay. We simply do not see humanity as a nexus of self-interested individuals who give mutual consent to certain economic and political arrangements, such as the free market or the absolute state, in order to protect their property rights. Albeit we gave those patron saints of the present-day libertarian think-tanks, Adam Smith and David Hume, to the world, it must be remembered that they consciously embraced the dominant English social vision of their time and rejected the older Scottish social tradition. In the words of Alasdair MacIntyre, 'What Hume represented in almost every respect, what indeed Smith too was to represent... was the abandonment of peculiarly Scottish modes of thought in favour of a distinctively English and Anglicizing way of understanding social life and its moral fabric.'

We are now witnessing the return of Hume and Smith's ideological stepchildren, intent on carrying through their social revolution in Scotland with a brazen arrogance that would have horrified David Hume, careful never to allow his subversive social philosophy to mar his social intercourse with his many friends in the bastions of the native social tradition, the Kirk, the law courts and the universities. Now the gloves are off, such social niceties as consensus have been dispensed with, and we are confronted by an adamantine will determined that Scotland should be recreated in the image of those twin foreign gods set up by the English philosopher Thomas Hobbes: the atomised, privatised, property-preserving individual, and a state endowed with absolute power, the 'mortal God' he called the great Leviathan and we call the British Parliament. This confrontation of mutually exclusive social philosophies is the root reason for the crisis of human identity that we are witnessing in Scotland today.

The **second** reason for the crisis of human identity lies with the would-be defenders of the Scottish tradition against this predatory attack of alien social norms. The very intellectual thinkers and cultural leaders that we might rely on to defend and revitalise our own ways of understanding social life, share with their opponents one common belief of the European Enlightenment that enervates their capacity to respond effectively while it energizes the attackers. Christopher Harvie has called this Enlightenment conviction 'Voltairean scepticism'. It is the conviction that religion can offer humanity no certain knowledge or understanding of life. As Voltaire himself wrote, 'It is only charlatans who are certain. We know nothing of first principles. It is truly extravagant to define God... and to know precisely why God formed the world, when we do not know why we move our arms at will. Doubt is not a very agreeable state, but certainty is a ridiculous one.'

This doctrine of doubt about any underlying first principles and scepticism about a providential God energizes the secular libertarians of the New Right. Further inspired by the scepticism of David Hume, they believe that in such a moral vacuum, only the autonomous individual pursuing his or her own self-interest can be the final arbiter in society, under a sovereign state with the absolute powers to guarantee the security and property of such individuals.

Paradoxically, this same Enlightenment doctrine of scepticism seems to have paralysed those humanists who do not accept the dominant social and political philosophy of the New Right in contemporary Britain. How can you find the inner resources to resist such triumphant individualism in the face of its electoral success in recent British history and remain hopeful about the possibility of a more humane society in the face of the persistent triumph of evil in human history, if you are committed to a fundamental scepticism about life? Describing his own journey from such scepticism to Christian faith, Christopher Harvie has spoken of how he 'realised that scepticism was less a liberating than a constraining force, narrowing both the range of human experience and, more seriously, the range of sympathy.' He went on to say:

> Moving to Germany, moreover, prompted a preoccupation with evil and the power of faith to conquer it, because here was a country where, for twelve appalling years, evil had been allowed to have its way in a sophisticated and complex modern society. This had stimulated a response by committed Christians which gave them solidarity with the persecuted, but the cost of the process had been terrible.

At the heart of Scottish intellectual life there now exists the conviction, perhaps as yet no bigger than one man's mind, that the sceptical humanism of the Enlightenment, embraced by both the Left and the Right, is no adequate foundation for historic Scottish convictions about the social nature and moral purpose of human identity.

Tom Nairn may have brilliantly turned the French revolutionary slogan into his own Scottish version, strangling the last minister with the last copy of the Sunday Post, to expose the dead weight of Kailyard religion and social conservatism on human identity in Scotland. But it was a Dutch Calvinist historian who beat him to the satirical use of the quotation by over a century and highlighted a far greater threat to our humanity, coming from Nairn's own Enlightenment philosophical tradition of scepticism and unbelief. Delivering a series of lectures in the mid-1840s on the subject of the philosophy of sceptical unbelief in the French Revolution, Guillaume Groen van Prinsterer wryly observed that, 'Judged by revolutionary standards even Diderot's barbaric yearning "to strangle the last king with the guts of the last priest", so far from being excessive, represents the purest love of humanity.'

Groen was making his prophetic point over a century before the revolutionary standards of sceptical unbelief were fully exposed at Auschwitz, in the Gulag and the killing fields of

Cambodia. Having swept the European house clean of the demon of religious superstition, Enlightenment scepticism has found itself letting in to the twentieth century seven more demons worse than the first, which it has proved singularly powerless to exorcise.

In the absence of the kind of absolute moral values that were essentially derived from Christian belief and worship, MacDiarmid looked to a Nietzschean Superman of god-like power and strength of will to forge a new order out of the social chaos and moral relativism resulting from the death of God in Western thought and culture. No such native superman has emerged. As we noted above, the Will to Power seems to lie with the prevailing philosophy of the New Right as it advances to attack the last citadels of Scottish society resistant to its claims.

The sceptical outlook of the Scottish Left and wider intellectual circles has proved an Achilles' heel in their fight against this philosophy of self-interested individualism and state absolutism. Where do you stand against such an onslaught, if you lay no claim to absolute beliefs or fundamental convictions, and if you have lost confidence in MacDiarmid's revolutionary will to power? Electoral success, as in the 1988 Govan by-election, can be a temporary shot in the arm but the effect on morale can quickly wear off, as the earlier electoral victories of the 1970s remind us. The long march through a decade like the 1980s has to be sustained by something more than the vagaries of the British electoral system. Movements to unite Scottish opinion around a common policy on constitutional reform are to be welcomed but they are also high risk operations with as much potential to deepen divisions as to create effective majorities. Christopher Harvie has suggested that faith offers the firm ground for human solidarity that scepticism has failed to provide. But here too, among the upholders of Christian faith in Scotland, we find a crisis of identity.

An Imagined Community, a Common Identity

Twentieth century Scottish literature began with a harsh, cold vision of our national life, George Douglas' *The House with the Green Shutters*. Not only was the novel a dark repudiation of the sentimental portrayal of small town Scottish life beloved by the

Kailyard school of popular fiction. It also represents the colli-
sion between the predatory individualism of the small town
trader and the Christian tradition of social solidarity. At the
climax of the novel the dominant figure, John Gourlay, is
murdered by his weak-willed son. Gourlay is a brutal, arrogant
man, standing aloof from the small-minded community of
Barbie and driven further into his chosen social isolation with the
collapse of his business ventures. But the women in his family
hang on to the last vestiges of Christian compassion and community.

As the novel nears its end, Gourlay's widow and daughter
contemplate the path of suicide taken by Gourlay's son. The
daughter Janet chooses to die with her mother rather than face
being left alone in the world. Even in death, she rejects the
isolated individualism that was her father's creed and embraces
the solidarity of suffering humanity. In the midst of her state of
mental frenzy, a strange calm comes over Mrs Gourlay. She
reaches for the big family Bible and reads from the 13th chapter
of the 1st Letter to the Corinthians, Paul's great passage on
charity (love) - when all else has failed or passed away, the
greatest virtue, charity, will remain. Even while reading these
sublime words, Mrs Gourlay remains in an abnormal state,
detached from her own humanity and possessed by the spiritual
power of her fatalism. Her daughter clings to the Bible reading
'as the one thing left to her before death' and for a brief moment
they pull back from the abyss: 'She turned and looked at her
daughter, and for one fleeting moment she ceased to be above
humanity.' It is not enough to save them, and, together, they take
their own life.   Why did the warm Christian humanism of
Paul's hymn to charity fail them at the end?   Although the
Christian faith is seen to hold out to them the hope of loving
social fellowship, in stark contrast with Gourlay's competitive
individualism, Mrs Gourlay is finally uncertain of such love.
Why?   Because of her vision of Jesus Christ.   In that final
moment of true humanity she says wistfully to her daughter: 'I
have had a heap to thole! Maybe the Lord Jesus Christ'll no' be
owre sair on me.' Once more we encounter 'the Scottish Christ'.
Mrs Gourlay sees Christ as her judge. Her only hope is that the
weight of her human suffering, a heap to thole, may yet move

Christ sufficiently to make him mix his wrath with mercy. Christ is seen as a remote, divine figure -the **Lord** Jesus Christ - who is hardly touched by all that suffering humanity has to thole. She doubts his fellow humanity and the extent of his love for her. Therefore, finally, she doubts her own humanity and is driven to the all-or-nothing despair of suicide.

The dark picture of Scotland to be found in *The House with the Green Shutters* is a paradigm of the problem we face in grounding a social vision of our human identity in Christian faith. The several Scottish Christian traditions acknowledge our social identity, and then present it with a profound source of instability.

Both the medieval Catholic and the Reformation traditions in Scotland have affirmed the social nature of human and Christian experience. In the late medieval celebration of the Mass in Scotland, a 'paxboard' was kissed, symbolising the kiss of peace among the worshipping, reconciled community, living in social harmony with one another. The concern of the Reformed Kirk Session to exercise discipline over the whole life of the parish reflected a conviction about the social solidarity of sin and grace, as much as a moralising authoritarian legalism. As Samuel Rutherford put it, at the start of his classic work of Scottish Calvinist political theology, *Lex Rex* (1644), 'God hath made man a social creature'.

The eighteenth century Moderate party in the Kirk may have paid only lip-service to the Calvinist doctrine of men like Rutherford, but it did not abandon their central notion of humanity's social identity. Writing on the crisis of identity in eighteenth century Scottish literature, Kenneth Simpson states in his recent book, *The Protean Scot*: 'The promptings of Calvinism in its Scottish form ensured the prolonged existence of an almost medieval sense of community within the Scottish value-system.' For example, Adam Ferguson, a Gaelic-speaking minister and central figure in the Scottish Enlightenment, in his *Essay on the History of Civil Society* (1767), stressed the importance of the community for human identity and progress, even in an emerging capitalist economy. For all that Thomas Chalmers accepted laissez-faire economic doctrines, he held passionately to his social vision of Scotland as a Christian community. And even while they were dropping Chalmers' vision of the Godly Commonwealth, grounded as it was in religious belief, secular Scots still thought in the social terms of a moral community, grounded in a common Christian social ethic. Only in community could human beings find peace and salvation, their true humanity.

This reflects the rich Biblical insight that for human beings to be made in the image of God (Genesis 1:26,27) means that we find our humanity only in and through relationships - with God and one another. In the light of the Biblical tradition, it is impossible to define human identity apart from mutual relationships of love, trust and communion among God and humanity; with humanity understood inescapably in social terms, as the community of man and woman together. Human identity and knowledge are essentially to do with persons, understood as those who live in personal, dynamic and ultimately mysterious relationships of mutual self-giving with one another in community. This personalist understanding of human identity and knowledge, deriving from the Biblical and Christian traditions, has continued to influence twentieth century Scottish philosophy and social thought; as the recent writings of Ronald Turnbull and Craig Beveridge have shown, in their studies of the personalist ideas and influence of modern Scottish Christian thinkers such as John Baillie, John Macquarrie and John Macmurray. The Scottish Christian vision of our humanity as the social identity of persons in community, persons in relationship with one another, is a rich heritage as we face the contemporary crisis of human identity in Scotland and an alternative human vision of competitive individualism.

The Roots of our Fear

What, then, is stopping contemporary Scots from embracing that warm, personalist Christian social vision of our humanity? I believe there is a deep rooted fear that any return to a Christian social vision will bring us back to the kind of mistrust and despair of our own frail humanity that we can find within the pietism of both medieval Catholic and Calvinist Christianity in Scotland. In his insightful book *Christian Spirituality and Sacramental Community*, the German theologian Wolfhart Pannenberg argues that the Protestant Reformation doctrine of justification by faith (that we are put right with God through faith in his grace and not through our own good works) brought great relief to the sensitive medieval conscience, weighed down by personal guilt, endless penance and the oppressive burden of the church hierarchy. However, precisely because it was medicine for the problem of moral guilt, Protestant piety through time proved equally enmeshed in the problems of sin, anxiety and guilt-consciousness from which it originally promised liberation. This led to the kind of penitential piety which deliberately cultivated a sense of guilt as the necessary prelude to experiencing the grace of divine forgiveness. This in turn led to the destructive Protestant psychological tendency to self-aggression and hatred, fed by a moralising style of preaching.

Pannenberg's analysis of his own Lutheran tradition of penitential piety applies equally well to Scottish Calvinism. As Professor James Torrance has argued, the early Calvinist tradition of the Scottish Reformation was taken over by a later school of Calvinist theology, known as 'Federal Calvinism'. The doctrines of this movement led to the kind of introspective, legalistic piety which remains the popular image of Calvinism today. Federal Calvinism, according to Torrance a significant distortion of Calvin's own theology, had a profound effect on the Scottish religious consciousness from the seventeenth to the nineteenth centuries. We live with it today, even in secular Scotland, as part of our cultural inheritance.

From this Federal Calvinism (so called after the Latin word for a covenant, *foedus*) we got the idea that Christ died only for some people, while the rest were predestined to hell. To be sure that you were one of the elect, you had to keep looking within your own soul and search your conscience for the moral evidence that proved your salvation. As those twin masterpieces, James Hogg's *Confessions of a Justified Sinner*, and Robert Burns' *Holy Willie's Prayer*, brilliantly expose, such Calvinist piety could lead either to amoral despair or ludicrous hypocrisy. For most Presbyterian Scots, it led to a deep distrust of their own humanity, arising out of an intrinsic uncertainty about whether Christ in his humanity was for you, as one of the elect, or against you, as one of the damned. Thus the cry of Mrs Gourlay, at the fall of *The House with the Green Shutters*: 'Maybe the Lord

Jesus Christ'll no be owre sair on me.' That this fundamental mistrust of our human existence has gone deep into our Scottish identity can be seen from Alastair Reid's poem, *Scotland*:

> It was a day peculiar to this piece of the planet,
> when larks rose on long thin strings of singing
> and the air shifted with the shimmer of actual angels.
> Greenness entered the body. The grasses
> shivered with presences, and sunlight
> stayed like a halo on hair and heather and hills.
> Walking into town, I saw, in a radiant raincoat,
> the woman from the fish-shop. 'What a day it is!'
> cried I, like a sunstruck madman.
> And what did she have to say for it?
> Her brow grew bleak, her ancestors raged in their graves
> as she spoke with their ancient misery:
> 'We'll pay for it, we'll pay for it, we'll pay for it!'

This notion that we must pay the price of retribution for any good human experience is deep-rooted in our Scottish identity. We cannot trust ourselves or the universe because at any moment we may be struck down by the hand of God, the whim of Fate, or the unseen hand of the Market.

There are several contributing factors to this national pathology. A particular kind of Calvinist religion forced many Scots to doubt God's love for them. In the Federal Calvinist scheme of things, God loves not all humanity but only the Elect. Therefore, for the Scottish Calvinists, their human experience became the entrails that had to be dissected for evidence that they were of the Elect, not the arena God himself had entered to assure them of his love. God's love for them became conditional upon their own moral performance, proving that they were saved and not damned.

If the enjoyment of their humanity was dependent on God's love for them, and if that love was conditional and not certain, then the effect was to make their own humanity something precarious and conditional upon their own constant moral striving. If Jesus Christ did not 'pay' for the sin of **all** humanity on the Cross, but only for the sin of the Elect, then **we'll** pay for it. And we cannot be sure how sair the Lord will be with us on the

Day of Judgement. In this particular tradition of Scottish Calvinism, God's love and, therefore, the security of our human identity and worth become very conditional and uncertain things - except to the unco' guid!

This alone is not a sufficient explanation for the deep-rooted social and cultural sense that human dignity and worth are something the Scots can never take for granted. Through the precarious economic and political history of Scotland, the Scots, especially the poor, the Highland peasants and the Lowland working class, came to see their very humanity as something precarious and uncertain. Again, this sense of the insecurity and capriciousness of our human identity is well expressed in Scottish poetry. Joe Corrie was a Fife miner and socialist poet and playright writing earlier this century. His poem *The Image o' God* reflects on the miner's working experience and compares it with the Biblical definition of our humanity:

> Crawlin' aboot like a snail in the mud,
>   Covered wi' clammy blae,
> ME, made in the image o'God -
>   Jings! but it's laughable, tae.
>
> Howkin' awa' 'neath a mountain o' stane,
>   Gaspin' for want o' air,
> The sweat makin' streams doon my bare back-bane
>   And my knees a' hauckit and sair.
>
> Strainin' and cursin' the hale shift through,
>   Half-starved, half blin', half-mad;
> And the gaffer he says, 'Less dirt in that coal
>   Or ye go up the pit, my lad!'
>
> So I gi'e my life to the Nimmo Squad
>   For eicht and fower a day;
> Me! made after the image o' God -
>   Jings but it's laughable, tae.

If any post-industrial entrepreneur is tempted to point out that deep mining is now almost extinct in Scotland , and dismiss this poem as the proletarian romanticism of a past industrial era, that is to miss the point. This poem expresses the de-humanised despair arising from human social conditions experienced by many Scots today, trapped in the social underground of poverty, unemployment, debt, single-parenthood or addiction. That despair was articulated by the novelist William McIllvaney, in his essay on *Being Poor*, published in a recent study of poverty and deprivation, *Scotland: The Real Divide*. Describing the life of a single parent in Livingston, he wrote:

> Kathy's case is unremarkable. It is at least partly the result of personal experiences no one could have legislated for, but its most definitive element remains insufficient money to live anything like a reasonably fulfilling life and no apparent possibility of getting any more. She is one of very many trying to fight a rearguard action of personal decency against the economic odds in society where the principles behind the distribution of the available wealth have developed, it should be acknowledged, beyond the logic of the fruit machine and the morality of the Monopoly Board, but not far enough beyond them.

The conditional love of God, only for the Elect? The human condition, ruled by the economic logic of the Fruit Machine? A warped religious tradition and oppressive social conditions have left us very unconfident about our human identity in Scotland. It is never something upon which we can rely. The problem is made worse by the precarious nature of our national identity as Scots. If our sense of human identity is fundamentally a social sense, then the social experience of being Scottish must also bear upon our sense of human worth.

This is not a problem with which our southern neighbours are troubled. When Samuel Johnson arrived back in Glasgow, after his trip round the Scottish Highlands with James Boswell, he sat in his inn, warming his legs at the fire, and declared, 'Here am I, an Englishman, sitting by a coal fire!' As his biographer John Wain commented on this revealing remark, the great Englishman spoke 'as if he were resuming his familiar identity like a favourite coat that had been hanging in a wardrobe.' If familiarity with their own national identity breeds contentment for the

English, it can often breed self-contempt among the Scots. Too often our 'inferiorist' sense of national identity has served only to reinforce doubts about our human worth. Faced with the effortless presumption of the superiority of English rather than Scottish history, culture or institutions, the inferiorist Scot also cries, 'Me! In the image o' God - Jings! but it's laughable, tae.'

Recovering our Humanity

Religion, class and wounded nationalism unite to dispossess the Scots of their humanity. As one elder declared, upon being asked whether he had understood that morning's sermon, 'Ah wudnae presume!' Too often the glad, confident affirmation of our common humanity has been seen as sheer presumption. Like the woman from the fish-shop in Reid's poem, any spontaneous expression of joy at the wonder of human life on earth is met by the ancestral rage and fear that we'll pay for it. The experience of human suffering and injustice has served to distance us from God rather than draw us closer to him. The Scottish Christ stands far above our humanity, whether in joy or suffering, administering his eternal decrees of election and damnation, scarcely touched by all that we have to thole.

How far this Scottish Christ is from the real Jesus of history and Biblical faith! If we are to explore the human condition in Scotland through verse, then we must complete our trilogy of poems on humanity with this early Christian hymn of faith in Christ Jesus (Colossians 2:6-8):

> Who, being in very nature God,
>   did not consider equality with God
>   something to be grasped,
>   but made himself nothing,
>   taking the very nature of a servant,
>   being made in human likeness.
> And being found in appearance as a man,
>   he humbled himself
>   and became obedient to death -
>   even death on a cross!

The Christian Gospel is that God has taken on **our** humanity in Jesus of Nazareth, and through his incarnation, shared in **our** suffering and death. God is not remote from our human joy and suffering. Through the incarnation God affirms our humanity in the fullest way imaginable. I use the word imaginable deliberately. If humanity is made in God's image, then God himself took on his own image, and **our** own human image, through taking flesh in the fully human nature of Jesus of Nazareth. God has visited his human creatures by becoming one of them in the person of his son. As the hymn of faith to Christ in Colossians makes clear, this meant for God nothing less than embracing our human suffering and death. If we embrace this good news without reserve, then we embrace our own humanity, in both its joy and suffering, as something unconditionally loved and affirmed in Jesus, God made flesh among us. To paraphrase the Boys' Brigade hymn, 'We have an anchor that keeps our human identity, grounded firm and sure in God's incarnate love.'

As I suggested in chapter five, **this** Christ is not unknown in Scottish Calvinism. We find him in the theology of John Macleod Campbell, Edward Irving and Patrick Brewster. This Other Scottish Christ - the Christ who embraced **our** fallen humanity, and healed it from within, by his sinless, holy, fully human life in **our** flesh - does affirm the reality and meaning of human experience for us **all**. Making himself the servant of all, he is to be found among all whose suffering makes them doubt the dignity and worth of their human experience: 'For you know the grace of our Lord Jesus Christ, that though he was rich, yet for our sakes he became poor, so that you through his poverty might become rich.' (2 Corinthians 8:9)

This is not the Lord Jesus Christ that Mrs Gourlay feared, at the end of *The House with the Green Shutters*. This is the Christ who took upon himself **all** she had to thole. This is the God who was owre sair on himself, at the Cross, for **all** our sakes, in order that we might **know** for certain his grace towards us **all**. In the Incarnation we see the unconditional love of God for all humanity. The Incarnation is our anchor for the unconditional acceptance of our own humanity before God. We are human because we are unconditionally created in his image, healed in his incarnate human life, with its atoning death and resurrection, and fully restored in his coming rule on earth. The implications of this Gospel of The Other Scottish Christ for our vision of humanity are profound and far-reaching. If we put **this** Christ at the centre of our Christian social vision, then we must re-think what it means to be human in Scotland today.

In chapter six I suggested that nations should be seen Biblically as 'imagined communities' (adapting a description used by Benedict Anderson in his book on nationalism, *Imagined Communities*). Nations are human communities that define their sense of national identity through shared images of their common life. Apart from all the left luggage of miscellaneous cultural and historical images - thistles, lions and tartans, etc - one of the key images for our Scottish sense of national identity has been the human image itself. It is because we have seen that human image in a particular way in Scottish religion, philosophy and culture, as inseparable from human community and a social identity, that we have maintained a distinctive sense of our Scottish identity.

The human image has been both the strength and the weakness at the heart of our national identity. In *The Protean Scot*, Kenneth Smith quotes Francis Russell Hart's comment on the moral primacy of the community in Scottish fiction: 'It is implied that true community nurtures genuine individuality... a denial of community is a threat to personal integrity. Idolatrous self-hood destroys community.' If the community is the place where we discover our genuine individuality in human experience, it is also the place where personal integrity is most threatened. There is an idolatrous human image destroying the heart of that community - the notion that a person's humanity is social but conditional on asserting itself over against others in society.

This often takes the form of the self-righteous assertion of moral superiority within a Church or social class 'that's no' for the likes o' us.' We have turned the human image from God's unconditional gift, enjoyed in mutual relationships of trust, into an idolatrous self-hood, caught, in Neal Ascherson's brilliant perception of our national identity, between self-assertion and self-distrust within the Scottish community.

Judged from a Biblical perspective, we have rightly seen the human image in the social terms of persons in community. But our inadequate Scottish experience of the humanity of Christ,

and our precarious social experience of the human condition
have together led us to see the human image as something
conditional on the outcome of impossible demands: we are only
human if we are good enough, or successful enough, or normal
enough - but we can never be sure. In the words of Anthony Ross,
'the Scottish community has created, and still creates, conditions which will further strain its psychiatric hospitals and
already overcrowded jails, exhaust and frustrate understaffed
social services, and stimulate emigration.' I have already quoted
at the start of this book Ross' call for an act of contrition for
ourselves and the community in which we live, as the necessary
prelude to a renewed vision of what it means to be Scottish. As
a first step, he suggests that, 'It might help if we could set aside
for a time the image of Scotland presented in the glossy maga-
zines... looking instead on the... roll-call of those people in
Scotland whose tragedy is buried in statistics but who challenge
all the conceit with which we brag about our great traditions...
(including) an obsessive puritanism to which Protestant and
Catholic have both contributed...' But if we replace the glossy,
tartan images of Scotland with the human image, what do we
find?

Ross paints a moving portrait of the other human image of
Scotland: '... the young man with a history of baby home,
orphanage, approved school, borstal, young offenders institute,
and prison, who repeats dutifully that of course it has all been his
own fault; or the defeated woman who longs for the day when
another of her fourteen children will leave school and she can tell
him to go and look after himself...' This is our 'imagined
community' of Scottish nationhood: a nation imagined in terms
of a human identity whose security and worth is made conditional on moral or social or national demands which are impossible to meet. Caught up in the impossible tension of these
several imperatives, we oscillate between Ascherson's self-
assertion and self-distrust. Bound by such a conditional sense of
our human identity, we never find the grace of self-acceptance.
That can come only from a new, unconditional sense of our
human identity. Such an identity will be grounded in the celebration of God's unconditional love for us rather than ground down
by impossible conditions demanded of us.

We receive that unconditional sense of our human identity from the Incarnation of God among us. As Robert Bruce, minister of St Giles in the late sixteenth century, put it: by taking **our** humanity, 'He delivered us from the disorder and rotten root from which we proceed. For, as you see, Christ Jesus was conceived in the womb of the Virgin, and that by the mighty power of His Holy Spirit, so that our nature in Him was fully sanctified by the same power.' If our human identity is guaranteed for us through the human nature of Jesus of Nazareth, God incarnate among us, then we are set free to enjoy and accept the gift of our own humanity, healed through him.

What it means for us to be human can no longer be determined by the impossible demands made on us by religious tradition, socio-economic injustice or cultural imperialism. Our human identity is determined by the way God has anchored himself to us in the humanity of his Son. Our humanity is not something we must either assert or distrust. It is something we enjoy and accept, as a community of relationships he created and restored for us through Jesus Christ. In this way the human image at the centre of our social identity can become something unconditional and liberating. The incarnation opens up for us a new kind of imagined community - one in which what we share in common is the image of God, unconditionally and universally.

All other possible images of our nationhood are divisive and potentially idolatrous, destroying our sense of community and social identity. Particular ethnic, cultural, religious or historical images can be shared only by sections of the Scottish community - Protestant but not Catholic, men but not women, middle but not working class, Lowland English-speaking but not Highland Gaelic-speaking, urban but not rural, white but not Asian, and so on. Particular images may be of a certain value and significance in creating a shared sense of national identity. But ultimately they must exclude some within or outwith our Scottish community. The same holds true of any conditional image of our human identity and worth. It excludes those who do not meet the conditions set, and who are judged to have failed, morally, socially, economically or culturally. By restoring the unconditional, universal humanity of Jesus Christ to the centre of our thinking about what it means to be human, we shall create a new sense of common identity in Scotland.

What we all share in common is the divine image made sacred in us all through the fellow humanity of Jesus Christ - with women and men, handicapped and able, poor and rich. When we start to imagine our Scottish identity in terms of the human image of our common humanity, then all the national images that would divide us in Scotland are smashed for the idols they are. In their place, we imagine our fellow Scots to be all who share God's image, without exception.

This not only overturns any narrow, xenophobic images of our national identity. It must also lead us to a more inclusive sense of community, bound together in the common image of our shared humanity and responsible for one another because bound together in relationship to God: 'Whatever you did for one of the least of these brothers of mine, you did for me.' (Matthew 25:40) It must bring into question all relationships within our Scottish community, whether cultural, economic, political, religious or social, which deny the unconditional human identity of all its members, especially those relationships which are exploitative, sectarian, sexist or racist.

But where will that re-thinking of our human identity around the humanity of Jesus Christ begin? There can only be one place - around the Lord's table. It is in the celebration of the eucharist, the Lord's Supper, that the Church symbolises the social restoration of our common humanity through the broken, suffering humanity of Christ crucified. In his broken body and shed blood we are all reconciled into one new humanity. As Pannenberg has stressed, it is the social nature of the eucharist that we have neglected, concentrating too much on the penitential meaning of the sacrament for guilty individuals. When the Church gathers around the Lord's table and shares in the meal together, it is anticipating and symbolising the reconciliation of humanity to God and to one another through Jesus Christ - and celebrating that new common social identity in Christ.

So the Church must be the troubling universal community within the particular community of the nation, calling into question all the national images with which it imagines itself a nation, and re-thinking them according to the universal image of God in the man Jesus Christ and all women and men. But is the

Church that kind of universal community and disturbing presence within Scotland today?

Chapter 10

THE CHRISTIAN IDENTITY CRISIS -
A Confessing Church

The Christian identity crisis can be put simply. Is Scotland any longer a Christian country?

The Church of Scotland, in the Declaratory Articles of its Constitution, claims to 'represent the Christian faith of the Scottish people'. This reflects the historic relationship between church and nation that has existed in Scotland since the thirteenth and fourteenth centuries and the nation's struggle for independence. We shall explore that relationship in the next chapter.

Today we are confronted by a paradox in the relationship. On the one hand we see the church, particularly the Church of Scotland, hanging on to its historic national identity. It would be easier for some to give up the doctrine of the Trinity than the Treaty of Union's recognition of Scottish Presbyterianism! On the other hand we see a profound reluctance to think theologically within a Scottish context in order to develop a theological understanding of the nation. It would be easier for some to see the relevance of the Gospel to the liberation of the oppressed in Latin America or South Africa than to a theology of Scottish nationhood! We are too sure of our national identity as Christians but not sure enough of our Christian identity as Scots.

No church faces a greater identity crisis than the Church of Scotland. Since the Reformation of 1560 the Reformed Kirk has been the national church, claiming spiritual continuity with the earlier Catholic and Celtic churches in the history of the one Kirk of Jesus Christ in Scotland, the *Ecclesia Scoticana*, the one Church of Scotland before and after the Reformation. In the Articles Declaratory of the Constitution of the Church of Scotland, adopted in 1926, the Kirk was described as 'a national

Church representative of the Christian Faith of the Scottish people', in the words of the third article which asserted the continuity and identity of the Church of Scotland.

Two factors make it hard for the Church of Scotland to sustain such a view of its identity today. First, the existence of a large Scottish Roman Catholic community among several other Christian denominations makes it increasingly implausible to claim a unique symmetry between the Kirk and the 'true face' of the one Christian Church in Scotland. Not all Christians in Scotland would regard the Church of Scotland as representative of their Christian Faith. The ecumenical dimension brings the Kirk's national identity into question, as does the reality of living in a multi-faith society, especially in urban Scotland.

An even greater challenge is presented by the Scottish people themselves. The implicit assumption of mass adherence to the Christian Faith by the Scottish people must seriously be brought into question as well. Membership of the Church of Scotland has dropped from around 1.3 million in 1956 to a figure that will go well under 800,000 by the end of the century, if present trends continue. While there may be some evidence of an implicit Christian faith and adherence to Christian values in the wider society, the Church of Scotland embraces in its formal membership a declining minority of Scots. Secularisation affects the Kirk's national identity at two levels. On the level of its formal religious beliefs, the prevailing secular outlook undermines the Kirk's credibility as an authoritative voice in Scottish society. On the level of its membership's perception of their standing in society, it becomes increasingly implausible sociologically to claim that the Kirk is an influential national institution if its members experience the social reality of being a declining minority. And yet, despite all this, the Church of Scotland clings to its national identity as just such a representative national institution, the Kirk and her Scotland.

The Kirk and the Post-War Devolution Debate

No one issue exposed the weakness of the Kirk's asserted national identity more than the postwar debate about devolution for Scotland; especially its outcome in the 1979 referendum on the Scotland Act, setting up a Scottish Assembly with legislative powers over matters already largely under the devolved administrative control of the Scottish Office. Since 1946, the General Assembly of the Church of Scotland has consistently supported a larger measure of devolution of legislative and administrative powers in Scottish affairs by Parliament. Since the 1960s, it has been convinced of the need for an effective form of self-government for Scotland under the Crown and within the framework of the United Kingdom, through an elected assembly.

When a Royal Commission on the Constitution of the United Kingdom was set up in 1969, the Church of Scotland was one of the bodies which submitted evidence to it. The Kirk was in a strong position to do so, given its unbroken record in advocating the case for the devolution of legislative powers over national affairs to a Scottish Assembly, conceived of as a 'parliament with powers'. Significantly, the grounds on which it chose to build its case were those derived from its representative identity as a national institution.

When the Church of Scotland spokesmen made their opening remarks to the members of the Constitutional Commission they were careful to make clear 'the base from which we speak'. As members of the Church and Nation Committee of the General Assembly they could only articulate the views of that Assembly, views that were only established after independent debate in that Assembly. The views presented to the Commission on the Constitution were, therefore, the views of the General Assembly. A further point was stressed about the base from which they spoke. It is worth quoting in full:

> The third point I would make is the widely representative character of the General Assembly. The Church of Scotland has a membership of just under one and a quarter million adults, out of a total Scottish population of around five million, which is a sizable proportion of the people of Scotland. The General Assembly is widely representative of the Church. It is not a clerical or hierarchical assembly: fifty per cent of the members are laymen or laywomen, and the Assembly also contains a quarter of the ministers, each of them with an elder from the different parishes of Scotland

drawn in rotation, so that it represents the Kirk, from the Borders to the Shetlands and from the Western Isles to Aberdeen and Edinburgh in the east. The point I am making is not that the Assembly is entirely representative of the people of Scotland, nor that it is an assembly of experts in political economy or social theory; nor am I claiming that, because it is the Kirk which is speaking, it claims an infallibility in its judgement. What we do claim is that the General Assembly is widely representative of public opinion in Scotland, more so than any other body in Scotland at the present time, and it is for that reason that many people are of the opinion that the Assembly of the Kirk is the nearest approach we have had so far to a parliament in Scotland.

There could hardly be a fuller or franker statement of the identity of the Church of Scotland, in its General Assembly, as a representative national institution, however carefully qualified that representative role might be. As the established Church in Scotland, the Church of Scotland was concerned with the welfare of the Scottish people, the whole nation. Devolution was seen as a matter affecting the welfare of the Scottish people and therefore worthy of comment by the Kirk. But the base from which the Kirk chose to speak on this issue was the national identity of the General Assembly as a body 'widely representative of public opinion in Scotland'.

There were at least two other bases from which the Kirk might have addressed its views to the Commission, a constitutional one rejected by the Kirk at the outset and a theological one raised by the Commission itself.

In its opening statement to the Commission, the Church and Nation Committee concluded that 'The Church claims no competence in devising political constitutions.' While showing a healthy rejection of the old Calvinist theocratic pretensions of the Kirk to dictate to the state, this statement displays an alarming loss of memory about the Kirk's own highly developed constitutional theory of church and state and a loss of nerve about its possible relevance to the question of devolution. A national Church that has fought for centuries to establish its competence to devise its own constitution, on the basis of constitutional principles that are universally recognised as part of the common inheritance of Western constititutional thought and which are as applicable in the secular sphere as they are in ecclesiastical matters, has surely something worthwhile to say when the nation itself seeks to devise its political constitution! But no, the Kirk decided not to speak from its strong base in constitutional theory and practice, to the regret of at least one member of the Constitutional Commission.

This member tried in vain to press the Church witnesses to consider more detailed constitutional questions concerning the powers of their proposed Scottish Assembly; but the Kirk spokesman would only reiterate the representative base from which they offered their evidence: 'What the Assembly has tried to do is to give expression to the dissatisfaction which is widespread throughout the country and to give expression to the two poles along which we think a solution should be found, namely, that it should be self-government within the framework of the United Kingdom.' As stated, it was not up to the Church, through its Church and Nation Committee to formulate a constitutional model. It did not have the expertise. In as much as it made proposals for constitutional change in Scotland, it was only expressing what Scottish public opinion seemed to want.

To this, the Commission member replied, 'I am sure that as witnesses, representing a Committee of the General Assembly of the Church of Scotland General Assembly, you are solely concerned with the welfare of the Scottish people. But where difficulties arise I am sure you should have a hand in sorting them out. This is not simply a matter that can be put aside as an expert one.' Clearly the Commission on the Constitution recognised that it was legitimate for the Kirk to speak from a constititutional base. The Kirk did not.

The refusal of the Kirk to speak from a second, theological base puzzled the Commission even more. Another member asked whether, if the Kirk's recommendations on devolution were accepted, the Church would expect its situation 'to be better as regards witnessing to the Gospel?' To this question, the reply came, 'I do not think this is an element which has entered into our calculations at all. We have put forward these suggestions not in the interests of the Kirk but in the interests of the Scottish people.' Again, this statement may express a healthy rejection, by the Kirk, of the use of political means to proselytize on its own behalf. But it does reveal a worrying lack of connection, in the Kirk's thinking, between what the Commission member saw as the fundamental work of the Kirk, that 'of maintaining and spreading the Christian faith', and its views on important national affairs like the government of the country.

When the Church representative replied as above, the Commission member responded, 'I do not think that I have had an answer.' We must also wonder whether, if the fundamental task of the Kirk is to witness to the Gospel, some account should have been taken of the social context for that witness, as it might be affected by devolution.

The Church and Nation Committee itself, in its written submission to the Commission, listed six reasons for self-government identified by the General Assembly, including the view that the value of self-government was psychological, cultural and even spiritual. It is the profound insight of both the sociology of religion and contextual theology that just such a social context may affect the Church's witness to the Gospel as much as witness to the Gospel may influence society. A curious dualism seems to have operated in the Church's comments to the Commission at this point. The Kirk's representative role as a national institution allowed it to hold views on devolution as an expression of Scottish public opinion, without any reference to its fundamental evangelical task of witness to the Gospel; while its missionary role of witness to the Gospel did not require it to consider the political context as something that aided or hindered its mission.

When we remember the damage done to the witness of the Church of Scotland to the Gospel, and to the welfare of the Scottish nation, in the nineteenth century, by the refusal of the British Parliament to consider distinctively Scottish concerns in the events that led up to the Disruption of the Kirk in 1843, the neglect of the Gospel in its social and political context by the Church of Scotland in 1969 shows a disturbing lack of theological and historical awareness. Just how disturbing that was to prove, is shown by the events of ten years later, in 1979.

The Events of 1979

Having rejected both a constitutional and a theological base from which to speak on devolution in 1969, and having clearly adopted a representative basis for its position, the Church of Scotland went into the 1970s confident that it was representing the growing tide of Scottish opinion that seemed to favour devolution, in both election results and opinion polls. Therefore, when the Labour Government finally passed its Scotland Act, setting up a Scottish legislative Assembly, but made its implementation dependent on at least 40% of the Scottish electorate voting in favour of its proposals in a referendum, the Church and Nation Committee was in no doubt as to what it should do in the referendum campaign of 1979. It drew up a statement on devolution with the recommendation that it be read in all pulpits of the Kirk on the two Sundays before the referendum polling day, March 1st.

This statement reminded church members of the consistent position of the General Assembly in favour of devolution but did not tell them how they should vote in the referendum. It did, however, encourage Kirk members to use their vote and gave the warning that failure to vote would be treated as a No vote in the referendum, given the 40% ruling. This was too much for one leading churchman, Dr Andrew Herron. At a meeting of the Commission of the General Assembly on February 22nd, Dr Herron successfully proposed that the Commission recall the statement and forbid any minister to read it from the pulpit.

Herron argued that the statement favoured the Yes side in the campaign and that its claim that a failure to vote would be treated as a No vote was grossly misleading. In moving against the Church and Nation Committee's statement, he believed that the referendum debate had no Christian implications. He was reported as saying, '... if I hear of any minister who reads this statement from the pulpit on Sunday and who knew of the Commission ruling then I will have him up for contempt of the Commission.' In this way was the Church of Scotland's long held mind on devolution officially silenced in the last days of the referendum campaign.

How could a Church that had consistently supported devolution for over thirty years get itself into that position at the crucial moment when its voice should have been heard in the nation? One overriding reason must be the base from which the Kirk had chosen to speak, its representative national identity as an expression of Scottish public opinion. By January 1979 it was clear to many that public support in Scotland for devolution was wavering and that even among its committed advocates there were doubts about the proposed Assembly. An article in The Scotsman newspaper on January 29th by Arnold Kemp identified the mood of the time. He argued that Scotland had become bored with devolution as early as 1977, when the first Labour devolution bill had foundered. The whole debate had gone on too long, after the heady excitement of constitutional debate in the early seventies. 'Thus', he wrote, 'as we go into the March 1 referendum, perhaps the most important moment in Scotland's history since the Union, apathy is everywhere and even the friends of devolution brood about the Scotland Act's inconsistencies.' It is little wonder that Dr Herron found it so easy to silence a Church that claimed to represent Scottish opinion on devolution.

If the national opinion which the Church of Scotland claimed to represent on the devolution issue was seen to waver in its support, where did that leave the Kirk? A Church that chooses to build its arguments on a representative national identity is building on sand. 'And the rain descended, and the floods came, and the winds blew, and beat upon that house; and it fell: and great was the fall of it.' Only a strong base in the Biblical Word of God, interpreted in terms of theological and constitutional principle, would have proved a rock on which to stand firm in public support for devolution and weather the conflicting currents in public opinion and the storm of internal church debate raised by the referendum campaign. But the Kirk had abandoned that solid ground ten years earlier and by early 1979 it was too late.

The verdict of both secular and church academics on the wider role of the Church of Scotland in influencing national opinion on devolution, rather than simply expressing it, is also sobering. It might naturally have been imagined that a national institution which consistently supported Scottish self-government over so long a period, long before the stunning SNP by-election and General Election victories of the late 1960s and early 1970s brought it to the top of the British political agenda, must have had some influence on Scottish public support for devolution in the postwar era. Not so, according to political scientist Jack Brand or church historian Henry Sefton.

In a study of the rise of modern Scottish nationalism, Brand argues that while the Church of Scotland has held a consistent stance of support for a considerable measure of devolution for Scotland, it has done so only in response to events in Scottish political life. As in the 1950 General Assembly deliverance, which referred to the fact that over a million people had signed a national covenant in favour of home rule, 'It seems clear from the timing... that this was not a case of the Church leading the nation but the Church following an existing lead.' Referring to Brand's analysis in his own essay on the Church of Scotland and Scottish nationhood, Sefton has written, 'It is difficult to resist the conclusion of a recent commentator that the church has followed rather than led opinion on this issue. The general assemblies have reacted to nationalism, the Scottish covenant, the Hamilton by-election and the various royal commission reports and government white papers.' For a Church that chooses to speak from a representative base, this seems an inevitable fate and an unerring conclusion.

Both the Church and Nation spokesman addressing the Commission on the Constitution in 1969, and Dr Herron, addressing the Commission of the General Assembly in 1979, declared in different ways the same conviction - that the democratic control of Scottish affairs had nothing to do with the beliefs or mission of the Church of Scotland. It had everything to do with the representative national identity of the established Church. For the Church and Nation Committee this identity led it, and successive General Assemblies, to support devolution. For Dr Herron, it led him to the view that the Kirk should not pronounce on these matters during the course of the devolution referendun campaign, in order to maintain its integrity and carry out its ministry of reconciliation as the national church in a nation divided on the issue.

We see here a clear crisis of identity for the Church of Scotland, but it is one that goes far deeper than just an inner conflict over the nature of its national identity. Though few recognised it at the time, the sorry story of the Kirk and its representative approach to the devolution issue was also symptomatic of a crisis of Christian identity for many Scots.

One Kirk minister saw the point clearly. In a letter to The Scotsman in late February 1979, part of the correspondence arising from the Herron episode, the Rev J.M. Ritchie wrote, 'The Kirk has too long been saddled with the incubus of being the voice of Scotland, and "representing Scottish nationality" which is quite inaccurate. Once an Assembly is formed it will then represent Scotland, and the Kirk in partnership with other Christians, can then concentrate on being the Kirk of Christ in this land with no ambivalence or confusion or distracton.'

A Theology for Export Only

It is precisely here, in being the Kirk of Christ, representing Christ in this land of Scotland, that we find so much ambivalence on the part of Scottish Christians. As part of a representative national institution, the national Church representing the Scottish people, Kirk members feel free to consider national and global questions with equanimity. They pronounce on the affairs of southern Africa or support the contextual liberation theology of Latin America with ease and enthusiasm. Groups like 'Scottish Christians for Nicaragua' spring into existence, just as a hundred and fifty years ago, Scottish Christians were active in the campaign against black slavery in the southern states of America. And rightly so. But 'Scottish Christians for Scotland' is almost unthinkable, and certainly tainted with chauvinistic nationalism! Scottish Christians find it very hard to take a Scottish context for the universal Church and Gospel of Christ with any great seriousness, and will consider Christian questions from a Scottish perspective only with self-conscious and apologetic unease. Discuss Scottish issues, yes, by all means, but keep the Gospel out of it!

That this is part of a wider British phenomenon is shown by an observation made by the English theologian John Kent at the close of an essay on the failure of a serious English political theology to develop since 1945:

... it is time to end the favourite English middle-class game, no doubt a substitute for the lost empire, of

vicarious imperialism, which is reflected at the religious institutional and pressure-group levels as an
obsession with pseudo-action in South Africa or South
America - any place which is a long way from the
Welsh mining valleys or the quiet hells of outer
London. It is time for the English to come home
imaginatively and set about the transformation of their
own society, which they have put off for a hundred
years while they interfered with the societies of other
races.

Substitute Scots for English, industrial Lanarkshire for the
Welsh valleys and Glasgow for London, and you have described
this aspect of the Christian identity crisis in Scotland exactly. It
is indeed time for Scottish Christians to come home imaginatively and set about the transformation of their own society,
which they have put off for a hundred years while they have
concerned themselves with the societies of other races, not least
the English!

That last reference is not a frivolous one. One reason for the
flight of the Scottish Christian imagination from radical concern
for their own nation may well be a similarly displaced and non-
threatening need to express that social concern in countries
safely far away, whether in the old Empire or the modern Third
World. The American historian C. Duncan Rice, for example,
has suggested that the middle class Seceder Presbyterian evangelicals who were so prominent in the Scots Abolitionist societies, campaigning for the abolition of black slavery in America
from 1833 to the outbreak of the Civil War, may have been
projecting their own sense of moral guilt for the conditions of
their employees in the Scottish working class at home, safely
across the Atlantic. They may also have been transposing their
own fierce national debates about religion and politics in the
turbulent decades of the Reform Act and the Disruption into the
veiled terms of a divided American society. This is a familiar
pattern in the social psychology of groups who find it too
threatening to discuss their own internal problems directly.
Domestic conflicts are carried out in coded form, using foreign
actors and dramas. But nineteenth century Scots faced the added
dilemma of interference from a society much nearer home,

England. This too may be a reason for the Scots' imaginative flight from their own country.

As part of a wider Scottish culture, Scottish Christians since at least the mid-nineteenth century have felt ambivalent and confused about expressing their Christian identity in contemporary Scottish terms. They have lost their nerve about a distinctively modern Scottish context for their faith under the impact of a globally ascendent English culture and the traumatic break-up of their own Scottish institution, the national Kirk, at the 1843 Disruption. Struggling or ambitious to make their way in that wider world, their distinctive Scottish church history, theology and public culture were either romanticised or stripped of any peculiar national characteristics.

In particular, the Scottish Reformed tradition, in coming to terms with the urban, industrial, post-Enlightenment, secular and pluralist modern world, never attempted, after 1843, to renew itself from within the resources of its own theological tradition in a way that owned its national origins or was specifically applied to its own national context; unlike the Calvinist tradition in the Netherlands in the same period which did undergo such a process of theological and national renewal in an explicitly Dutch context. We have explored that historical comparison in part two. Here it is enough to note the phenomenon and the way it has affected the Christian identity of the Scots.

We can make the same point about Scottish Christians that the philosopher George Davie has noted about Scottish literary and intellectual figures in the nineteenth century. In his book, *The Crisis of the Democratic Intellect*, Davie shows how David Masson, an influential mid-nineteenth century Scottish professor of Rhetoric and English Literature, suggested that Scottish writers who wished to reach a wider audience for their work should detach the presentation of their ideas from the Scottish linguistic, cultural, historical and social traditions in which they had originated. The parade of the peculiarities of Scottish speech, history and customs, so evident in the works of Robert Burns and Sir Walter Scott, had been overdone, and, if not discarded or cut back, would result in a provincialism which would stifle the very ideas that Scottish writers wanted to get over, according to Masson. In its place, Masson promulgated the principle of the internalisation of Scotticism. The kernel of universally intelligible Scottish ideas could be expressed without the unnecessary husk of their national context. The writings of Thomas Carlyle are a classic example of this development. They are steeped in Scottish Calvinist and philosophical ways of thought but with few explicit references to their Scottish origins.

I suspect that something similar happened to the Reformed Christian tradition in Scotland as occurred in the Scottish literary tradition in this period. An internalisation of the Scottish context for Christian thought took place. Distinctively Scottish theological ideas and concerns were maintained, but detached from the Scottish philosophical, ecclesiastical, cultural and national traditions in which they had originated and by which they were still sustained. While such national Christian documents at the 1320 Declaration of Arbroath, the 1638 National Covenant and the Kirk's 1842 Claim of Right are explicit about their Scottish context, you will find only the odd passing reference to Scottish society or the Scottish theological tradition in the Baillie reports on *God's Will in our Time* accepted by the General Assembly in the 1940s. However, there is no mistaking the implicit Scottish theological perspective of its author!

George Davie considers the impact of Masson's principle of the internalisation of Scotticism upon Scottish literature in the context of his study of Hugh MacDiarmid's struggle with Scots as a literary language capable of expressing in poetry the ferment of modern intellectual thought in philosophy, politics, science and the arts. At first MacDiarmid rejected Scots as a viable medium for his poetry. But later experiments with the language convinced him that he had been wrong. In Davie's words, 'The result was astonishing to the poet himself and to his friends, since in using the new medium of an externalised Scotticism devised by himself, he had managed to produce philosophical poetry of a far higher quality, both in regard to the profundity of its ideas as well as the graphic precision with which they were put over, then he had ever been able to put over in English in the mode of internalised Scotticism...'

I have suggested earlier that MacDiarmid's Nietzschean solution to our human identity crisis in Scotland is no acceptable or credible answer. However, as unlikely as it may seem, I do believe that MacDiarmid   offers a solution to the Christian identity crisis in Scotland.

His discovery of an externalised Scotticism, the explicit use of Scottish language, culture, history and ideas in his poetry, shows us the creative potential and universal significance in such a transition. Far from becoming parochial, MacDiarmid's use of Scots liberated his mind to roam on a global scale and catch a vision of the Infinite. In a classic Scottish way, he sought to contemplate universal questions through his own particular Scottish experience. I dare to suggest that Christians in Scotland need to undergo a similar conversion experience to their own Scottish context, like MacDiarmid. We need an externalised Christian Scotticism in Scotland today. In other words, we need to express and relate the universal truths of the Christian faith in the explicitly Scottish terms of our history, theological and religious traditions, philosophy, culture, society, economy and politics. We need to understand the Gospel in our Scottish context and let the Gospel shape that Scottish context. If we do that I believe that we shall discover a new power and range in our Christian understanding and practice that will far surpass anything that is currently offered by the Anglo-Saxon Christian world of irrational, spiritual experience, authoritarian leadership techniques, and how-to-do-it pragmatism.

A Choice for Christians

It may be a shock for some Christians to realise that such fashionable religious movements are based ultimately on the same old Nietzschean philosophy of the primacy of the will in a relativist universe. Scots brought up in the shadows of Nazism would instinctively recoil from any religious movement that exalted the power of the human will to shape life according to its own designs. But Nietzsche's philosophy in its religious form has not reached us in its dark, pessimistic European guise. It has travelled to our shores via America, where its sojourn there transmuted it into a typically optimistic American version. Not the Will to Power but Power Healing and Power Evangelism, the power to get results!

The same battlelines are being drawn in the Church today in Scotland that George Davie has shown were fought over in

Scottish education in the 1920s. Then, it was a straight choice between two different educational philosophies. On one side of the debate was a pragmatic approach to truth, inspired by the American John Dewey's philosophy that the truth of an idea lay in its practical efficacy. Such a philosophy resulted in the breaking up of education into narrow specialisms to equip people for specific tasks in society. On the other side of the debate stood the older Scottish philosophical tradition with its metaphysical understanding of truth, where knowledge was pursued for its own sake, prior to the question of its practical efficacy. This led to the characteristic Scottish generalist philosophical education which sought to equip people for life in society, irrespective of their later specialised studies or careers.

Today the Church faces the same stark choice. On the one side beckons a pragmatist Christianity that sees truth as that which demonstrates its practical effectiveness in successful results, and has little connection with doctrinal questions or historical tradition. The Gospel is seen to work in terms of specialised techniques derived through business and sociological theory from the kind of pragmatist philosophy espoused by John Dewey. On the other side stands an older theological Christianity that seeks to know the One who is the truth, God as he has uniquely disclosed himself in Jesus Christ. The Scottish church tradition is rich in that theological understanding of truth. Yet it is in danger of being either neglected or despised by so many Scottish Christians.

As MacDiarmid rediscovered Scots and its literary depths, so we must rediscover our own Scottish theological language and its living depths. Only in this way can we hope to resolve our Scottish Christian identity crisis in such a way that the faith which alone can sustain our common human identity may flourish in contemporary Scotland.

As with our human identity crisis, we face a crisis of Christian identity for two main reasons. We have based our Christian identity on a representative role within the nation, and we have not dared to base our national identity on a Scottish contextual theology. Neither position is tenable in Scotland today. While historical and cultural forces may have led the Church of Scotland into such an impasse, its own third Declaratory Article in its 1926 Constitution must bear some of the responsibility for this situation. A Church that sees itself as 'a national Church representative of the Christian Faith of the Scottish people', can easily slip into being a national institution representative of the opinions of the Scottish people, as the devolution saga sadly demonstrates.

The notion of the Church as a body representative of the Christian faith of the Scottish people may be a reference to the historic adherence of the Scots to Christianity. That is no longer a plausible sociological identification to make in contemporary Scotland. Therefore, the whole historic representative basis on which the Kirk seeks to be the national Church must be brought into question. We must seriously ask whether it would not be better to move to a theological definition of its national role, as a national Church representative of Christ and his mission to the Scottish people. This would require us to take more seriously both the nature of the distinctive Christian identity of the Church and also the importance of understanding the Scottish context of the Church's life and witness: as something distinct from itself, that the Church does not represent but rather seeks to identify with and yet see transformed by the Gospel.

Sometimes of course, in churches as in nations, change does take place, and only later are constitutions brought into line. This may now be happening slowly in the Church of Scotland, whose 1989 General Assembly appointed a new Board of National Mission, with effect from 1st January 1990. But there may be a more urgent theological reason for changing the third article of the Kirk's Constitution. It may be heretical!

A Racist Model?

In every family cupboard there is a skeleton. The family of God is no exception. Certainly not the Church of Scotland branch of the family. One particular skeleton rattles around the 1926 definition of the Kirk's identity as the national Church, in the third Declaratory Article of its constitution. As I have just suggested, the phrase 'representative of the Christian Faith of the Scottish people' may largely be a formulation to express the historic links between Scotland and Christianity, and the self-understanding of the Kirk to be a Reformed branch of the

Universal Church in continuity with the Catholic and Celtic Churches prior to 1560. But if the statement is put in the context of the Church of Scotland's official thinking about its national identity in the period in which this definition was adopted, the 1920s, then it takes on an altogether more sinister meaning.

In 1926, the same year in which the Declaratory Articles were adopted by the Church of Scotland, the convener of the Church and Nation Committee of the Kirk's General Assembly, John White, himself a principal architect of that Constitution, reported to the General Assembly on a letter he had written to the Secretary of State for Scotland. The subject of the letter was Irish immigration into Scotland and the need for its restriction on racial grounds. Two years earlier, in 1924, the General Assembly had described this Irish influx as a 'menace to Scottish nationality and civilization' because of the inferior quality of the type of Irish who emigrated to Scotland and the marked contrast between their social and moral conduct and ideals and those of the 'native Scots'. In 1925 the Church and Nation Committee, having been instructed to watch over the racial situation in Scotland and to confer with the Secretary of State on 'the Racial Problem', wanted a government committee to inquire into the situation, 'with a view to the preservation and protection of Scottish nationality and civilization.'

Why this should be the explicit concern of the Church of Scotland was made evident in the 1927 Church and Nation report. Calling for the regulation of Irish immigration, it stated:

> The Church of Scotland, whose interests in the past have been so intimately associated with those of the Scottish people, has clearly an obligation to defend Scottish nationality such as no other organisation or institution has. The Church has reacted on the nation, and the nation has impressed its own genius on the Church in a most notable way. If ever there was a call to the Church of Scotland to stand fast for what men rightly call dearest - their nationality and their traditions - that call is surely sounding now, when our race and culture are faced with a peril which, though silent and unostentatious, is the greatest with which the Scottish people have ever been confronted.

Seen in the context of these reports, the Declaratory Article definition of a national Church takes on a racial as well as a historical and ecclesiological character. Given the vigour of expression in the Church and Nation pronouncements on the 'Irish Menace' to 'Scottish nationality and civilization', the phrase 'the Scottish people' in the Declaratory Articles must have had clear racial overtones among those who used it at the time. What is unquestionable from these statements is that the Church of Scotland saw itself as the guardian of Scottish nationality: defined as a particular racial and cultural identity whose purity was threatened by the immigration of one particular race, the (Catholic) Irish. The Kirk could not have adopted a more explicitly racial and ethnic identity for itself as the national Church or for Scotland as a nation. Biblical injunctions to make the stranger welcome among God's people seem to have been forgotten.

The Church of Scotland was not in any way inciting the 'native Scots' to racial violence or hatred and its call for action on the 'Irish Menace' was limited to formal requests to government for the regulation and restriction of Irish immigration. Somewhat patronisingly, it drew a distinction between the Irish people in Ireland, of whom it thought highly, and the so-called more inferior sorts who emigrated to Scotland and were seen as a threat to the Scots' racial and cultural purity, jobs and welfare resources. However, if the word 'Irish' was replaced with the word 'Jewish', and the source had been the German Church, not the Kirk, then these reports would take on an even more disturbing quality, given events in Germany in this same period, especially in the Nazi era of the 1930s.

The Church and Nation Committee continued to report on the 'Irish Menace' regularly up to 1939 and the outbreak of the Second World War. With bitter irony, its final appeals for the restriction of Irish immigration appeared alongside reports on extremely limited relief work among 'Non-Aryan' refugees (Jews) from Nazi Germany.

I must stress that there is a vast difference between the murderous intent of German Nazism and the racial hatred of their anti-semitism and the plodding legalism of the Kirk's opposition to the immigrant Irish community within Scotland.

Mercifully, that racial attitude and approach to Scottish nationality did not reappear after 1945 in Church and Nation reports, nor did any references to the 'Irish menace'. However, it is a matter of some shame and public record that the Church of Scotland adopted a racial definition of church and nation during the 1920s which must have affected in turn its understanding of the Declaratory Article definition of its identity as a national Church representative of the Christian faith of the Scottish people - clearly excluding the Irish immigrants from that definition of the Scottish people.

An Acoustic Community, a Confessing Identity

In Nazi Germany, faced with the move to impose upon the German Churches a racial definition of the Church's message, membership and mission, some Christians, including Dietrich Bonhoeffer and Karl Barth, signed the Barmen Declaration. This document opposed such developments as profoundly antithetical to the Church's confession that Jesus is Lord. Its confession made them look at the Church and world in such a way that no racist divisions or definitions could be accepted by Christians. The Barmen Declaration was linked to the rise of the Confessing Church movement in Germany which distinguished itself from the institutional Church's identification with the Nazi racialist creed in its call for a clear Christian confession of faith.

There is of course no straight comparison between the Church's response to the Jewish question in Nazi Germany and the Kirk's views on the Irish question in the 1920s and 1930s. What the comparison does is to throw into sharp relief the danger of the kind of approach to the identity of church and nation adopted by the Kirk over the question of Irish immigration. To that extent at least, we may need to consider a 'Confessing Church' type of response to the third Declaratory Article. If it appears that twentieth century Church of Scotland thinking on its Christian and national identities - as the national Church upholding the nationality as well as representing the Christian faith of the Scottish people - is partly rooted in a racial and ethnic definition of both identities, then that must be repudiated as a matter of fundamental Christian confession. The tendency of the Kirk to see itself as a representative national institution in the devolution debate of the 1960s and 1970s may, however indirectly, owe as much to the context of racial fear and suspicion in the 1920s as it does to the claim that its General Assembly has been a surrogate Scottish parliament since 1707.

A Church for the Nation

The skeleton of the 'Irish menace' should serve not to scare-monger but to concentrate minds on the serious nature of the Christian identity crisis faced by the Church of Scotland in the 1990s and beyond. Put simply, what does it mean in distinctively Christian terms for the Kirk to be the national Church on the eve of the twenty-first century? Most of the Church's energies are directed towards thinking about that question in terms of the problems of numerical and institutional decline and a lack of ministerial or material resources. Much more thought needs to be given to re-thinking its distinctive Christian identity and purpose in the nation's life. I believe that this will involve a fundamental shift away from being the Church **of** Scotland towards becoming the Church **for** Scotland, for three reasons.

The **first** reason is a Biblical one. In chapter six I suggested that while the nations of Biblical history could be seen theologically as 'imagined communities', constituted by humankind in the course of history as provisional human communities, the people of God (both Israel and the Church) were seen in Scripture as 'acoustic communities', constituted by God through the hearing of his word. As such, the people of God could only hear God's word and maintain their distinctive acoustic identity in as much as they accepted that God had chosen them to be his holy nation, set apart for his missionary purpose to all nations. If the people of God tried to become like the imagined communities of the nations, and abandoned their identity as a separate people amid the nations, then they could no longer be effective transmitters of God's word to these same nations.

Understood in this way, as part of the holy nation of God's people, the Church of Scotland has been in grave danger of abandoning its distinctive Christian identity for the sake of a national identity. This can only distort its existence as an acoustic community, hearing and obeying the word of God. It also leads to a breakdown in what I have termed the Biblical ecology of nationhood, where the holy nation of God's people live in a particular set of missionary relationships with the historic nations within the total environment of the coming Kingdom of God. If the Church abandons that missionary relationship and separate acoustic identity then it fails the very nations it was called to serve and to address with the Gospel.

As the sociological distinction between the Christian community and the wider secular, pluralist community of Scotland becomes more apparent, it would be liberating for the Church of Scotland to see that gap as a dawning evangelical opportunity to fulfil its Biblical mission to the nation, as the Church to Scotland, rather than as the crevice down which the old national kirk will disappear. It is only when the Church of Scotland recognises the gap between itself and the nation as a healthy distinction, that it will recover its authentic identity as an acoustic community and re-discover its purpose: to make Scotland an acoustic community through the word it brings to the nation.

The **second** reason for this fundamental shift away from its old identity as the national Church is a practical theological one. As the Church of Scotland goes into institutional decline it will increasingly face the tension between two classic types of church community and ethos. As the established national Church, it may try to maintain the appearance of a *Volkskirche* or broad Church embracing the whole nation as its parish and potential membership. Or it may come to terms with its numerical decline and become much more of a sect-type of religious body, existing with a more tightly-defined membership and concern for its own internal life.

Both options are highly undesirable. By maintaining a facade of being the Church of the Scottish people, it could lose its Christian distinctiveness within the nation. By retreating into its own dwindling membership and internal concerns it could lose its relevance and concern for national life.

There is, however, a **third** option or church model, suggested above in the analysis of the significance of the 'Irish Menace' skeleton. If the Church of Scotland finds itself compromised by its twentieth century attempts to stress its ethnic identity and yet increasingly challenged by a society hostile to its Christian message, then perhaps it is time to see itself more as a Confessing

Church to the nation rather than the common Church of the nation.

This would require the Kirk to re-think its Christian identity as the community of those who confess Jesus as Lord, with a distinctive life from the rest of the secular community and yet with an overriding sense of responsibility for that nation in mission, social criticism and service. In that sense, a Confessing Church would remain very much a national Church in its mission and concern but from within the circle of a more self-consciously separate Christian community. As a minority within the nation, such a Confessing Church would be made more aware of the distinctiveness, not to say the deviant nature of some of its beliefs and practices and the need to sustain its outlook against social pressure as well as intellectual unbelief. And yet, such a Confessing Church might also be freed from various existing social constraints acting on the national Church, in order to speak out more forcefully in a prophetic way within society.

Finally, there is a sound national reason for this shift in the Kirk's identity. As we noted in chapter three, too often in Scottish history, and partly under the impact of the covenant nation thinking of the seventeenth century, genuinely secular, national interests have been confused with church interests and transposed into an inappropriate ecclesiastical key. In other words, people have felt that guaranteeing the interests of the Kirk as a national institution has ensured the nation's welfare as a whole. This happened at the time of the Union of Parliaments in 1707 and at the Disruption of the Kirk in 1843, and to a much lesser extent, at the reunion of the Church of Scotland in 1929.

If the Church were, with patience and wisdom, to disinvest itself of its role as a representative national institution in order to be perceived more as a community representative of Jesus Christ to the nation, then that might help the nation to clarify its needs and wishes concerning its own representative national institutions. It would help to create movement and space in Scotland's institutional life and open up the possibility of another 'Knoxian paradox'. That is to say, by concentrating on being an acoustic community of the Word, speaking to the nation out of a faithful hearing of that Word for today, the Church might yet again in its history give rise to a whole new set of distinctive Scottish institutions and traditions arising out of a new obedience to that Word within Scotland.

By taking seriously its Biblical and Reformed theological identity as an acoustic community, the Church of Scotland will have to re-think its Christian identity as the national Church. Central to that revision will be the meaning and purpose of its increasing separation from the majority in Scottish society. Far from being a prescription for despair or retreat, it may be God's gift. It may be the catalyst for a more confident, if humble confession of Jesus Christ as Lord of Church and nation.

Why should this be the case? Well, we have seen within the human life of Jesus a spiritual movement through separation from human sin towards identification with human suffering. His dedication to God's will led him apart from all human idolatry. But the clear knowledge of God's will thus gained, led him back into a profound identification with God's loving plan to liberate humankind from that sin and idolatry. First it led him away into the desert, and then back to the villages of Galilee to preach the Kingdom, to heal the sick, to cast out demons. Finally it led him to Gethsemane, and from Gethsemane to the Cross.

Gethsemane is the place of resistance. There Jesus wrestled with the temptation to reject his Father's will. He was alone, apart from his disciples and from the nation that could not accept his identity as a suffering messiah. But in that place of resistance he saw clearly his identity and pupose. And it led him back out into the nation, to lay down his life at the Cross, the place of identification.

A Church that confesses Jesus the suffering messiah as Lord will be led into that same spiritual dynamic in its identity and purpose. Socially separate from aspects of Scottish culture that reject God, it faces the spiritual temptation and sociological pressure to compromise its faith. By resisting, in the place of separation, it will see more clearly God's will for both Church and nation. The Church will be led back into a new sacrificial identification with the nation's well-being in mission and service. The experience of being a minority within the nation can lead a 'Confessing Church' to recover its Biblical identity as a community of resistance to national idolatry, a holy nation, but also, inexorably, through the logic of the Gospel, its identity as a community identifying with the nation's life in unconditional love and critical solidarity.

These reflections on a new confessing identity for the national Church of Scotland lead us on to reflection about Scotland itself, and to the task of re-thinking our national identity.

Chapter 11

THE NATIONAL IDENTITY CRISIS -
A Constitutional Nationhood

The nature of the national identity crisis in Scotland can be put even more succinctly than that of our Christian identity - 'How big is big?' That is to say, is Scotland big enough to exist as a nation and can it co-exist with its bigger neighbours without losing its own national identity?

This question has always been recognised as central to the Scots' dilemma over nationhood. Perhaps the first recorded expression of it can be found in the Declaration of Arbroath in 1320. This document is an appeal to the Pope to recognise the Scottish claim to independence from England. It includes the call, 'that you will deign to admonish and exhort the King of the English, who ought to be satisfied with what he has, since England used to be enough for seven kings or more, to leave in peace us Scots, who live in this poor little Scotland, beyond which there is no dwelling place at all, and who desire nothing but our own.' From the beginnings of Scotland's history as a nation, it faced the problem of its small size and limited power as a peripheral European country in proximity to a much larger and more powerful nation, England. The Scots have never had a self-sufficient sense of nationhood. We have never been big enough to sustain our nationhood without reference to the wider world. We have always had to look to the wider world to maintain and develop our national life.

Scots looked to the rest of Christendom, especially to the Pope and to France, to support their political independence during the medieval period. Scots looked to Protestant England to establish their Reformation in 1560, while still drawing on continental thought and practice to evolve their own distinctive traditions and institutions in religion, education and law. After their own

226

ill-fated attempt at establishing a trading colony in Central America, in the failed Darien scheme, Scots in the 1700s looked to a political union with their southern neighbour to resolve their economic and political crisis and give them access to the larger common market of England and its overseas colonies. During the later eighteenth century the leading figures in the Scottish Enlightenment sought intellectual eminence on a European scale. Victorian Scotland depended on world markets as one of the first and leading heavy industrialised economies. Genera- tions of Scots since the 'British' unions of 1603 and 1707 embraced the opportunities offered for careers in England and in the wider British empire. And, in the last decade of this century, the Scots are weighing up the political, economic and social implications of belonging to the European Community and its single market, for their life as a nation within the United Kingdom and within Europe.

What kind of nationhood does that give the Scots? The post- 1945 cross-party government policy of regional development in Britain has now been abandoned but it offers us an incidental clue to our national identity. One planning concept considered in the postwar strategy for the economic development of the Scottish Highlands was that of the 'linear city'. Rather than build a large concentrated urban development in one area of the Highlands, the various economic and social developments that make up such a city could be spread out in a line through various Highland communities, from an aluminium smelter in Invergor- don, through a university in Inverness to a pulp-mill in Fort William- a linear city.

Here is the clue to our national identity as Scots. We are **a linear nation**. While the landmass of Scotland, its history and society are the essential endpoints and centrepoint of our nation- hood, the line in between runs through many different centres around the globe. You cannot understand medieval Catholic Scotland without tracing the line to the great continental centres of learning and the brilliant Scottish minds of scholars like Duns Scotus and John Major who flourished there. You cannot map the boundaries of Reformation Scotland and the development of the Scottish Kirk, universities and legal system, without tracing the line to Calvin's Geneva or the Dutch universities of the seventeenth century. The sources and influences of the Scottish Enlightenment lie far beyond our own shores. The cultural, intellectual, social,economic and political boundaries of eighteenth, nineteenth and twentieth century Scottish national identity require to pass through nations and events across the face of the earth, from colonial and revolutionary America to the parliaments of Westminster and Brussels.

Of course, this is all a truism, in as much as every people and country are interdependent on wider movements in history and culture. But it is a particularly acute and significant truism for a small nation like Scotland which has sought to establish and maintain its nationhood precisely through its relationships with the world beyond its own small borders. As this linear nation, we have never been able to contain or comprehend all that we mean by Scottish nationhood within the limits of our own land or experience. We have understood ourselves as Scots only as we have learned from others and shared with them in larger circles of community, through which we have traced the line of our own identity. And so we return to our initial question, that takes us to the heart of our crisis of national identity in present-day Scotland. How big is big? What contemporary forms of wider association and larger identity will ensure the wellbeing of the Scottish people and their historic national identity up to and beyond the year 2000? For three hundred years and more, that wider association has been the United Kingdom and that larger identity has been British. It is precisely these points in our linear identity that are in question today.

Out of the Empire and into Europe

It is more than coincidence that two distinguished historians in Scotland, Dr William Ferguson and Professor George Shepperson, should choose the same quotation to sum up their thoughts on the present state of Scotland within the United Kingdom. Ferguson, writing on the history of Anglo-Scottish relations, concluded:

> The United Kingdom has undoubtedly achieved great things and contributed much to the development of the modern world. The snag is that the United Kingdom's greatest achievements belong to a particular phase of

history that has vanished beyond recall... The problem now really is (as Dean Acheson, a former American Secretary noted some years ago) that Britain has lost an empire and failed to find a role in the world. Can the United Kingdom find a new *Staatsidee*, complicated as that must be by membership of the European Economic Community? If not, it is doubtful if the union of England and Scotland can continue unaltered on the old eroded assumptions.

Shepperson, reflecting on the history of the Scots abroad, part of what I have called our linear identity, quotes with approval first the view of the Scottish jurist Professor Andrew Dewar Gibb, that 'the existence of the empire has been the most important factor in deciding the relationship of Scotland and England in the last three centuries.' Then, in his own conclusion, he writes:

> In 1962 Dean Acheson made his famous comment on contemporary British history: 'Great Britain has lost an Empire and not yet found a role.' Of no part of the United Kingdom, in the opinion of the present writer, is this truer than of Scotland, now that the epic of the Scot abroad has come at last to an end.

The question now is whether the epic of the Scot at home has come to an end as well. The loss of the empire has meant for the Scots a search for new landmarks in our wider, linear identity, and a questioning of 'the old eroded assumptions' of Scotland's union with England in the United Kingdom.

For three centuries, since 1707 and the end of Scottish political sovereignty, the most significant fact about Scottish nationhood has been that it has survived at all. It has done so for most of that period within two larger political and economic frameworks, the United Kingdom and the British empire. Access to the benefits of that empire was one of the main motivations and guarantees of Scotland's acceptance of the British union in 1707 and thereafter. With the loss of the empire after the Second World War and the related decline of the United Kingdom from a world power to a middle-ranking European state, the original attraction of the British connection has waned. At the same time the appeal of a continuing Scottish identity has grown and manifested itself culturally and politically in the rise of a modern Scottish nationalist movement. The electoral successes of the Scottish National Party in the late 1960s and 1970s, and their resurgence in the late 1980s, along with the conversion of the still dominant Labour Party in Scotland to devolution, all demonstrate the political survival of a Scottish national identity within the United Kingdom; and that despite the inconclusive 1979 devolution referendum result and the subsequent dominance of a unionist government at Westminster that refused to countenance any measure of self-government for Scotland.

In the 1990s, the new factor that must inevitably cause the Scots to consider the re-alignment of their national identity is the prospect and reality of a closer union with the European Community, within or outwith the existing boundaries of the United Kingdom. The lines of our linear identity are now being drawn politically between the alternatives of a unionist Scotland in the United Kingdom or an independent Scotland in Europe, with several devolved or federalist options in between.   Before considering this present dilemma over the best boundary marks for our linear nationhood in the future, it is worth considering the reasons for Scotland's survival as a nation in the period since the last time our constitutional boundaries were re-drawn, in 1707.

Scotland's Survival as a Nation

After the creation of the United Kingdom parliament through an incorporating union with England, Scotland was able to participate in the emerging British economic and political order of industrial revolution and imperial expansion while maintaining a large measure of autonomy in its own national and local life. It did this through the distinctive national institutions of its civil society that survived the loss of statehood; its established Presbyterian national Church and its own systems of law, education, public welfare and local government. These institutions were the main and, until the mid-nineteenth century, the sufficient carriers of national identity for most Scots.

By the second half of that century, however, the state was playing a greater and more dominant role in Scottish society than it had ever done before or since 1707. For example, it took over the responsibility for local welfare provision and education, previously in the hands of the established Kirk and its local parishes, in 1845 and 1872 respectively. This was part of a wider expansion of government involvement and powers in response to the increasingly complex and related problems of an advanced urban, industrial society; further complicated in Victorian Scotland by the break-up of the Church of Scotland as a comprehensive national institution and its self-absorption in denominational rivalries after the Disruption in 1843.

It is from this period in mid-century, with the growing involvement of the British state in Scottish national and local life, and the collapse of such a key national institution as the Kirk, that political as well as civil institutions began to be seen as a key part in Scotland's survival and future as a nation. From the 1850s, public voices were raised demanding the recognition and strengthening of the Scottish dimension in the operation of the British state's increasingly pervasive and centralising rule north of the border. The national sentiment that had its roots in Scotland's long history as an independent nation, that had survived the unions of crown and parliament and been sustained by its separate religious and secular civil culture, was now being transmuted into demands for a greater political autonomy. Such demands were in response to the perceived threat posed to the Scottish identity by a British state whose actions in Scotland were too often shaped by English criteria.

The last point should not be underestimated. As the historian William Ferguson has written, doubts about the union began to arise from about the middle of the nineteenth century; 'Their causes were many and varied, but possibly the most potent was the one that is hardly ever mentioned - the continuing assertion of English nationalism... in its quiet purposeful way, the most potent in the British Isles: it calmly took over the United Kingdom, as Henry VII had put it, "the greater drawing the lesser".' Even the shared fruits of empire were not enough to stop Scottish recognition of the English face so often identified behind the British mask of state.

A growing number of Scots began to press for the recognition of a Scottish face within the British government instead. From 1885, when the office of Secretary for Scotland was established, the Scottish political dimension within the United Kingdom has grown to the point where, today, the Secretary of State for Scotland, as a cabinet minister, and the other junior ministers in the Scottish Office are responsible for the devolved administration of government policy affecting wide areas of Scottish life. However, along with the growth of administrative devolution over some Scottish affairs in the last hundred years, there has been a related demand for the devolution of legislative and executive powers over Scottish affairs from the British to a Scottish parliament.

The Scottish Home Rule movement that found support in the dominant Liberal Party and aspiring Labour Party before 1914, split in the decades after the First World War into a nationalist movement calling for independence, eventually emerging in 1934 as the Scottish National Party, and those who continued the earlier call for self-government within the United Kingdom, often operating within the existing political parties or cross-party campaigns for home rule. This modern movement, from the 1920s onwards, related the argument for self-government to the need to tackle the country's chronic economic and social problems, yet with little electoral support from the Scottish people (although well over a million signed a 1949 national covenant calling for a Scottish parliament within the framework of the United Kingdom). By the 1960s and '70s, when the postwar consensus policies of successive British governments were seen to be failing to find lasting remedies for an ailing Scottish economy and social fabric, many more Scots were willing to consider the Scottish National Party's assertion of a Scottish political solution, even if they would not go as far as the SNP's own policy of complete independence. SNP success at the 1974 General Elections forced the Labour Government to pass an Act setting up a Scottish Assembly with devolved powers, subject to support from at least 40% of the Scottish electorate in a referendum held on March 1st, 1979. While a majority of those voting favoured the proposed Assembly, it fell short of the required percentage of the total electorate, and the Scotland Act fell, as did the Labour Government and electoral support for the SNP in the subsequent General Election.

From 1979 Scotland was ruled by a UK Conservative Government and Scottish Conservative Party resolutely set on maintaining the unionist constitutional status quo, despite the marked decline in the number of its Scottish MPs in the 1980s. Labour remained both the dominant party in Scotland and, with some hesitations, committed to its policy of devolution. However by the late 1980s, the SNP found increasing support through a combination of its new, less separatist policy of independence within the European Community, the electorate's frustration at Labour's powerlessness to prevent Conservative policies being implemented in Scotland, and a growing alarm at the perceived erosion of Scottish control in the economy, local government, education and the public arts.

In 1988 the Campaign for a Scottish Assembly issued 'A Claim of Right for Scotland', identifying a crisis of democracy in Scotland, and proposing a Constitutional Convention to resolve the problem by coming forward with an agreed new constitutional settlement. That Convention held its first meeting on March 30th, 1989, and issued a stirring Declaration acknowledging 'the sovereign right of the Scottish people to determine the form of Government best suited to their needs', and stating its intention to draw up a scheme for a Scottish Assembly or Parliament.

As we approach the three hundredth anniversary of the Treaty of Union in the year 2007, it is clear that a sense of Scottish nationhood survives and that the recurring question of its proper political and economic boundaries will be debated with renewed passion in the 1990s. A national identity has survived because of the survival of distinct national institutions and a growing support for a political and constitutional expression of that separate identity.

In the opening chapter I described the Scots' nationalism as one of principled calculation. Intellectual and democratic reflection upon first principles and the common good has always been central to any understanding of the Scottish identity, but deciding the proper boundaries within which to apply them in our national life has been a matter of rational discourse and careful calculation. The current crisis of national identity has come about because once more in our history we are calculating the compatibility of our constitutional boundaries with our principles and perception of our national welfare. As the late

John P. Mackintosh observed, this is something inherent in the nature of our dual identity, as both Scottish and British.

Our Dual National Identity

In 1974, at the height of an earlier surge of support for the SNP, Mackintosh, an authoritative academic participant in British politics, wrote an article in The New Statesman that offered an illuminating analysis of the nationalist phenomenon. He argued that the Scots have a dual sense of nationality. The shared experience of going to school, living and working in a country with common systems of education, local government, law and religion imbued people with a sense of being Scottish, 'with perhaps an incomplete, but none the less definite element of national identity.' Parallel with that Scottish experience was a British dimension that for over two centuries had given the Scots the sense of being part of a great country which led the world. For Mackintosh, 'the two sides of this dual nationality co-existed with the emphasis changing from time to time, from one aspect to another.' The changing fortunes of either nationality meant a careful calculation of where the emphasis should be laid in defining the boundaries of the Scots' national identity and interests. For the Scots, 'with the dual nationality, there is a simple alternative if the pride in being British wanes: just be Scottish.'

Mackintosh used this concept of a calculated dual nationality to explain the rise of the SNP in the context of the postwar decline of Britain as an imperial power and the failure of its governments to solve the accompanying economic and political decline. His proposal for halting growing nationalist support in Scotland, as a strongly pro-devolution Scottish Labour MP, was a period of successful British government which would cause a satisfied electorate 'to vote positively for a party that has once again restored the feeling that Britain is a successful, worthwhile country to belong to for those who do have other places they can go and other traditions and titles to which they can turn.' I doubt if the 'successful' Thatcher governments of the 1980s were quite what Mackintosh had in mind! Nor, it would seem, has the Scottish electorate felt that Britain is a successful, worthwhile country to belong to under such a rule, judging by their voting preferences. As Mackintosh discerned, a British government which is deeply unpopular in Scotland serves to remind the Scots that they have other places they can go and other traditions and titles to which they can turn.

Someone once said that morality is like art, a question of drawing the line somewhere. We might say the same about the Scots' sense of national identity. As a linear nation, our identity crisis has always been a question of deciding where to draw the line; not just in the sense of the physical borderline from the Solway to the Tweed, but far more in the sense of the imaginative line and the coordinate points in human history and society that set the moving boundaries of who and what we are as Scots.

This can be argued from two historical case studies that illustrate and illuminate my proposition and its relevance to the contemporary national identity crisis in Scotland. In the mid-sixteenth century, in Reformation Scotland, and in the mid-nineteenth century, in Victorian Scotland, the Scots were inescapably confronted with this question of where to trace the lineaments of their national identity - around an autonomous Scotland within Europe or around an imperial England within a greater Britain? In each case there was a principled calculation between the alternative places they could go and competing traditions and titles to which they lay claim in tracing the imaginative line and significant reference points of their national identity.

The line between the old medieval Catholic Scotland and the new Reformed Scotland, before and after 1560, is so set in the popular imagination that it is difficult to conceive of any other significant fault lines in the topography of our national identity in the sixteenth century. Both Protestant and Roman Catholic partisans in Scottish culture have so emphasised this great divide and its consequences for our national identity, that we have been blinded to any other contours in the minds of Reformation Scots. The novelist Fionn MacColla, for example, a convert to Catholicism, drew his creative inspiration from a burning sense of outrage at the damage done to Scottish culture and history by the break with the life-affirming Catholic and Celtic identity of pre-Reformation Scotland, and its replacement with the life-denying and anglicising Calvinism typified by John Knox. Presbyterian

Scots have, not surprisingly, offered a different interpretation of events! As the inscriptions on the nineteenth century statues to John Knox in the courtyard of New College, Edinburgh, and the Necropolis in Glasgow, testify, they were conscious only of the benefits he conferred on his native land. I do not wish to deny the importance of this dividing line and its bearing on our Scottish identity. But it was certainly not the only significant fault line in the Scottish national consciousness of the period, as the work of the American historian Arthur H. Williamson has brought to light.

In his study of that Scottish national consciousness in the age of James VI, Williamson has identifed among the Scottish reformers two very different understandings of their national identity. On the one side were those Scots like John Knox himself, who had spent time in England and on the continent with their fellow English reformers. Williamson contends that Knox had imbibed from some of these English Protestants an apocalyptic theological and political interpretation of the times in which they lived that identified England with its Protestant monarch as an elect nation, chosen by God in the 'latter-days' to bring in the reign of the true church and dethrone the Antichrist of Rome within Christendom. The English proponents of this identification of the Elizabethan state with the prophecies of scripture based their claim on the long and unbroken religious and secular history of England, made to seem plausible by the ancient pedigree of English institutions and the possession of a wealth of public documents going back over centuries. England's history and destiny were seen as central to the divine purpose for the world, to the extent that one propogandist even claimed that the Almighty himself was an Englishman! On a slightly more modest scale, the English monarch was seen as the sacred successor to the Christian emperor Constantine whom scripture prophesied would reign at the end of the age.

Where did that leave those exiled reformers who embraced this political theology and yet were not Englishmen, but rather Scots returning to carry out the work of reformation north of the border? In Williamson's words, 'What would the Christian apocalypse mean for the Scottish Church and for Scottish public culture?'

Any Scot wishing to interpret Scotland's history and destiny in similarly apocalyptic terms was faced with insuperable problems. Although an ancient Christian kingdom like England, its institutions were much weaker, its public records far scarcer, and its monarchy had never been strong enough to foster pretensions of imperial grandeur. This lack of a well-documented history and impressive, ancient institutions, had far-reaching consequences for Knox and other Scots of an apocalyptic frame of mind. According to Williamson, 'it led Scottish thinking in two potentially exclusive directions.' One way would lead the Scots to define themselves as a covenanted nation: 'If Scotland possessed no truly imperial past to be re-written and re-interpreted, the present moment in itself might achieve a spectacular, indeed apocalyptic significance. Scotsmen might covenant with their God to create a church and a kingdom central to the historical redemption... A Scotland covenanted... would endow the ancient kingdom with new purpose.' This line of thinking about Scottish nationhood took several decades to unfold, until it led, in 1638, to the National Covenant. One of the most significant but least discussed causes of this slow development of the notion of Scotland as a covenanted nation was, for Williamson, 'the existence of a competing political vision, already broadly shaped before 1560':

> Scotsmen could covenant with themselves (and God) to establish a Scottish Church and a redefined Scottish nation. But they had another alternative which many Scotsmen could find intellectually more appealing and politically more persuasive. For they might instead covenant with Englishmen (and God, needless to add) in the latter days and thereby create an altogether new state. This proposed British covenant long antedated the purely Scottish conception.

Williamson argues persuasively that, 'Since the mid-sixteenth century Scotsmen have been disproportionately exercised in determining what "Britain" and a "British Empire" might mean.' Not least among them was John Knox himself, who appears to have believed in and worked assiduously towards the union of Scotland and England under a British crown and within a British realm. By hitching its star to England's, in a new British galaxy,

Scotland would share in its heavenly destiny and earthly prosperity. By wishing to map Scotland's identity along these
British lines, Knox and his successors were following in the
course set by medieval Scottish apologists like John Major for
a British union of the two realms. However, other Scottish
reformers like John Erskine of Dun 'were little attracted to the
lure of Great Britain.' Or, like John Napier of Merchiston, they
contested the English imperial interpretation of the Biblical
apocalyptic literature. Napier's own Biblical interpretation
stressed the need for the Scottish king 'to proceed with the social,
legal, and spiritual reform of Scotland' without reference to a
British union.

It can be seen, then, that a serious and sustained theological
and political debate took place in Reformation Scotland, concerning where the lines of the Scottish national identity should
be drawn. The choice was between an autonomous Scotland,
given new purpose and direction through a reforming national
covenant, and an imperial Britain, within which Scotland would
share with England its elect destiny in the world. As a key
element in that debate, the Scots fashioned a particular notion of
'Britain' that enabled them to imagine a common destiny with
England, an identity which the English themselves were not
always as enthusiastic about or as willing to adopt.

While the notion of a covenanted nation gained the as-
cendency in the mid-seventeenth century, in defining Scottish
identity, the cumulative effect of political, ecclesiastical and
economic debacles later in that century led to a loss of nerve
about the viability of an independent Scottish nation. After the
disaster of the overseas trading venture in Darien and under great
pressure from England, the competing political vision of a
greater British union finally triumphed in 1707. Yet there was
already an earlier loss of nerve on the part of those late medieval
and early Reformation Scots who favoured a British union with
England. Faced with the victory of the English state under Henry
VIII at Flodden, the success of the Protestant cause under the
young King Edward, and the imperial might of Elizabethan
England, many Scots believed that their own native institutions,
polity and traditions were no match for those of their southern
neighbour in the one British isle.

Although the Scottish reformers shared the same fundamental theological principles, and none can doubt their patriotism, they disagreed in their political calculation of the places to which the Scots should go and the alternative traditions and titles to which they should turn in tracing the imaginative line and significant reference points of their national identity. Both a covenanted autonomous Scotland and an elect greater Britain were considered as competing mental coordinates for the Scots' sense of national identity in the years between 1560 and 1707. Crucial to that choice was the loss of nerve on the part of some Scots about their own public culture, which made them defer to English models within an imperial British union. Those who kept their nerve about the native culture, like John Erskine of Dun, and yet who saw the need to reform Scottish national life according to Scottish and European principles, favoured a continuing Scottish independence. Rationally argued and principled assessments of the relative merits of Scotland's institutions, culture and constitution were all part of the calculation of where the country's future lay.

A Loss of Nerve

The debate over 'where to draw the line' of the Scottish identity did not cease, just because of the Union of the Parliaments in 1707, as the following case study demonstrates. The tensions between a Scottish or an English orientation in public life were evident throughout the eighteenth century and the age of Enlightenment, nowhere more so than in the anglicising life and work of the philosopher David Hume, who even changed his surname from his native 'Home'. Yet the Scots experienced a more acute and damaging crisis of national identity in the mid-nineteenth century, in a secular version of the earlier theological debate.

Once again in Scotland's history we can see a profound loss of nerve over the worth of indigenous national traditions and institutions when compared with those of imperial England. Like the Scottish reformers before them, Victorian Scots were confronted with a self-confident English culture embarked upon another phase of imperial expansion and conquest. The impact of this unequal encounter can be traced through several areas of mid-century Scottish life. The historian Marinell Ash and the philosopher George Davie have identified a loss of nerve in the national tradition of scholarship in this period.

Ash has described this loss of nerve among those engaged in serious historical scholarship as 'The Strange Death of Scottish History'. In the early nineteenth century there was a growing movement that was concerned to recreate a credible picture of Scotland's past, 'through the recovery of historical materials such as documents, and the rigorous study and analysis of them.' The model and inspiration for this scholarly enterprise was the work of Sir Walter Scott. In his romantic desire to understand the past, Scott had written historical novels that 'had recreated past societies which worked on their own terms, not modern preconceptions.' Scott had a clear, and on the whole correct, vision of the past and of the historical needs of the nineteenth century, according to Ash. Yet by the second half of the century this critical and informed study of Scotland and its history had given way to a sentimental clamjamfry of 'meaningless or highly selective images of Scotland's past whose symbols are bonnie Scotland of the bens and glens and misty shieling, the Jacobites, Mary Queen of Scots, tartan mania and the rise of historical statuary.' Contrary to received opinion today, Ash argues that it was not Scott who was to blame for this strange death of serious Scottish historical scholarship. Its demise was brought on by Scottish society's own 'historical failure of nerve' in mid-century over its national identity.

In response to the tensions created by the country's transition from 'a distinctively Scottish society to one (or several) societies with a British or imperial orientation', Scots reacted in two distinct ways. As we have seen, some called for the expansion of Scottish political rights through a greater say in the expanding powers of the British state, as they affected Scotland. From the founding of the National Association for the Vindication of Scottish Rights in 1853 to the present-day SNP and Campaign for a Scottish Assembly, the nationalist and home rule argument has been a persistent modern response to the perceived crisis of national identity.

The other reaction was more to do with the Victorian Scots' loss of intellectual will than any nerving of a political will in defence of national interests. This failure of nerve occured when Victorian Scotland ceased to be distinctively and confidently itself, in Ash's phrase, and felt it increasingly necessary to emulate the successful, dominant cosmopolitan model of imperial Britain. In practice that meant assimilating the culture, values and historical perspective of metropolitan England. The result was a typical sundering of the Scottish mind and heart.

The educated Scot began to see his own country's history as parochial. As George Davie has argued in *The Democratic Intellect*, his classic earlier study of the demise of the Scottish intellectual tradition, even the Scottish universities were anxious 'to accommodate themselves to the expansive epoch of Durbars and Jubilees':

> Thus at the very time when our neighbouring countries were becoming increasingly 'history minded', the Scots were losing their sense of the past, their leading institutions, including the universities, were emphatically resolved - to use a catch phrase fashionable in the Scotland of the twentieth century - 'no longer to be prisoners of their history.'

Davie himself calls this 'a failure of intellectual nerve among the Scots', as their own educational tradition of democratic intellectualism, based on a generalist, philosophically grounded training for university students from a relatively wide range of social backgrounds, came under unfavourable comparison with the English Oxbridge system of specialist and elitist education geared to producing the civil servants and administrators of the empire. It was nothing less than the abandoning by the mainstream of the Scottish establishment of the sober and critical study of their own nation's history, within a European and metaphysical intellectual tradition, for the attractions of another history and educational ethos, with a British form but an English substance.

The effect of this wilful labotomy on the national brain was, ironically, to make Scotland all the more a prisoner of its history. Without a cool, discriminating and informed understanding of Scottish history and society, the Victorian mind collapsed 'into emotional or excessive manifestations of a vanished past'. This collapse was evident in the huge public appetite for the Kailyard school of popular literature, with its commercially lucrative portrayal of an idyllic, mythical Scottish past of godly, if eccentric rural parish life. It could also be seen in the Victorian passion for the Highlands and a Celtic past that had been skilfully reinvented once the real Highland Gaelic culture had been destroyed militarily at Culloden and economically in the Clearances. All of this was a flight from the real Scotland of harsh urban poverty, industrial discipline and emptied northern glens. It was a nostalgic escape from the confusion felt over the modern meaning of national identity for 'North Britain' in England's triumphal imperial age.

It was therefore an age when the Scottish dimension of the Scots' dual identity was weighed and found wanting while the British dimension was heavy with prestige and glittering prizes. The coordinating first principles of the Scottish religious and secular traditions were thrown away and a new calculation of national interest was made by drawing the line of national identity firmly through the capital and outposts of empire to mark its head, and through the mists and myths of romance to mark its heart. The choice between confidence or loss of nerve over our native social philosophy and institutions has therefore been a crucial one in deciding the future of Scotland. The recovery of nerve about our own history and intellectual traditions had to await the twentieth century, and its renaissance in the study of Scottish history and writing of Scottish literature.

Where Now?

We can see, therefore, that the present debate over the proper boundaries of our national identity, with England or Europe, is not some novel aberration in our national life due to the rise of modern Scottish nationalism. The debate is a very old one going back at least to the disputes among the several claimants to the Scottish throne in the late thirteenth century. The debate is intrinsic to Scotland's historic existence and identity as a nation. The Scottish Reformation, for example, cannot be understood adequately except in the context of the contemporary debate over whether Scotland's geo-political future lay with England or France.

We are thus engaged in a normal and typical Scottish debate when we question where and with whom our future lies as a nation, whether in a renegotiated United Kingdom or European Community. As we go on, in the 1990s, to explore the human, Christian and national dimensions of the present crisis of Scottish identity, we must do so in the full knowledge of this recurring feature of our national identity.

Scottish nationhood has always been a social and cultural phenomenon capable of rational debate over the benefits and disadvantages of its several possible imaginative and actual boundaries. There has never been one sacrosanct settlement of the nation's political life that has had to be preserved in perpetuity to ensure Scotland's survival. Only our social principles and moral values, and those religious, legal and educational institutions that have been seen to incarnate them, have been granted that place and degree of continuity in our national life. That being so, it is nonsense for a Scottish unionist or nationalist to make metaphysical claims for the self-evident, unnegotiable truth of a national identity within either the British Union or a separate statehood. Both cases, and any in between, have to be argued through a rational public discourse over Scotland's past, present and future; one that is open to challenge and refutation concerning the nation's welfare and common good.

To say that Scotland is British is to repeat a relatively recent political definition of our national identity, not some natural truth like the force of gravity or the wetness of our Scottish climate. Nations are historical communities with a temporal and provisional existence. They rise and fall. They are created or re-created and disappear within time and space. They are also 'imagined communities' in the sense that the historian Benedict Anderson has defined this useful term, in his book on nations bearing the same title. Any community of people larger than a face to face one requires certain shared images of their communal identity to unite them across the separating distances of space and time. Nations are those imagined communities which perceive themselves to be nations and share common mental or physical boundaries and reference points as to their national identity.

It is both conceivable and historically proven that such communities can shift the ways in which they imagine their shared national identity. Catholic Scotland in alliance with France became Calvinist Scotland in alliance with England. Covenanting and zealous Scotland became Moderate and enlightened North Britain. It would be folly and a modernist hubris to assume that somehow, at the end of the twentieth century, we had reached the ordained and fixed end of that road. We are only at the next step, with no certain path or guarantees of our future. It is essential that we graft into our understanding of nations a strong sense of their mutability and impermanence as historical and not natural communities.

A Tangible Community, a Constitutional Identity

The one thing that gives the Christian that sense of the provisional nature of nations is a belief that the Kingdom of God is not yet. God's rule has come into human history in the person of its unlikely king, Jesus of Nazareth. There are many tangible signs of the coming of God's rule in the life of the Church amid the nations, as it witnesses to the good news of the Kingdom. But the full, tangible community of the Kingdom on earth has not yet come. Therefore no human community or cause can be identified with that Kingdom. At best they may show signs of the coming reign of God's justice and peace but they will always fall short and be judged by the terms of that Kingdom. However, that is never a reason to abandon the struggle for the coming of the Kingdom of God. Rather, it is to set the nations within the constitution of that Kingdom.

Historically, in Scotland, such a Kingdom framework has been developed to define the identity of the national Church in relation to the state. The Reformed Kirk especially defined and refined its relationship with the State over five centuries, arguing that Christ's kingship and headship of the Church meant that it should be free from state control. The earlier and later seventeenth century Covenanting movements, the eighteenth and early nineteenth century struggles over patronage, culminating in the 1842 Claim of Right and Disruption of the Kirk the following year, these conflicts were all fought in terms of the Crown Rights of the Redeemer over his Church.

What has not been done, with a few honourable exceptions, has been to bring the secular affairs of the state under the searching light of that coming Kingdom. We have already come across one of the few prophetic voices in the history of the Church of Scotland who did see Christ's kingship in broader social terms, Patrick Brewster, minister at Paisley Abbey at the time of the Disruption. Calling him 'The Unique Exception' to the lack of prophetic Christian social criticism in this period, Donald C. Smith has written: 'Alike on biblical and historical grounds, Brewster claimed that it was the privilege and the imperative duty of ministers of the Church of Scotland to subject the laws and activities of governments and all the affairs of national life to the criticism of the sovereign Word of God.' And so he preached in a sermon:

> To preach Christ crucified... without preaching the UNIVERSALITY of God's law, which Christ 'came to fulfil', would not be to preach 'the truth as it is in Jesus'. To preach a mere fraction of revealed truth without preaching obedience to the divine law in all the affairs of life, would neither be preaching the word of God nor the Gospel of Christ. Christ is 'PRINCE OF THE KINGS OF THE EARTH'; and his kingdom, though not of this world, yet ruleth over all. This is the true HEADSHIP of the Son of God... He must be acknowledged and served as the 'King of kings, and Lord of Lords'. We must take the law of his word as our guide and director in the affairs of life, holding and asserting its SUPREMACY over every other law, and demanding that all the acts, whether legislative or executive, of RULERS AND MAGISTRATES, shall be tested and judged by his supreme will, and that all human statutes by which nations are governed, shall be brought into harmony and accordance with his holy and unerring requirements.

It is that voice and political vision which must be recovered today, in the judging of all national affairs, including governments and laws, according to God's sovereign Word in Jesus Christ. That will not mean simplistic panaceas or the crude identification of the Kingdom of God with particular social and political programmes. It will mean bringing questions of government in national life under the scrutiny of Christ's lordship. Such a process of recovery is already underway in Scotland on the question of the country's constitutional future. In its 1989 General Assembly Church and Nation report on *The Government of Scotland*, the Church of Scotland re-affirmed its commitment to a Reformed tradition of theological reflection on constitutional matters.

> Fundamental to the Biblical view of the state embraced by the Reformed theological tradition is the notion of the legitimate but limited sovereignty of earthly governing authorities within the absolute sovereignty of God in his providential and redemptive rule over human affairs. It is, therefore, consistent for a Reformed Church and tradition shaped by such a theological understanding to favour a constitutional theory and practice based on the principle of the limited or relative sovereignty of the state. According to such a constitutional principle the state's sovereignty is not absolute but relative to the fundamental sovereignty of God, expressed within human society in fundamental law and the sovereignty of a people accountable to their Maker. The Scottish constitutional tradition, in both its secular and religious streams of thought and practice, has consistently favoured just such a 'limited' rather than an 'absolutist' notion of sovereignty. Historically, this meant that the ruler was seen as subject to the rule of law and consent of the people. In the original 'Claim of Right, made by the Scottish Parliament in 1689, it stated that King James VII was deposed because he violated 'the fundamental constitution of this Kingdom, and altered it from a legal limited monarchy, to an arbitrary despotic power'. The ruler's sovereignty was seen as relative to the legal limits set on his powers by the nation's fundamental constitution, a bulwark against arbitrary despotic power. In the Scottish constitutional tradition political sovereignty lay ultimately in the people and

not the state, both existing under the sovereignty of
God.

The report sought to apply the insights on the limited nature
of sovereignty and power in society which the Scottish and
Reformed constitutional tradition offered, to the questions raised
by *The Claim of Right for Scotland* (1988) about the future
government of Scotland. The same arguments were also being
used by Canon Kenyon Wright, an ecumenical church leader
who emerged as a leading figure in the Scottish Constitutional
Convention set up in 1989 to seek agreement on a new
constitutional settlement for Scotland. As he himself has written, the criteria of the Kingdom of God must apply in judging any
proposals for Scottish self-government:

> Finally there is a simple theology of justice which is
> also biblical. Bonhoeffer said in Nazi Germany,
> 'Whoever does not cry for the Jews, cannot sing
> Christian hymns'. For our society may we not say with
> equal conviction, 'Whoever does not cry for the **poor**,
> cannot sing Christian hymns'. If in the words of the
> United States Catholic Bishops' Letter, 'In any soci-
> ety the litmus test of its justice or injustice is how it
> treats its poor and powerless' - then we must ask the
> question, would a Scottish Parliament be more likely
> to pass this test than the *status quo*? The answer is a
> resounding yes.

All this serves to suggest that in any redrawing of the lines of our
linear nationhood, we must draw them through constitutional
and not institutional coordinates. For almost three hundred years
Scottish national identity has depended for its shared images on
the common institutions of the Church, Law and Education.
During that period Reformed Christians have been quick to
apply the constitution of Christ's Kingdom to the Church, using
the legal procedures of the Law to resolve its conflicts and the
moral education of schools and universities to inculcate its
values.

Such coordinates are now too faint to offer direction and shape
for our national identity. It is time to tackle the more awesome
coordinates of the sovereignty of God and the claims to sovereignty by frail, provisional nations. By embracing a humbler if

no less significant role in Scottish national life, as a more critical Confessing Church, it is now time, a *kairos*, a right time, to apply the constitution of Christ's Kingdom and the vision of the tangible community of justice and peace which it brings to the question of Scotland's government and future within Britain and Europe. The 1989 General Assembly report on *The Government of Scotland* points in this direction: it offers us a vision of a constitutional nationhood - Scotland seen as a democratic nation:

> . . . it is not possible to resolve the question of the democratic control of Scottish affairs and the setting up of a Scottish Assembly apart from a fundamental shift in our constitutional thinking away from the notion of the unlimited or absolute sovereignty of the British Parliament towards the historic Scottish and Reformed constitutional principle of limited or relative sovereignty. This is the only secure and lasting basis for any remoulding of democratic control of Scottish affairs within a British and a European context. Only such a constitutional principle can reflect the realities of Scotland as a nation and a democratic people committed to responsibility for its own affairs in partnership with other nations, through a Scottish Assembly or parliament.

We are now moving in the 1990s away from the old institutional national identity of post-Union Scottish civil society: into an understanding of our Scottish identity as a constitutional identity within a Scottish democracy, defined in the modern political terms of democratic constitutionalism. Christians must offer a vision of that constitutional identity from the reference point of the coming tangible community of God's Kingdom, with its litmus test of justice for the poor and powerless. The provisional nature of Scotland as a historical nation opens it up both to that constitutional possibility and to that constitutional judgement.

The Tragi-Comedy of Nations

Coupled with that awareness of the provisional identity of nations must be a strong sense of the ironic and the absurd, the tragic and the comic in national as in all human affairs. As we saw in chapter two, when Catholic churchmen penned the great Declaration of Arbroath, with its magnificent call to freedom, they could little envisage that their vision of Scotland would descend to Sir David Lyndsay's *Satire of the Three Estates*, with its biting lampoon of clerical folly. When Knox embraced Calvin's awesome doctrine of predestination, with its noble affirmation of the sovereignty of Almighty God, he could not have conceived of the comic degeneration of that terrible vision into *Holy Willie's Prayer*. When Thomas Carlyle thundered out his prophetic call for a devout and upright society, albeit one which had left behind the old God of the Bible, he did not have in mind the late twentieth century's devotion to Sunday shopping. And, as we have already noted, when Hugh MacDiarmid's poetic vision summoned forth revolutionary leaders of iron will, not even his Drunk Man could have dreamed up Mrs Thatcher. The imagined gods of our Scottish nationhood turn out to be impish satyrs.

The propriety of re-thinking our national identity as a linear nation cannot be in question if one accepts these two arguments - the historical precedents for it, and the constitutional necessity of it (given the provisional, historical and imagined nature of nations as human communities) - and the tragi-comic risks inherent in any such exercise. The question is more one of how we should go about such a re-thinking of who and what we are as Scots. That depends on where our ultimate loyalties and horizons lie. For Christians, that would require re-thinking what it means for the Scots to be human beings in the broken and healed image of a God who became a human being in Jesus the Jew from Nazareth. In facing the challenge of re-casting our national identity for the twenty-first century, we are called to a thorough re-thinking of all that we have ever meant by our human and Christian identity in Scotland.

When Anthony Ross issued that intellectual challenge in 1970, he was careful to stress its spiritual dimension. We must make at the start, he said, an act of contrition for ourselves and for our community. Pride is an intellectual as well as a moral sin. Christians have had a continuous hand in the shaping of that imagined community we call our nation since at least the days of Columba. If there is to be a penitent and humble re-thinking of our identity, then it should begin in the household of God, for the sake of the nation.

CONCLUSION

Chapter 12

THE CRUCIFIED VISION -
A Humble Nation

In the summer of 1988 I made a video programme on 'Christian Visions of Scotland', along the lines of the opening historical chapters in this book (part one). It involved filming in the Borders, in Ecclefechan and Langholm, the hometowns of Thomas Carlyle and Hugh MacDiarmid respectively. Sitting in Carlyle's chair, kneeling by MacDiarmid's grave, trying to think their thoughts after them, I was conscious of two great Scottish minds which wrestled Jacob-like with God, or with his absence. They would not let go until they had found the blessing of wisdom for their pains... and, for MacDiarmid at least, for his country.

Six months later a plane full of people returning home for Christmas was blown up by a terrorist bomb over the sky where we had been filming. It landed on Lockerbie, not Ecclefechan or Langholm. There too people wrestled with God, or his absence.

Where is the wisdom to be found that will give us a renewed vision of our Scottish identity? Not in Ecclefechan, with the Sage of Chelsea - the vein of secular Calvinism has long since been exhausted. Not in Langholm, with the Drunk Man looking at the Thistle - God-building supermen have become rather ridiculous figures in these days of *Perestroika*, *Glasnost* and the tumbling of the Berlin Wall. Not in these places, not in these minds, great and wise though they are and always will be. The God-shaped hole in our identity can be filled only by God.

No, wisdom is found in Lockerbie. Amid the tragedy of inhuman suffering and evil. James Whyte, then Moderator of the

Kirk's General Assembly, spoke at the Lockerbie memorial service. He quoted Martha's words to Jesus, on the death of her brother Lazarus: 'Lord, if you had been here, my brother would not have died.' (John 11:21) If you had been here, God... James Whyte's response was that God was there, in the suffering, sharing the tragedy, bearing the pain. We know that from Jesus, the Crucified God. He went through Lazarus' death, and Lockerbie's. God is here, in the midst of us, loving us by suffering alongside us - only then comes resurrection. The Crucified God is our Wisdom, the makar Scotland needs. There are no easy, triumphal Christian visions of Scotland with this God.

Calvin said that knowledge is of two kinds, knowledge of God and knowledge of ourselves. The two are inseparable and related. A new Christian vision of ourselves as Scots begins with a new vision of God. That vision comes through the humanity of Christ. There we see how God loves us unconditionally, as we are. He loves us so much that he laid down his own human life for us, and suffered and died. We do not have to become anything, or achieve anything, or prove anything to justify that love.

This love not only shows us what God is like, it actually does something in our lives; for the love of God is none other than God the Holy Spirit; his revealing of God within us leads to self-acceptance and an unconditional sense of our own human identity. This love is the personal knowledge of God that humbles the Church into being the serving community and not the triumphal crusade. This love is the knowledge of God that humbles nations and gives them wisdom about their true identity and purpose.

During the Second World War, after the Nazi conquest and occupation of France, an exiled Frenchwoman, Simone Weil wrote a spiritual manifesto for her country, *The Need for Roots*. Weil was a devout Christian, a French patriot who possessed a brilliant, critical mind. In her book, a Christian vision for France when it's glorious national identity lay in ruins, she wrote:

> One can either love France for the glory which would seem to ensure for her a prolonged existence in time and space; or else one can love her as something

which, being earthly, can be destroyed, and is all the more precious on that account... the latter is alone legitimate for a Christian, for it alone bears the badge of humility. It alone belongs to that species of love which can be given the name of charity... Let no one imagine either that a love of this nature would run the risk of ignoring or rejecting what there is of pure and genuine grandeur in the past history of France, or in the country's present hopes and ideals. Quite the opposite. Compassion is all the more tender, all the more poignant, the more good one is able to discern in the being who forms the object of it, and it predisposes one to discern the good. When a Christian represents to himself Christ on the Cross, his compassion is not diminished by the thought of the latter's perfection, nor the other way about. But, on the other hand, such a love can keep its eyes open on injustices, cruelties, mistakes, falsehoods, crimes and scandals contained in the country's past, its present and in its ambitions in general, quite openly and fearlessly, and without thereby being diminished; the love being rendered thereby the more painful... Just now it is the only sort of love that is suitable for the French... Compassion for our country is the only sentiment which doesn't strike a false note at the present time, suits the situation in which the souls and bodies of Frenchmen actually find themselves, and possesses at once the humility and the dignity appropriate to ...

Appropriate to what? Scotland. This is the sort of love that possesses the humility and the dignity appropriate to Scottish identity in the 1990s and beyond. This is the sort of love that any new Christian vision of Scotland must embrace. It is a compassionate love which can affirm the good and contemplate the bad in ourselves, without being diminished by self-assertion or self-distrust. The old name for it was charity. Charity is the kind of love described in Paul's first epistle to the Corinthians: 'Charity vaunteth not itself, is not puffed up...'

A Sober Woman looks at the Epistle

We began this book with one woman's vision of Christ and nation in the light of Paul's epistles - Margaret Thatcher's Sermon on The Mound. It is a vision I cannot accept as a Scottish Christian, for reasons which I hope are now clear. At the heart of this book's analysis of Scottish identity stands another woman's fearful vision of Christ, seen in the half-light of the first epistle to the Corinthians - Mrs Gourlay's last words in *The House with the Green Shutters*. These are sober women's visions that we can do without in Scotland.

I bring this book to a close with this third woman, Simone Weil's vision of Christ and nation. This is the vision we need for our Scottish identity. Here, that other sober woman looks at the epistle.

Weil, a Jewish Christian convert from communism, has a very different vision of the nation from Mrs Thatcher or Mrs Gourlay. What does she see as she contemplates the fate of occupied France in the light of the charity definitively expressed in the Corinthian epistle? It is a vision of God's unconditional love for a humanity sheltering within those frail, provisional communities we call nations - communities and identities which, being earthly, can be destroyed and are all the more precious on that account. It a vision of the nation that begins with a vision of God in the 'Christ on the Cross'.

In the Crucified God, the human Jesus nailed to the Cross, we find the clarity of vision to see our nation as it is, and yet as it can be. This vision is humbling. It is Micah's vision for his nation: 'And what does the LORD require of you? To act justly and to love mercy and to walk humbly with your God.' It leads to a Crucified vision of a humble nation - self-accepting and not self-destructive.

Looking at Scotland through Christ's humility, we will die to our old 'demiurgic identity', where our humanity was seen as conditional on our own efforts. We will see our humanity as God's gift. Then, it will no longer be laughable to be in God's image. Ours will be a **Common Humanity**. We will reject our triumphal national religion as idolatry. We will see the Christian community as a holy nation, set apart for Christ and his mission to the nations. Then, ministers of Christ will gladly be strangled daily to let Scotland be reborn! Ours will be a **Confessing Church**. We will reject the hubris of the British state's claim to absolute sovereignty over Scotland. We will affirm the state's limited sovereignty in a self-governing Scotland. Then, 'the government will be upon his shoulder'. Ours will be a **Constitutional Nationhood**.

It is time to paraphrase MacDiarmid . . .

> She canna Scotland see wha yet
> canna see the Christ
> and Scotland in true scale to him.

BIBLIOGRAPHY

Scotland, Nationhood and Nationalism

Benedict Anderson, *Imagined Communities* (London 1983)
Craig Beveridge and Ronald Turnbull, *The Eclipse of Scottish Culture* (Edinburgh 1989)
Jack Brand, *The National Movement in Scotland* (London 1978)
Kenneth Cargill, *Scotland 2000* (Glasgow 1987)
George Davie, *The Democratic Intellect* (Edinburgh 1961) and *The Crisis of the Democratic Intellect* (Edinburgh 1986)
Owen Dudley Edwards (ed.), *A Claim of Right for Scotland* (Edinburgh 1989)
Ernest Gellner, *Nations and Nationalism* (Oxford 1983)
Duncan Glen (ed.), *Whither Scotland?* (London 1971)
R.J. Hanham, *Scottish Nationalism* (London 1969)
Christopher Harvie, *Scotland and Nationalism* (London 1977)
James Kellas, *Modern Scotland* (London 1980); *The Scottish Political System* (4th ed., Cambridge 1989)
Neil MacCormick (ed.), *The Scottish Debate* (London 1970)
W.L.M. Mackenzie, *Political Identity* (Harmondsworth 1978)
Colin Maclean (ed.), *The Crown and the Thistle* (Edinburgh 1979)
Tom Nairn, *The Break-Up of Britain* (London, 1977 & 1981); *The Enchanted Glass* (London 1988)
P.H. Scott & A.C. Davis (eds.), *The Age of MacDiarmid* (Edinburgh 1980)
Hugh Seton-Watson, *Nations and States* (London 1977)
Jim Sillars, *Scotland: The Case for Optimism* (Edinburgh 1986)
Anthony D. Smith, *Nationalism in the Twentieth Century* (Oxford 1979); *Theories of Nationalism* (2nd ed., London 1983); *The Ethnic Revival* (Cambridge 1981)
Keith Webb, *The Growth of Scottish Nationalism* (Harmondsworth 1978)

Christianity and Nations, Nationalism

Paul H. Ballard & D. Huw Jones, *This Land and People: a Symposium on Christian and Welsh National Identity* (University College, Cardiff 1979)

Karl Barth, *Church Dogmatics III.4 Section 54.*3 (English tr., Edinburgh 1961)

Stewart J. Brown, *Thomas Chalmers and the Godly Commonwealth* (Oxford, 1982)

Keith W. Clements, *A Patriotism for Today* (London 1986)

Gordon Donaldson, *Scotland: Church and Nation through Sixteen Centuries* (Edinburgh 1972)

Bob Goudzwaard, *Idols of our Time* (Downers Grove, Illinois 1984)

Richard L. Greaves, *Theology and Revolution in the Scottish Reformation* (Grand Rapids, Michigan 1980)

John Habgood, *Church and Nation in a Secular Age* (London 1983)

Ian Henderson, *Power without Glory* (London 1967) and *Scotland: Kirk and People* (London 1969)

Daniel Jenkins, *The British: Their Identity and their Religion* (London 1975)

O.R. Johnston, *Nationhood: Towards a Christian Perspective* (Latimer House, Oxford 1980)

W.A. Klerk, *The Puritans in Africa* (Harmondsworth 1976)

Alan Kreider, *Journey Towards Holiness* (Basingstoke 1986)

Stewart Lamont, *Church and State: Uneasy Alliances* (London 1989)

Fearghas MacFhionnlaigh, *A' Mheanbhchuileag* (Gairm, Glaschu 1980)

Alasdair MacIntyre, *Whose Justice? Which Rationality?* (London, 1988)

Richard Mouw, *When the Kings come Marching in* (Grand Rapids, Michigan 1983)

Richard John Neuhaus, *The Naked Public Square* (Grand Rapids, Michigan 1984)

H. Richard Niebuhr, *Christ and Culture* (New York 1951)

W. Pannenberg, *Christian Spirituality and Sacramental Community* (London 1984); *Ethics* (Philadelphia, Pennsylvania 1981)

R.J. Schreiter, *Constructing Local Theologies* (London 1985)

Alexander Solzhenitsyn (ed.), *From Under the Rubble* (London 1976)

Bernard Thorogood, *The Flag and the Cross* (London 1988)

Robert E. Webber, *The Secular Saint* (Grand Rapids, Michigan 1979)

Simone Weil, *The Need for Roots* (London 1952 and 1978)

Arthur H. Williamson, *Scottish National Consciousness in the Age of James VI* (Edinburgh 1979)

David F. Wright (ed.), *The Bible in Scottish Life and Literature* (Edinburgh 1988)

ARTICLES and BOOKLETS

Peter Bisset, *The Kirk and her Scotland* (Edinburgh 1986)

British Council of Churches, *Devolution and the British Churches* (London 1977)

Alison Elliot & Duncan B. Forrester (eds.), *The Scottish Churches and the Political Process* (Edinburgh 1986)

Christopher Harvie, *Faith and Scottish Identity* (Radical Scotland, June 1988 - part of paper given at Carberry Tower)

Alastair Hunter & Steven G. Mackie, *A National Church in a Multi-Racial Scotland* (Scottish Churches Council, Dunblane 1986)

David McCrone (ed.), *What Scotland Wants: Ten Years On* (conference papers, Edinburgh University 1989)

David McRoberts, *The Scottish Church and Nationalism in the Fifteenth Century* (Innes Review, vol 19 1968)

John Peck, *National Identity* (Third Way, Oct 1989)

Jock Stein (ed.), *Scottish Self-Government: Some Christian Viewpoints* (Edinburgh 1989)

VIDEO

William Storrar, *Christian Visions of Scotland* (Church of Scotland, Edinburgh 1988) - a companion video to the author's book